DIALOGUES WITH CONVENTION

DIALOGUES WITH CONVENTION

Readings in Renaissance Poetry

R. D. BEDFORD

Ann Arbor
The University of Michigan Press

Published in the United States of America by

The University of Michigan Press

1992 1991 1990 1989   4 3 2 1

Library of Congress Cataloging-in-Publication Data

Bedford, R. D. (Ronald David), 1940 –
    Dialogues with convention: readings in Renaissance poetry / R.D.
    Bedford
        p.   cm.
    Includes bibliographical references.
    ISBN 0–472–10171–4
    1. English poetry—Early modern, 1500–1700—History and criticism.
2. Renaissance—England.   3. Literary form.   4. Milton, John,
1608–1674—Knowledge—Literature.   I. Title.
PR508.L58B4   1989
821'.309—dc20   89–20269
                                                                   CIP

To my Mother and my Father

CONTENTS

PREFACE

Renaissance poetry is made difficult to approach for modern readers partly by its recalcitrant notions of poetic genres and poetic conventions which often seem to govern a poet's usage and determine strategies. Renaissance poets habitually wrote 'genre poems', offering their own distinctive contributions in dialogue with recognised conventions of discourse. Of course, there is a sense in which any poet or writer, at any time, is also and always doing precisely this, but the *consciousness* of genres was particularly strong in this period and some of the conventions were themselves massively monumental and of many centuries' standing.

They might be the conventions of the Petrarchan love sonnet, or of revenge tragedy, or of the postures appropriate to devotional writing – how does one speak when literally or metaphorically on one's knees? – or the ancient and constantly practised conventions of pastoral, or of epic narration.

Most of the topics discussed here began life as questions – and not necessarily my own but those of my students, past and present. Why, for instance, does Sidney, who curses non-poets at the end of his *Defence of Poetry* and consigns them 'to live in love, and never get favour for lacking skill of a sonnet', so signally fail, in the person of Astrophil, to get favour himself, even though his 'skill of a sonnet' is unquestionably brilliant? Or why does Donne call some of his poems 'Elegies', and what might this be saying, or implying, about them? Or what did Milton, whom we usually think of as a card-carrying republican, suppose he was doing in Ludlow in 1634 offering an aristocratic masque to the royalist nobility? And, of course, the inevitable question on Milton's *Paradise Lost* (though now perhaps it has taken second place to questions about his apparent anti-feminism in the poem): why, if God knows exactly what is going to happen does he still let it happen? And if he is supposed to be a transcendent God, why does Milton give him a speaking part and so carelessly contaminate him in the narrative processes of the poem?

One way of approaching answers to such questions lies through the recognition and investigation of the genres and conventions in which these poets were working and what they may have been doing with them. And in dwelling on their dialogue with pre-decessors as well as on what is peculiar or different about them, 'we often find' (as T. S. Eliot reminded us), 'that not only the best, but the most individual parts of [a poet's] work may be those in which the dead poets, his ancestors, assert their immor-tality most vigorously' (*Tradition and the Individual Talent*, 1919).

As I have suggested, I am indebted primarily to the nagging and stimulation of my tutorial students over the years, and also to the wisdom of colleagues and former colleagues, especially the late Maurice Evans, the late Gāmini Salgādo, and Gareth Roberts in the School of English at Exeter.

R. D. Bedford
Exeter, 1989

ACKNOWLEDGMENTS

Some of the material in this book has been previously published in various forms, most of it here considerably rewritten and expanded. Part of Chapter 2 was first published as 'Ovid metamorphosed: Donne's *Elegy XVI*' in *Essays in Criticism*, edited by Stephen Wall and Christopher Ricks, vol. 32, July 1982, and part of Chapter 6 as 'Similes of unlikeness in *Paradise Lost*', *Essays in Criticism*, vol. 25, April 1975. A version of Chapter 4 first appeared as 'Donne's Holy Sonnet, "Batter my heart" ' in *Notes & Queries*, Oxford University Press, vol. 29, no. 1, February 1982. Chapter 5 is a revised version of 'Right spelling: Milton's *A Masque* and *Il Penseroso*', originally published in *English Literary History*, John Hopkins University, Baltimore, vol. 52, no. 4, December 1985. Part of Chapter 7 was first published as 'The ensanguind field of *Paradise Lost*' in *English Language Notes*, University of Colorado, Boulder, vol. 21, no. 3, March 1983; and a version of Chapter 8 originally appeared as 'Time, freedom and foreknowledge in *Paradise Lost*', by R.D. Bedford, in *Milton Studies*, vol. xvi, James D. Simmonds, editor (published in 1982 by the University of Pittsburgh Press; revised and reprinted by permission of the publisher).

I am grateful to the editors, journals and publishers for their permission to revise and reprint that material here.

INTRODUCTION

It has always been lawful, and always will be,
to issue words stamped with the mint-mark of the
day.

Horace, *Ars Poetica*

An artificial novelty is never as effective as
a repetition that manages to suggest a fresh truth.
Marcel Proust, *Remembrance of Things Past*
(Within a Budding Grove, 1919)

The studies in some English Renaissance poets that follow are
called 'dialogues with convention' first of all in the relatively
simple sense that each of the poets represented – Sidney, Donne
and Milton – is writing in, or participating in, specific conventions
of discourse. Among the examples taken are Sidney and the discourse of sonnet writing; Donne and the Ovidian elegy; Donne
and the peculiar discourse of devotional verse; Milton and some
conventions of epic writing. The poets, in each particular case,
are conspiring (and there may indeed often be something conspiratorial about their manipulations) with the distinctive elements, and hence the past practice, of the genres in which they
choose to write.

Genres here is not meant in any rigorously taxonomic sense, but
in the sense that it may be reasonably suggested that, for instance, an important dimension of *Hamlet* remains unappreciated
if we ignore the play's original, and disruptively questioning,
contribution to the genre of revenge tragedy: what happens if the
revenger asks all the wrong sorts of questions, or does not *want* to
revenge? Or we may miss the true and often sardonic richness of
Shakespeare's sonnets unless we are open to the probability that
Shakespeare had read a lot more Elizabethan sonnets than we
have and that it is on them, as well as on something we may wish
to call his personal experience, that he sharpens his pen. Similarly, without the recognition that Milton's 'Lycidas' is a pastoral
elegy and without some ideas about what a pastoral elegy is, we

may be unable to decipher what Milton is doing in his poem. When Marvell tells us that his poem about Cromwell and Charles is an Horatian Ode we may be tempted to think that he does not really mean it (it is in English after all) or that what he calls it does not matter to our reading of it. Nor, unless we are aware of genres and conventions, can we respond to an author's mixing of kinds, or of his modulations from one to another, or of his juggling with several genres at the same time.

That is to say, the texts may invite us to interpret poems or plays as statements about poetry or drama itself, and this self-referring 'writerly' activity is one to which all literature is, by its very nature, logically committed. The texts are also there to be made sense of, and part of that sense-making involves us in an act of recognition which is frequently more demanding than a mere appeal to conventions of plausibility or to a general knowledge of literature. To take an extreme case: a recent genre-study of Milton's *Paradise Lost* (Lewalski, 1985) has indicated what a vast repository of conventional forms that extended poem represents. Its narrative genres include autobiography, exemplum and epic (biblical, historical, hexamaemeral, philosophical, Homeric, Virgilian, Ovidian, Lucanic); its dramatic genres include comedy, pageantry, morality, mystery, pastoral, tragedy, tragi-comedy; its lyric genres embrace apostrophe, aubade, ballad, blason, canzone, complaint, dirge, eclogue, epicede, epigram, epithalamium, hymn, idyll, lament, sonnet, and many more; while its discursive genres include examples of debate, dialogue, encomium and sermon. There are also mixed genres which heighten further this sense of generic multiplicity. We might conclude that *Paradise Lost* is therefore little more than a huge mausoleum of dead forms and dismiss it as impatiently as Dr Johnson dismissed the pastoral of 'Lycidas' as 'easy, vulgar and therefore disgusting' (by which, of course, Johnson meant tasteless). But we might then be guilty of flushing away the poetic baby with the tired generic bathwater. As Barbara Lewalski points out, if Milton constructs his epic 'from many literary genres and models devised in accordance with normative Renaissance models and critical precepts, he also invests those forms with an imaginative energy and profoundly transforms them'.[1]

One possible effect of this situation may be to create the feeling that the literature of this period, while it has an extremely tenacious relationship with the 'literary' and the 'artistic', has only a very tenuous relationship to life and to what is actually so. The Elizabethan love sonnet may stand as a notorious example of that sort of artifice, but new readers of *The Faerie Queene* or of 'Lycidas' or of *Paradise Lost* may feel, though for different reasons perhaps, similar misgivings. It may be difficult (and certainly risks pedagogic disappointment) to persuade readers embarking on this literature that an understanding of the *literary context* in which a writer is participating is a vitally necessary ingredient of understanding. And in any case most of us feel our own sense of inadequacy, our inability to become, in Milton's searching and even menacing phrase, that 'fit audience . . . though few'.[2] Yet it is unlikely that a Renaissance writer would have been able to conceive of any written work of the imagination *without* a literary context. When they do appear to conceive of such an untethered piece of free enterprise, like Thomas Nashe's *The Unfortunate Traveller* (1594), they may actually be following, as could be argued in Nashe's case, a sort of Rabelaisian convention of literary anarchy. What is interesting about Nashe is the way he loses his nerve and is as bewildered, apparently, as his reader about the exact nature of his artefact: 'All that in this fantastical treatise I can promise is some reasonable conveyance of history and variety of mirth.' He pleads that he was egged on by 'divers of my good friends . . . to employ my dull pen in this kind, it being a clean different vein from other my former course of writing'. And he adds: 'how well or ill I have done in it, I am ignorant' ('Dedication'). Nashe is ignorant partly because he does not know what 'kind' he is supposed to be writing in anyway.

It is perhaps equally hard to imagine a Renaissance writer making much sense of Wordsworth's defence of poetry as 'the spontaneous overflow of powerful feeling', partly because such a poet would not share the modern romantic notion that self-indulged emotion, or even self-expression, is itself good and valuable, and partly because he would want to know – would in fact be much more interested in knowing – whether this 'powerful feeling' was to be rendered as 'tragedy, comedy, history, pastoral, pastoral-comical, historical-pastoral, tragical-historical, tragical-comical-historical-pastoral, scene individable, or poem unlimited' (*Hamlet*, II. ii. 402–5). Of course, he might also, as in this example, find in this interest material for literary jokes.

Such jokes suggest that by no means all these writers are really Rule-besotted pedants incapable of putting pen to paper without disappearing into their libraries for a fortnight, or at the very least without, as Sidney's Astrophil puts it (with nice self-mockery) 'oft turning others' leaves' to see what has been done in the genre so far. And for our approaches to this literature as readers, there may be parallel misunderstandings. It is very hard to be told (as we sometimes are) that we cannot, for instance, pretend fully to understand any one of Milton's poems until we have mastered all those studies of Milton's life and thought and religious and intellectual background (not to mention as much as we can lay hands on of what Milton himself may have read), as though we too are obliged to disappear into our libraries for a decade or two before venturing a judgement or a response. The sensible answer surely is that we are never, in fact, going to be 'ready' to understand any major poem; we contemplate its imaginative structures as best we can and are critically alert to the sorts of questions the work itself generates. Awareness of complexity may often be more fruitful than the assumption of understanding that complexity. Nevertheless, the Rules are there, and to ignore them and their implications for the poet submitting himself to them is to cut ourselves off from significant sources of understanding. We may, for instance, be content to sit back and read *Paradise Lost* as if it were some sort of versified fantasy novel. But Milton's search for an 'answerable style' (answerable, that is, to the Renaissance concept of epic) is a wholly serious undertaking in which he pits himself against and re-invents the *genus grande* of the Virgilian epic. Unless we are able to take this seriously we may miss both the point of Milton's revisions of that genre (his own 'argument/ Not less but more Heroic') and also the fact that Milton's style is (paradoxically) at the same time answerable to 'Things unattempted yet in Prose or Rime', that is, to the new and unique poem that he forges out of the raw material of the conventions of the genre.

In other words, the pursuit of 'literary history' involves an understanding of how each author is continually rewriting and entering into dialogue with his or her predecessors. The process of interpreting such texts is therefore contingent upon the perception of generic relationships which involves an appreciation of the synchronic interaction of texts as well as their diachronic progression. Authors rewrite what has already been written, and every writing is a rewriting. Just as in reality we as readers do not experience 'stories' singly but read each new one in the context of what we have already read, so Renaissance texts (like all texts perhaps) are generated in and by the experience of other texts. Sometimes it may be by translation, like Marlowe's of Ovid's *Amores*; or by imitation and recasting, like the *theoxenia*, or entertainment of a god by a mortal, of Raphael's vegetarian dinner with Adam and Eve, redolent of the story of Baucis and Philemon in Ovid's *Metamorphoses*; or it may be by verbal allusion, such as Milton's echoes of the Sybil's words *hic opus, hic labor est (Aeneid*, VI, 129) in 'though hard and rare' (*PL* III, 21), 'Sad task and hard' (*PL* V, 564), 'Sad task, yet . . . ' (*PL* IX, 13); or it may be by a more pervasive 'influence', a sort of osmotic percolation of texts and themes. Some, like imitation or allusion, imply conscious authorial design and strategy; others simply give evidence of a habit of mind which while not actually seeking anonymity nevertheless renders terms like 'originality' and 'plagiarism' irrelevant or incoherent.

In this sense the studies offered here may be broadly called 'structuralist' – a term that invites some comment. It is a confusing portmanteau of a word, repository of all manner of different ideas and applications, which derives in the first place from modern linguistics and the 'structural anthropology' of Lévi-Strauss, though it is evident that mathematicians, logicians, physicists, biologists and social scientists as well as literary critics have long been concerned with structure and were practising 'structuralism' before the coming of Lévi-Strauss or Roland Barthes. (A structuralist argument is very apparent, as we shall see, in the Elizabethan critic George Puttenham.) Structuralism is based in the first instance on the assumption that there are underlying conventions which govern the production of meaning, whether of human actions or of spoken or written language. For example, a British observer watching a game of American football on television (or indeed anything else on television) is very aware that the production of meaning and of intelligibility is dependent on a set of institutional conventions.[3] Thus, there are symbolic structures or conventions of linguistics that allow a collection of sounds to be a grammatical or an ungrammatical sentence; similar social conventions make it possible to score a touchdown, to get married or divorced, to vote in an election, or to write, or read, a poem. As Lévi-Strauss put it: 'Particular actions of individuals are never symbolic in themselves; they are the elements out of which a symbolic system, which must be collective, is constructed.'[4]

Analogously, appreciation of the conventions which govern the production of meaning in a 'love sonnet' or a 'revenge tragedy' are a vital part of that artefact's intelligibility. In this relatively simple sense of 'structuralism' it is evident that literary genres and modes provide *in advance* the kind of conventional codes for which the investigative linguist or the anthropologist has to search, and which he has to isolate, reconstruct and explicate. (However, we should also be aware that the literary critical activity of persuasion to a point of view or an interpretation is itself equally subject to conventions, to a shared sense, for instance, of what is central and what peripheral, and to common notions about how one should read. The critic's efforts at plausibility or acceptance depend on an often merely intuited sense of the nature of literary competence.)[5]

Moreover, this habitual tendency of Renaissance authors to cross-reference with others, to advertise constantly their work's formal literary categories, to write persistently within generic norms, may seem to leave in some disarray that very activity which we – for all sorts of complex cultural reasons – would tend to value most, that is, our personal, individual responding to what is written: either it is difficult to produce a response, a judgement, which we may confidently feel is in fact a properly *informed* one; or this habitual authorial tendency may seem to suggest that such 'personal' responding is probably irrelevant anyhow – just as it may for the creative activity of imaginative writing itself. Both this reader-insecurity and the recognition of writers' apparent enslavement to modes and models can generate resistance in us.

English literary criticism of the Renaissance is not, in its theoretical pronouncements, helpful in weakening such resistance. Generally they are packed with rhetorical figures, ornaments, devices, the trappings of 'style' as end rather than means. George Gascoigne's influential *Certain Notes of Instruction* (1575) on English verse recommend that 'The rule of Invention . . . of all other rules is the most to be marked', by which he means the 'conceit' or the 'idea' of the poem, what makes it novel and different from the ordinary or the merely literal, but also what makes it noticeable in comparison with other poets' 'inventions'. Thomas Wilson's *The Art of Rhetoric* (1553, revised and enlarged 1560), a popular handbook, is concerned again with expression only as form, and shows, by stacked examples and three-piled hyperboles, a crabbed enthusiasm for euphuism as the highest mode of fine writing.

But perhaps in George Puttenham's anonymously printed *The Arte of English Poesie* (1589, though written earlier and much revised) there are signs of strained perceptions of other possibilities for poets than the mere acquisition of a comprehensive stylistic tool-box. Certainly, the bulk of Puttenham's *Arte* is concerned with 'Proportion' and 'Ornament', and he is confident and at ease in dispensing his ample examples to such a word- and figure-loving generation. But the alliance of rhetoric with poetry was gradually being dissolved as Puttenham wrote and revised: the appeal and usefulness of 'precedence' and 'decorum', 'places' and 'figures', to what the most creative poets were actually exploring was minimal:

> The rhetorical conception of style as a shot and patterned material *applied to* a subject gave way before another which is exemplified, rather than defined, in the poems of Donne and the mature plays of Shakespeare.[6]

It is easy enough to see in Polonius's entangling himself in figures and Gertrude's reprimand, 'More matter with less art', a literary slogan or manifesto. In looking at Sidney we shall see not just that such attitudes may be discerned much earlier than Donne and the mature Shakespeare (Sidney's criticism of 'Pindar's apes' who 'flaunt they in phrases fine,/Enamelling with pied flowers their thoughts of gold' (*Astrophil and Stella*, Sonnet 3) is in a sense a commonplace) but that the tension between form and artifice and ornament and the putative urgency of some genuine human communication is always there for the poet if not for the poetaster.

Even in Puttenham himself there is the sense that, for all his commitment to his definition of the poet – 'A Poet is as much to say a maker' (1, i) – there is more to being a poet than to being a carpenter or a shoemaker or a gardener. He may not get as far as Sidney in perceiving the potential independence and self-sufficiency of poetry, but he has an extraordinary passage on the imagination (1, viii), comes close, in speaking of love poetry, to the idea of poetry as expression (1, xxii), and in his peroration he wrestles with the final paradox of the relation between Art and Nature, venturing beyond the cliché of an art which disguises art. He offers some accounts of this relationship: in some respects art may be an 'aider' of nature, a 'surmounter', or 'a bare immitatour of natures works'; but finally

> in another respect arte is as it were an encountrer and contrary to nature, producing effects neither like hers, nor by participation with her operations, nor by imitation of her patternes, but makes things and produceth effects altogether strange and diverse, & of such forme & qualities (nature alwaies supplying stuffe) as she never would nor could have done of herselfe.

He cites the carpenter building a house, the tailor a garment, the smith a lock and key, ' in which case the workman gaineth reputation by his arte'. Similarly

> Man also in all his actions that be not altogether naturall, but are gotten by study & discipline or exercise, as to daunce by measures, to sing by note, to play on the lute, and such like, it is a praise to be said an artificiall dauncer, singer & player on instruments, because they be not exactly knowne and done, but by rules & precepts or teaching of schoolemasters.

These all sound like good analogies for the poet, but Puttenham then develops this argument in a way which, for an instant, threatens to topple his whole edifice of rhetorical instruction:

> But in such actions as be so naturall & proper to man, as he may become excellent therein without any arte or imitation at all, (custome and exercise excepted, which are requisite to every action not numbred among the vitall or animal) and wherein nature should seeme to do amisse, and man suffer reproch to be found destitute of them: in those to show himselfe rather artificiall then naturall, were no lesse to be laughed at, then for one that can see well enough, to use a paire of spectacles.

It is clear that 'the actions' 'so proper & naturall to man' he has in mind are our human capacities for language and discourse:

> But what else is language and utterance, and discourse & persuasion, and argument in man, then the vertues of a well constitute body and minde, little lesse naturall then his very sensuall actions, saving that the one is perfited by nature at once, the other not without exercise & iteration?

The absurd spectacles that you do not need, the ear-horn when
you are not deaf, the elegant 'paire of ennealed glooves', seem to
stand for all the arts and figures of rhetoric: but 'though it be
better to see with spectacles then not to see at all' we do not
always trust the vision of the man with spectacles, 'no
more . . . that which a Poet makes by arte and precepts rather
then by naturall instinct'.

Perceiving the damage that may be done to the arts of rhetoric
by his position, Puttenham quickly reassembles his argument,
seeks to align the poet once more with the carpenter, and rests in
the reasonable compromise of moderation and tact:

> Therefore shall our Poet receave prayse for both, but more
> by knowing of his arte then by unseasonable using it, and
> be more commended for his naturall eloquence then for his
> artificiall, and more for his artificiall well desembled, then
> for the same overmuch affected. (111, xxv)

In a sense there is little new in this tension between Art and
Nature, the artificial and the natural, precept and natural instinct.
The most perceptive poets, hovering as they were between the
demands of 'Perfection of the life or of the work', had always
known about it, though not perhaps the literary theorists. Much
earlier, Petrarch had complained how, as a grand old man of
letters, he was forced to respond to a new generation of would-be
poets working to rule-books. He resents all this literary activity (is
he fully serious?) and wishes the young would do something
productive instead:

> Our sons formerly employed themselves in preparing such
> papers as might be useful to themselves or their friends,
> relating to family affairs, business or the wordy din of the
> courts. Now we are all engaged in the same occupation, and
> it is literally true, as Horace says, 'learned or unlearned, we
> are all writing verses alike'.

He finds himself every day victim of 'letters and poems shower-
ing down upon my devoted head', 'overwhelmed by floods of
missives, no longer from France alone, but from Greece, from
Germany, from England', and he complains that 'I am unable to
judge even my own work, and yet am called upon to be the
universal critic of others'. But what is the truth about all this
versifying? Real poetry is only understood by the rarest geniuses,

and experience teaches that 'in no branch of art can mere indus-
try and application accomplish so little'. 'How delightful,' he
adds, perhaps with a hint of self-satisfaction, or of envy of the true
rising poets, 'how delightful must this gift be to those who really
possess it'.[7]

While we may be encouraged by Puttenham's moments of
clear-sightedness or by Petrarch's irritation (reflecting perhaps
our own), we should also be cautious of wishing to liberate the
best of these writers into incipient romantics or symbolists or beat
poets. For in a sense there was worse to come. The freedom
enjoyed by Elizabethan and Jacobean poets, despite the Gas-
coignes and Wilsons, the Harveys and Fraunces, was in retrospect
very considerable and very real. In the middle of the seventeenth
century French influences tightened around critical thinking and
the neo-classical precepts, based not on the actual practice of
great poets but on abstract theorising, became the *arbiter elegan-
tiarum*. Poetry was rigidly divided into distinct categories and
classes, each 'kind' with its own subject-matter, aim, effect and
style: the epic, tragedy, comedy; the elegy, ode, sonnet, epigram,
satire. Boileau, for instance, treats all of these (the latter forms
very briefly, for he is mainly concerned with epic, tragedy and
comedy), but Rapin excludes these secondary forms altogether
from great poetry, describing them loftily as 'a little kind of verses . . . that have often made much noise in the world' and desig-
nating them 'mere products of the imagination'.[8] The idea was
that true genius was conveniently provided with rigid moulds
into which poetic thoughts were to be poured.

However, it would be surprising if the most creative poets of
any age actually saw themselves as constantly enslaved by forms
and figures which obliged them, whenever they contemplated a
blank page, to commit themselves to a pre-ordained set of rules
which effectively extinguished their individuality. Horace's 'we
are all writing verses alike' could be the incentive to a little
constructive anarchy, a creative manipulation of *imitation, art,
method* and *invention*. However strong our own resistance to the
characteristic Renaissance use of 'genres' and 'kinds' may sometimes be, it may often turn out to be a resistance shared by the
imaginative writer himself, who may display and decorate the
generic wrapping only to reveal something quite different. For
instance, there is detectable a studied ambivalence of tone and
effect at the heart of Astrophil/Sidney's famous ' "Fool", said my

Muse to me, "look in thy heart and write" ' (*Astrophil and Stella*, 1). Who, we may wonder, is hoodwinking whom? Or we may feel confident enough about the verbal register struck by Shakespeare's 'When in disgrace with Fortune' (Sonnet 29) – though we might have been forewarned by his initial stroke of anarchy in addressing his sonnets to a young man. 'When in disgrace with Fortune' apparently means in sonnet-lover's language (and this is a love sonnet) rejected by a lady (as in Samuel Daniel's 'This is . . . her triumphs prize / To tread me down with foot of her disgrace, / Whilst I did build my fortune in her eyes' Sonnet 20), until, as the subsequent 'and men's eyes' (rather than a tautological 'and her eyes') indicates, we realise Shakespeare actually means having a run of bad luck in the real world. It is a surprise expressive of that sort of counterpointing with sonnet norms that goes on throughout the collection. Donne's disarming and self-demeaning 'I am two fools, I know, / For loving, and for saying so / In whining Poetry' ('The triple Fool') provocatively mocks both activities: loving, and writing about it. Marvell opens the verbal chess game of *An Horatian Ode* with a move so outrageous it can catch us napping at the start:

> The forward Youth that would appear
> Must now forsake his *Muses* dear,

inviting us to devalue and dismiss the very activity in which the author is engaged. George Herbert's sophisticated / naive (which is it?) advice in the final '*Copie out only that, and save expense*' of 'Jordan II', or Milton's brutal response to pastoral wish-fulfilment in 'Lycidas' ('for what good could that have done?'), like Hamlet's rejection of the conventional expressions of grief –

> These indeed seem,
> For they are the actions that a man might play,
> But I have that within which passes show
> (*Hamlet*, I. ii. 83–5)

– are evidence of a revisionary willingness to engage in rhetorics other than those of the genre. We notice, in other words, a characteristic gesture simultaneously combining 'spontaneous overflow of powerful feeling' with a toughly, or sometimes mischievously, critical self-consciousness that is ready to exhibit the generic possibilities of the chosen form and to display inventions, disingenuities and surprises, often producing a conventional utterance that is subtly in dialogue with its own conventions. But the relationship of the artist with his model (the 'sugred love sonnet' or the pastoral elegy) remains a crucial and vibrant contact, whether we call the products of the encounter 'self-consuming artefacts', or 'detonations', or merely ' conventions of anti-convention'.

The point here of course is that unless we know *what* the convention is that the poet is exploring, or exploiting, we are only half reading the poem. And it is this sense of the 'dialogue with convention' that is the concern of what follows: that is, the way in which a writer like Sidney, demonstrating and dramatizing in the medium of the love-sonnet, those inconvenient insights of a Puttenham, can confront that problematic interface between fiction and reality, or Art and Nature. Sidney highlights the crucial disjunction between something we can call 'human experience' and another, different activity which we call 'writing-about-human-experience'. And Sidney adds, in his *Defence of Poetry*, a poignant dimension of his own to the disjunction. The nature of the difference (though without Sidney's exemplifying *tableau vivant* of *Astrophil and Stella*) is embedded in Puttenham's brief chapter on 'the amorous affections': how, is the question Sidney poses, does one reconcile an assertion like Puttenham's 'The first founder of all good affections is honest love', and (since one is going to write about that affection in a notoriously dishonest medium) the assertion that 'it requireth a forme of Poesie variable, inconstant, affected, curious and most witty of any others'? (*The Arte of English Poesie*, 1, xxii).

An analogous question can of course be framed to meet the impulse to religious devotion and that other (or is it the same?) impulse to write devotional verse. It is not a literary accident or coincidence that Herbert's 'Jordan II' precisely echoes Sidney's *Astrophil and Stella* 1. The paradoxes of this situation may be crudely expressed in the formula that devotion is a form of self-negation, the writing of verses a form of self-advertisement. Thus George Herbert is optimistically uncertain about the provenance of his poems ('*Yet not mine neither: for from thee they came*', The Dedication to *The Temple*); he is acutely sensitive to the bustling devices of 'groveling wit'; in taking his farewell of 'sweet phrases, lovely metaphors' he is prepared to shrug his shoulders in a gesture of good riddance:

> Yet if you go, I passe not; take your way:
> For, *Thou art still my God*, is all that ye
> Perhaps with more embellishment can say
> ('The Forerunners')

and he is constantly counterpointing the literariness of his activity with the unliterariness of his experience:

> Now I am here, what thou wilt do with me
> None of my books will show.
> ('Affliction I')

A similar debate is movingly rendered in Marvell's 'The Coronet' fatally tainted with its 'wreaths of Fame and Interest'. But the example explored here is Donne's well known Holy Sonnet, 'Batter my heart' – a poem which has traditionally been seen as at least immune from those particular self-deprecating paradoxes and even as a positive orgy of self-advertisement. Yet beneath its surface of vividly rendered actual experience, apparently unmodified by overt 'literariness', a triumph of personal spontaneity over artifice, there are submerged metaphorical sub-texts dependent upon biblical and typological conventions which rigorously structure and articulate this rendered overflow of powerful feelings.

The analogy between authorial and reader activity implied or expressed so far – that is, the sense in which each of the parties to the literary transaction, the addresser and the addressee, is conditioned by conventional expectations; is writing, and reading, from a shared awareness of models and *exempla*, and where the trick may be for the author to lay out, and the reader to perceive, modifications, revisions and re-workings of conventional materials – is an analogy which stresses not only authorial competence and knowingness but also reader competence. The implications of this are interestingly reflected at both ends of the spectrum of current literary discourse, from the higher reaches of post-structuralist criticism to the new approaches to literary study being made by many school examining boards.

By using the term 'post-structuralism' I do not mean an abstract critique of the metaphysics of meaning nor an equally abstract theory of 'the text' (neither of which in the end are likely to be of much practical use to the critic of literature). I mean only to suggest that sort of literary criticism which holds a theoretical belief in textual semiotics as the key to meaning, which insists on the pure, unsettling play of significations in an open, unauthored and therefore unauthoritative text amenable to an infinity of unforeseeable meanings, and whose optative critical judgements respond to a work's generation of an indefinite number of senses, a plurality of possible readings. Italo Calvino's author, Silas Flannery, painfully and whimsically identifies the dilemma. He watches from behind his typewriter a distant woman in a deckchair reading a book – perhaps *his* book. He looks at her with a spyglass, then wonders what would happen if *she* were to train a spyglass on him while he writes:

> Readers are my vampires. I feel a throng of readers looking over my shoulder and seizing the words as they are set down on paper. I am unable to write if there is someone watching me: I feel that what I am writing does not belong to me any more.

Flannery senses his own redundancy and acquiesces in the dream of authorial anonymity: 'How well I would write if I were not here! . . . If I were only a hand, a severed hand that grasps a pen and writes'.[9] In this parable of post-structuralist perceptions Flannery seeks not only anonymity but dehumanization. Oddly, a Renaissance writer, poised at his writing desk and training an optick tube on a distant reader, would want to turn this whole formulation on its head. The throng of readers are not vampires but the necessary 'fit audience'; far from being unable, the author can *only* write when someone is watching him, nor could he feel that what he was writing did not belong to him because he never supposed that it did in the first place.

There may be perceived here (as with much recent literary-critical language) the bones of an old debate, an important part of which may be reduced to the notion of the 'author's intention'. Authorial intention, and with it authorial temporality and demarcation, is not part of that sort of 'open text' which lives on in the Barthian or Kermodian reader's unqualified creativity.[10] The drift of the studies that follow is in opposition to that aspect at least of post-structural thinking. When Silas Flannery complains that 'style, taste, individual philosophy, subjectivity, cultural background, real experience, psychology, talent, tricks of the trade: all the elements that make what I write recognisable as mine seem to me a cage that restricts my possibilities'[11], he is both expressing and accounting for a sense of abandonment, the death of the author and with it the extinction of any authorial authority – an extinction which he seems to welcome or, rather, to fantasise about. But what he is diagnosing can also be inverted: if we substitute 'what I read' for Flannery's 'what I write' we may be saying something equally pertinent. Yet we do not need to pretend (or have anybody else pretend) that we (or they) don't know of a particular work that it was, for instance, composed, like Milton's *Comus*, in the 'cage' of performance (on 29 September 1634); or of another work that it is the product of editorial patchwork; or of another that its author had a declared communicative intention. We do not either (to use the inevitable jargon) necessarily delight in a text's 'surplus of signifier over signified'. We may prefer to rest in the simple notions that a reader must try to learn the language and the cultural context of his or her text, and that every reading (even of a recent work) is more or less an act of translation. No one of course can prevent the reader or critic taking over from the author as the creator of meaning, though there is no reason why readers who report their personal experiences with a text should assume that others will be interested in their fragments of autobiography.

Although the critical language of post-structuralism has not yet made a significant appearance in the vocabulary of sixth-form students of literature, there are evident pedagogic pressures, reflected in the strategies of examining boards, designed to move students away from a relatively passive 'listening and writing' posture to one involving a more active, participatory role in which there is a strong emphasis on personal response. Coursework elements (rather than old-fashioned sit-down examination papers) encourage readers to choose what to read and how to write about it, and emphasis is placed on individual sensitivity and judgement. There is clearly much to welcome in such an emphasis and the change from fustian teaching methods it presumes; but there are also apparent in the polarities its debaters generate echoes of those rhetorical valuations which oppose 'ancient' to 'modern' 'closed book' to 'open text', 'limited answers' to 'infinite questions', 'dead' to 'alive', 'authority' to 'plurality'.[12] Another analogy may indeed be apparent here: instead of the 'authority' of an authorial and generically-based text is the 'authority' of the teacher or of received opinion, both of them ultimately set against, and even hostile to, individual perception and response.

In this confrontation may be discerned too elements of the polarity between 'the scholar' and 'the critic', both of whom may be in their several ways admired but only one of whom is to be emulated.

This emphasis upon 'independence of mind' may be supported by sophisticated ideologies:

> Independence of mind implies confronting the difficulties of epistemology, for there is no case for independence unless the ideal of freedom of thought can be accepted, and this in turn implies a conviction that knowledge is constructed by thought rather than revealed by authority.[13]

The quest involved here is one that seeks the emancipation of teachers and students from 'the instrumentality imposed by a conception of authoritative knowledge' and in which intellectual autonomy is opposed to intellectual authority.[14]

While some teachers may regret that in practice such tantalising images of independence are belied by didactic teaching, there is perhaps a cautionary tale to be read in the example of our contacts with the poetry, prose, and artistic forms of the Renaissance. For the 'ideal of freedom of thought' which 'implies a conviction that knowledge is constructed by thought rather than revealed by authority' is a rhetoric which omits to say that thought is about something, and that what that something is determines appropriate and relevant modes of thinking. The supposed 'freedom of thought' immediately encounters the necessary limitations imposed by the inherent demands of the item of knowledge or topic of thought. One might speculate on the possible meaning attributable to the phrase 'freedom of thought', or 'knowledge constructed by thought', in relation, for instance, to the proposition that two and two equal four, or that sulphuric acid is H_2SO_4, or that Machiavelli died in 1527, or that Milton's 'Lycidas' is a pastoral elegy. Nobody is free to think otherwise or to offer alternative constructions, though one may have to *understand* principles of numbers, or chemical relations, or literary categories. I can independently think about two and two as if they did not make four and I might mount an argument to demonstrate my independent thought, but I would be completely wrong. I may independently argue that Machiavelli did not die in 1527. Unless I can provide novel documentary evidence to confirm it, my item of knowledge constructed by thought is valueless. I might, similarly and independently, vouchsafe that 'Lycidas' is a comic poem.

Of course, if one were talking not about *thought* but about *feeling*, then one might be saying something. There might be an ideal of freedom of feeling (within the limitations of one's psychoneurological, socio-economic, racial, etc. make-up), though it would be difficult to see how such a freedom could actually be tampered with. What might be intended, then, is that such free feeling should be properly *valued* as a faculty of discrimination, judgement and insight. But the creation of an ambience in which inarticulated and visceral responses such as 'I like this', 'I don't like that', 'this moves me', 'this bores me' prevail, is hardly one of which we would want to say that we have produced 'pedagogies and resources that support growth of independence of mind.' Nor is it clear why such solipsistic judgements should be of any great interest to anyone else apart from the critic's relatives and friends. Oddly, part of our proper objective might turn out to be the *suppression* of independence of mind or of feeling in the interests of an appropriate dependence on the demands of the material. And it seems absurd that a teacher, or a literary critic, cannot find a proper role in attempting to elucidate this paradox.

Much of the 'work' in sixth-form, or university, or in any learning situation, is of this order: the acquisition of relevant information, the collection of data, the prior requirement (prior, that is, to acts of judgement) of a recognition of the nature of the material with which one is dealing and its peculiar properties. It would be misleading and also irrelevant to say of two and two equals four that it has been revealed by authority, that is, an authority over and above the authority of the principles of numbers. It might be equally misleading and irrelevant to say of the proposition, 'Swift's *A Modest Proposal* is a scathing satire' that it has been revealed by authority when it is a discoverable property of the work which is revealed by correct reading, just as the merging of two plus two into four is revealed by correct addition. Once we introduce the idea that there may be right or wrong, correct or incorrect, relevant or irrelevant, appropriate or inappropriate modes of thinking-about, then we have to be more rigorous about what we mean by 'independence of mind'. Perhaps the slogan could be rephrased more philosophically as 'knowledge is constructed by thought about what is revealed by the authority of the object of thought'.

Such a formulation still leaves ample room for free individual critical enterprise, just as the neo-classical moulds or norms into which creative genius was to be poured were (theoretically at least) capable of sustaining originality and individuality. Not that what follows makes any claims to critical originality: its questions, on the whole, are those which simply ask what we can know about, or see in, the text offered which is revealed by the authorial–authority of the texts. And most often this knowledge is dependent on consideration of the generic norms, or conventions, that are implied in the chosen forms of discourse. Thus the account of Sidney's *Astrophil and Stella* turns on the paradox of the author's decision to write in the mould of the sonnet sequence and to call himself both 'Astrophil' and 'I', as if to conceal himself or to pretend that 'I am not I' (Sonnet 45), while by the very fact of writing 'I' the author is driven to put into this 'I' something of himself, of what he feels or imagines he feels. And just as the image of the writer in the text acts as a double for the real writer, partly disclosing, partly concealing his life and thoughts, so the image of the reader is also present in the text – partly constructed *by* it, partly fictive and partly actual, and very often interacting ironically with real live historical readers, whether sixteenth-century courtly wits and gossips or a modern Flannery/Sidney young woman reader sitting in a deckchair. The question that emerges is not so much, what does this text mean? but rather, what does Sidney say, or imply, about some of the things that it *might* mean, and particularly for the activity of writing sonnet-poetry itself?

The account of Donne, limited to two or three poems, is offered partly as a counter to the view that this author is one whose authorial 'I' is more or less transparently illustrative (despite his dramatic stances) of what the writer feels and thinks, or imagines he feels and thinks, or would like to feel and think. Donne is the sort of writer who attracts attention, a *personality*, no anonymous presence against an anonymous background. While certainly not claiming for him a self-effacing submersion in genres and imitative exercises, I would claim for him more purely *literary* sophistication and playfulness than has frequently been accorded him. Much of this receives correction in Arthur F. Marotti's recent book on Donne, *John Donne, Coterie Poet* (1986), a socio-literary study of the cultural environments which generate the poetry and into which it is projected. 'All the basic features of Donne's poetic art,' Marotti argues, 'are related to its coterie character.'

Donne's compulsive literary 'performances' expect a sceptical agility and connoisseurship in his best readers, as in his best friends, for Donne was 'obviously most comfortable when he knew his readers personally and they knew him.'[15] And together with knowledge of his readership, allowing that unbuttoning expansiveness, that drollery and even slyness, go assumptions about what that readership would already know and have read and what they would expect to hear.

The studies on Milton seem to suggest a change of direction, as though they are addressing a different set of questions from those of the earlier chapters. In a sense they are, since Milton does not on the whole project himself as an authorial enigma, nor (which regrettably cannot be said of many of his current critics) does he habitually wink knowingly at an assembled audience of friends and cronies. On the contrary, he addresses Christian Humanist European society at large and is autobiographically present as the heroic poet or seer wearing his bardic robes. The emphasis, however, is still on genre or conventions of discourse, and recent Milton criticism seems increasingly aware of the extent to which Milton manipulates, and often breaks, generic boundaries.[16] Since Milton's sense of generic distinctions was unusually strong and well-informed, his 'games' with genre are especially conscious. What, for example, is the man we know as the puritan-republican poet-prophet doing in Ludlow putting on a masque in celebration of the aristocracy? Among the essays that follow one, picking up a phrase of Milton's own in 'Il Penseroso', is concerned with the question of 'right spelling' not only of the 'text' but of the occasion, the setting, the participants, the audience, the medium of *A Masque presented at Ludlow Castle*, just as it does in a different way with the 'spelling' of the Companion Poems, 'L'Allegro' and 'Il Penseroso'. At the same time there is plenty of speculative kite-flying (some readers may think far too much). Yet it is hoped that speculations are derived from a perceptible Miltonic dialogue between the conventions of the genre of aristocratic entertainment and the demands of Milton's own emergent reforming instincts, or, in the case of the Companion Poems, his conversation with the pagan and hermetic material of those poems and their relation to the 'conventions' of Christian dogma.

Paradise Lost is of course a poem energetically and committedly participating in the genre of Heroic Poem, which Dryden described as 'undoubtedly the greatest work which the soul of man is capable to perform'. And Dryden insists on conformity in such poems to epic norms: 'even the least portions of them must be of the epic kind: all things must be grave, majestical, and sublime' (Dryden, *Dedication of the Aeneis*, 1697). Among the generic conventions of the form is that of epic similes, and Chapter 6 on Milton's similes explores Milton's complication and subversion of those conventions. This complication may be perceived as part of his larger strategy of subverting the values embodied in the epic model itself, as the recurrent confrontations between 'epic' and 'pastoral' modes of discourse and valuation in *Paradise Lost* seem to suggest.

Chapter 8 deliberately extends the idea of 'convention' to try to say something about Milton's handling of our more intractably conventional notions of 'time' and 'history'. One great span of Milton's architecture in *Paradise Lost* holds in its curve the rise and fall of epic; another span has its foundations in a more diffusely located area of *myth*, a form of narrative discourse which simultaneously denies sequential narrative, which has no 'beginning' and 'end', and which, while using time, obliterates time. And somewhere beneath this span in enacted a human drama of disobedience whose intelligibility seems crucially dependent on temporal notions of cause and effect, choice and sequence, acts of determination and responsibility, and which is yet overlooked, as it were, by a being who is outside time. This means, in effect, yet another nagging at the theological and philosophical conundrums which are trussed up in Milton's epic of the Fall of man, though I hope to show, through consideration of the nature of the debate in which Milton is participating and of the distinctively poetic and artistic strategies he employs, both the intellectual and poetic response of his poem to the deep puzzles it so freely exhibits.

These discussions of topics and texts, culled apparently at random here from the vast and rich poetry of the period 1580 to 1667, undoubtedly have a strong air of indulgence about them. I am not about to defend myself from the charge that I have merely written about the this or that which interests me, since every author might want to preserve that right. Nor would I suggest some false thread or sophistical principle of coherence knitting these studies together in an approved consecutive manner. Nevertheless, in the spark of whatever it was that made these topics and not some others interest me enough to want to write about them is detectable a principle of sorts; and that is, a concern

with the fascinating truism that the recognition of literary conventionality, whether of form, mannerism, or attribute, strikes us
simultaneously with recognition of an authorial voice. Thus our
question is not only what is the voice saying, but why is it saying
it like this? To ask such questions of a Mozart aria or a Wagner
duet is to open up the history, conventions and functions of the
distinctive form of 'opera', yet the task may be little different
when the voice is saying 'I can love both fair and brown', or 'I
think it mercy, if thou wilt forget', or 'Within the navil of this
hideous Wood/Immur'd in shades a Sorceror dwels', or 'Necessitie and Chance/Approach not mee, and what I will is Fate'.

NOTES

1. Barbara K. Lewalski, *Paradise Lost and the Rhetoric of Literary Forms*,
   Princeton: Princeton University Press, 1985, pp. 16–17.
2. *PL* VII, 31. Milton's phrase should not perhaps be taken too literally:
   the gesture he is making is in fact a commonplace (like the dedication of Donne's *Poems* of 1633 to 'The Understander') which is
   actually encouraging and whose exclusivity is complimentary.
3. See Roland Barthes's fascinating discussion of the differences between boxing and wrestling and their different cultural conventions,
   Mythologies, 2nd edn, Paris: Seuil, 1970, pp. 13–24.
4. Lévi-Strauss, 'Introduction á l'oeuvre de Marcel Mauss', *Sociologie et
   Anthropologie*, Paris: PUF, 1950, p. xvi.
5. See Jonathan Culler, 'The Linguistic Basis of Structuralism', in
   Structuralism: An Introduction, ed. David Robey, Oxford: Clarendon
   Press, 1973; also Culler's *Structuralist Poetics*, London: Routledge,
   1975.
6. Introduction to Puttenham's *The Arte of English Poesie*, ed. G.D.
   Willcock and A. Walker, Cambridge: Cambridge University Press,
   1936, p. lxxxiii.
7. *Petrarch, The First Modern Scholar and Man of Letters*, ed. J.H. Robinson and H.W. Wolfe, New York and London: Puttnam, 1898.
8. Quoted in *English Literary Criticism: 17th and 18th Centuries*, J.W.H.
   Atkins, London: Methuen, 1951, repr. 1968, p. 12.
9. Italo Calvino, *If on a Winter's Night a Traveller*, trans. William Weaver,
   London: Picador, 1982, p. 135.
10. See, for example, the theoretical assumptions of Frank Kermode's
    The Classic (the T. S. Eliot Memorial Lectures), London: Faber,
    1975, in which the figures of Barthes and Derrida eclipse that of
    Eliot. The debate on authorial intention is pursued in E. D. Hirsch,
    Validity in Interpretation, New Haven: Yale University Press, 1967,
    and *On Literary Intention*, ed. David Newton-De Molina, Edinburgh:
    Edinburgh University Press, 1976.

11. Calvino, *If on a Winter's Night a Traveller*, p. 135.
12. These polarities have been picked from the argumentative thread of Frank Kermode's *The Classic*.
13. 'Academic sixth-form courses, the library, and perspectives on independent study: a report on a project', by David Hopkins and Jean Rudduck, *Educational Research*, 26, 2, June 1984.
14. See, for instance, Lawrence Stenhouse, *Authority, Education and Emancipation*, London: Heinemann, 1983. Even the Committee of Vice-Chancellors and Principals is capable, in describing the general aims of the new GCSE examination, of the self-defeating ambition that 'the application of knowledge should take precedence over the acquisition of knowledge', Annex to Note N87/47, 'Access and University Courses', 21 May 1987.
15. Arthur F. Marotti, *John Donne, Coterie Poet*, Madison and London: University of Wisconsin Press, 1986, introduction.
16. New books and articles are constantly appearing on Milton. Among those which highlight generic approaches, Barbara K. Lewalski's *Paradise Lost and the Rhetoric of Literary Forms*, noted earlier, is seminal. *Composite Orders: the Genres of Milton's Last Poems*, ed. Richard S. Ide and Joseph Wittreich, (*Milton Studies*, 17), Pittsburgh: University of Pittsburgh Press, 1983, is a collection of original essays particularly on biblical genre-expectations in Milton's texts, and on the way in which Renaissance genres, especially drama, provide interpretative contexts. Claes Schaar's difficult and learned *The Full Voic'd Quire Below: Vertical Context Systems in Paradise Lost*, Lund Studies in English 60, Lund: Gleerup, 1982, is a useful compendium of possible sources, parallels, generic analogues and allusions. Two very recent books emphasise genre: Charles Martindale's wholly delightful *John Milton and the Transformation of Ancient Epic*, Beckenham: Croom Helm, 1986, and Christopher Kendrick's undelightful *Milton: A Study in Ideology and Form*, London and New York: Methuen, 1986, whose Marxist machinery creaks obliquely through a generic approach to *Paradise Lost* as the epic of emergent capitalism, and whose Babylonish dialect ('There is . . . what we might term a systematic theological homogenization of epic gestures in *Paradise Lost* effected at a distance by the ontological–representational space of its hexameral content') is frequently impenetrable.

1

CONVENTIONS OF ART
Sidney and the idea of the sonnet

> Every poem is in a sense a kiss bestowed
> upon the world, but mere kisses do not pro-
> duce children.
> Goethe, conversation with Ortlepp, 1825

The 'love sonnet' is a profoundly and teasingly paradoxical form, for it is at the same time the most personal and confessional of modes and the most heavily encrusted with, and indebted to, conventions. Every poet who attempts it (and there were aspiring poets by the dozen in the latter years of the sixteenth century who attempted it, frequently knocking up centuries or more) seems forced either to acquiesce in its inherited conventions or to struggle against the carapace and reform it.

The sonnet itself is, too, a technically taxing form, a metrical and verbal carapace, and it is salutary when reading (and perhaps wilting under the attrition of) successive sonnets to take time to try writing a sonnet oneself. It may not then be so surprising that some sonneteers, like the feeble *Sonnets to Coelia* by William Percy, 1594, or the extraordinarily inept and mercifully anonymous *Zepheria*:

> When I emprised, though in my love's affections,
> The silver lustre of thy brow to unmask,
> Though hath my muse hyperbolised trajections,
> Yet stands it, aye, deficient to such task

seem relieved merely to have sorted out some rhymes and to have closed the thing up with a semblance of decency. The important point here is that the sonnet, in English, is a verbal artefact requiring considerable skill and is consequently, whatever its appearance or relaxation or spontaneity, always in a state of tension: it is, as of a musical instrument, highly strung. In this important respect (important because its tension of form is part of its meaning, in its efforts, for instance, to find the word 'fit' not only to convey 'meaning' but to fulfil the technical obligations; its formalized, frequently antithetical *structuring* of the moment to be recorded; its destination in some kind off closure) the English sonnet is quite unlike its Italian forebears. Petrarch does not have to search for rhymes, or forge quatrains out of resolutely intractable material, for rhymes are native to the language he is using; so much so that Dante can spin off chains of *terza rima* throughout the *Divina Commedia* without especially drawing attention to this as a feat of extraordinary difficulty – one might compare the difference between Dante here and the density of Spenser's elaborate stanzas multiplying themselves through *The Faerie Queene.*

The sonnet form not only draws attention to its character as a verbal artefact, a thing made, constructed against the odds. Its fashionable and inevitable cultivation by poets wishing to explore the pains and joys of the experience of human love also draws attention to, and confirms, its public and 'artificial' nature. It is quite possible to put this last point the other way about: that poets, in their desire to explore and write about love, may be directed into the discursive playground laid out by Petrarchanism and hence organised into writing sonnets; or they may wish simply to write sonnets, and hence find themselves necessarily writing about love. Or, of course, they may wish to do both at the same time.

Some implications of this possibly trite observation may be drawn out by asking of the Sidneyan or Spenserian or Shakespearean sonnet such deceptively simple questions as: why did the poet write it? what does he think it is for? who is he talking to? who is supposed to be listening? or reading? It is not necessary, in considering the first of these questions, for us to become involved in intentional fallacies, or in the fallacies of the intentional fallacy, since the poets themselves provide a rich fund of motives and reasons for writing the poems and quite deliberately draw attention to the necessity of asking those sorts of questions. As Sidney asks, 'Doubt you to whom my Muse these notes entendeth?'[1] And the answers that they generate to service these doubts can be extraordinarily complex.

Sidney's *Astrophil and Stella* sequence was first printed by Thomas Newman in 1591, in a very corrupt text, five years after its author's death. But the sonnets circulated earlier in more than one manuscript, and from one of these Newman got the copy for his piratical edition (including the form 'Astrophel' for 'Astrophil'). Some of the sonnets may have been written before 1581, and Sidney may have expanded, and certainly revised, the sequence after his marriage in September 1583. *Astrophil and Stella* is the first real sonnet sequence in English. Thomas Watson had published his *Hekatompathia or Passionate Centurie of Love* in 1582, mostly translations from Italian sonnets, and John Soowthern published thirteen clumsy and worthless Ronsardian sonnets in his *Pandora*, 1584. It was undoubtedly Sidney who started the sonneteering craze, though it is interesting to note that Newman's edition of *Astrophil* included twenty eight sonnets by Samuel Daniel, who published his *Delia* the year following the Newman edition. Sidney's close friend Fulke Greville wrote some of his *Coelica* probably at the same time that Sidney was writing *Astrophil*; and another friend, Spenser, may well have written some of his *Amoretti* years before its printing in 1595. The earliest practitioners of the form were connected with Sidney and his circle: Daniel was a protégé of the Countess of Pembroke, Sidney's sister; and Henry Constable may well have seen *Astrophil and Stella* in manuscript, certainly knew Sidney himself, and also addressed a sonnet to Lady Rich. Thus there is clear evidence of a coterie of writers, both mutually encouraging and critically competitive, providing material for one kind of answer to the questions why they wrote their sonnets and whom they were addressing.

Focus upon this dimension of the poetry produced will emphasise the role of the reader: 'each reader brings his or her preconceptions, aesthetic and socio-cultural, to bear on the poems'; and the most important readers and audiences of the poems are 'the ones unnamed', that is, their contemporary courtly readers within whose aesthetic and socio-cultural ambit the sonnets are generated (and of course ourselves, the poems' future readers throughout history). Like texts for performance, the poems are circulated in manuscript, both springing from and inhabiting the world of their audience, and dependent for their full meaning upon interaction with that audience.[2]

Material for another kind of answer is of course provided, in Sidney's case, by the fact that in 1581 Penelope Devereux, the Earl of Essex's daughter, married Lord Rich. Six years before, in 1575, a match had been proposed between Sidney and Penelope Devereux, but came to nothing – as did the proposed match in

1577 with William of Orange's sister. Sidney, it would seem, fell in love with Penelope only when she was out of reach; the snarling Sonnet 24 ('Rich fooles there be') shadows the marriage that ended his hopes. Or, to put the matter another way, Sidney writes, via a screen of indirections and distances, of Lady Rich (how could she not be flattered by the compliment?) because he wishes to anatomise and render 'actual' the humiliations and excitements of unrequited passion, drawing on the stock of literary *topoi* that have accumulated around that familiar position of the sonneteer-in-love. The way of putting it is crucial. In the first we read the sequence as the outpouring of personal emotion, subjected to and restrained only by the disciplines of the medium; in the second we respond to the nature of the medium and what Sidney is doing with it.

In the Elizabethan hierarchy of poetic genres the sonnet is the 'personal kind', in which sort of verse the poet was expected to speak in *propria persona*. But we are often reminded that we should not take that too literally, no more than we should take Ovid's Corinna or Petrarch's Laura too literally. Poets would seem to respond to this invitation as though to an *exercise* in first-person writing. Thus J. W. Lever can remind us of the normality of this (as it were) deception by pointing to Spenser's *Amoretti* 86–89 and their basis in some actual occurrence in Spenser's life which, if true, 'would certainly mean a departure from his usual practice and a break with the classical conception of poetry as a public offering rather than an outlet for private emotion'.[3] Most often we are advised, in order to lay the biographical ghosts, to take to heart Milton's sensible sort of advice in the fifth chapter of his *A Defence of the English People*:

> But you must know . . . that one is not to regard what the poet says, but what the person in the play speaks, and what that person says; for different persons are introduced, sometimes good, sometimes bad; sometimes wise men, sometimes fools; and such words as are put into their mouths, as it is most proper for them to speak; not such as the poet would speak, if he were to speak in his own person.

Milton is talking specifically about drama, but his point is relevant to all kinds of fictional or 'dramatic' writing, even, as it had been practised, the 'personal kind' of the love sonnet. It is impossible to miss, in *Astrophil and Stella*, the piquant relationship

between the incompetent and confused Astrophil, biting his pen
and beating himself with frustration, and Sidney the literary the-
orist showing him how to do it and elegantly turning out those
paradoxically witty sonnets about the impossibility of writing sonnets. In other words, it is an important ingredient of our response
to what Sidney is doing that we should understand the *difference*
between Sidney and Astrophil. But we may feel that this situation
of poetic self-denial, or of personal detachment, cannot be the
whole story.

Sidney's stance in *Astrophil and Stella* appears to be one of
directness and spontaneity. The poems stand as the intimate
record of a man known personally to hundreds, probably, and
admired by a whole nation. He continually proclaims the sincerity
of his passion as well as the inspired originality of his verse. But is
he really wearing his heart on his sleeve? This is not, of course,
generally thought of as either a fashionable or a useful question to
ask, as though the framing of the question itself betrays a fatal
critical naïvety. The standard answer would seem to be that Astrophil no more reveals Sidney's heart than Hamlet does Shakespeare's. But, as Sidney's biographers and editors have all noted,
Sidney himself certainly so arranges things in *Astrophil and Stella*
that it is possible to think that question a good one. There is, for
instance, the steady infiltration of circumstantial, factual biographical and autobiographical material into the romance world of
Astrophil and Stella: that Sidney intended to represent himself and
Penelope is apparent from reference to his coat of arms (Sonnet
65), the Devereux coat of arms (Sonnet 13), the puns on his own
name, the vicious wordplay on the word 'rich', and so on.

Responses to the existence in the poems of autobiographical
material are various. William Ringler, in his edition of Sidney's
poetry, draws attention to how much Sidney *omits* of his real
interests and activities and how 'everything in his experience
during those months which did not directly relate to his central
theme' (that is, his relations with Stella) 'he ruthlessly ex-
cluded'.[4] Views may polarise in interestingly incompatible ways.
One will simply pretend that there isn't any autobiographical
material and assert that 'Sidney was thinking of no particular
woman at all . . . Stella merely represented the platonic ideal of
love, courtliness and beauty – a symbol of the Renaissance poetic
idea of perfection.[5] Another will accuse Sidney of an impure, self-
regarding rhetoric whose sole and single-minded purpose is the

seduction of Penelope Devereux.[6] Each of these views seems to me equally wrong, for what Sidney is involved in is far more complex than either allows. Similarly, the view that the principal *reader* of these poems is not an historical or ideal audience but only Penelope Devereux Rich, is in danger of turning the poems into enigmatically coded but ultimately impenetrable exchanges between two courtly and politic lovers.[7] Sidney's procedure, at various moments or in individual sonnets, may be adequately described by recourse to a straightforward biographical decoding of his 'I'; and other times and places it may be a purely fictive and dramatic 'I'; at others, a purely formalist persona, mask, synechdoche or emblematic figuration. Such varieties and combinations of converging and distancing, authenticating and fictionalizing, devices create interactions in which identities are both revealed and veiled, in which an actual human story, embedded in a matrix of social and political restraints, is rendered in a discourse of fictional poetry which is itself embedded in its own matrix of artistic conventions. It is partly our inability to know or to decide at what point fiction 'becomes' fact, or fact 'becomes' fiction that makes these poems so successfully strenuous in their engagement with the mysterious issue of the relationship beween art and life. Not least among the effects of the autobiographical documentations in the poems is the way in which Sidney, participating in the art world of Petrarchan love poetry, involves both his poet (Astrophil) and his readers in an awareness of a surrounding and impinging world of the conditional and the problematic. His territory is both the landscape of the 'heroick mind' with its golden images *and* the circumstantial world of Philip Sidney. Sidney's original audience would clearly have felt this continual pressure in the poems of 'real' people and 'real' events; they would be aware too, as it seems to me Sidney intends, that the 'purpose' of *Astrophil and Stella* (the winning of Stella) cannot be fulfilled in the realms of art but only in personal and social life.

William Ringler's conclusion is that in Sidney's case art wins out over life – or, rather, that 'though the substance of his poem was autobiographical, mere fact was made subservient to the requirements of art'.[8] One of the things I wish to do here is to question this formulation, and even to turn it on its head, by arguing that Sidney shows an acute and often damaging awareness (damaging, that is, to the clarity and status of his poetic figurations) that 'mere fact' will not always be so easily subservient, and that art may ultimately be subservient to 'mere fact'. But first we should look at some instance of Sidney's commerce between the two realms.

A good example of convergence between the persona Astrophil and author Sidney occurs in Sonnet 83 ('To a Sparrow'), for the punning 'Good brother Philip' (sparrows being traditionally called Philip or Pip or Phip) advertizes its author. It also of course refers to Astrophil – but not to a character called Astrophel, which was the spelling used by Newman and the 1598 printing of the poems at the end of the Folio of the *Arcadia* apparently under the supervision of the Countess of Pembroke. In his Oxford text of the poems, Ringler spells it Astrophil – star-lover – and rightly points out that the form 'Astrophel' makes no sense. Why then does the form occur in so many versions? Is it part of the game of now-you-see-me, now-you-don't? However, our route to the conclusion that Sidney is here obviously abandoning the persona mask is rendered hesitant by the recognition that the poem is a very literary piece indeed, related to Skelton's witty *Philip Sparrow* and deriving ultimately from Lesbia's sparrow in Catullus. It is an example of a figure used by many sonneteers: the poem of sexual envy at the freedom enjoyed by the lady's pet, and may even be detected, in a neat variation, in Shakespeare's multiple parody, Sonnet 128, where the envied keyboard jacks kiss 'the tender inward of thy hand' as the lady plays the virginals. Sidney is doing two things at the same time: he is asserting the 'actuality' of the moment ('Good brother Philip' – that's me of course, or I wish it were) and also the literary fictionality of the moment.

Sometimes the coincidence of Sidney and Astrophil may be very deliberately provocative. Most readers have felt the shock and incomprehension of stumbling upon Sonnet 30 after experiencing, with reasonable security, the manoeuvres of the first twenty nine sonnets. In them Sidney had laid out his programme of Astrophil's confessional, his passion for and praises of Stella, his wrestles with language and with finding his own authentic voice, just beginning to modulate into an awareness that his friends are watching him and shaking their heads ('The curious wits, seeing dull pensiveness / Bewray it selfe in my long setled eyes', Sonnet 23), the whole movement interlarded with commentary on the literary activity of the writing of sonnets themselves, eschewing 'enamelling', classical bordering, 'poore

Petrarch's long deceased woes', the 'Dictionarie's methode' of rhyming, 'sugred sentences', 'allegorie's curious frame', and so on. And then Sidney offers us this, engineering the inevitable puzzled response:

> Whether the Turkish new-moone minded be
>> To fill his hornes this yeare on Christian coast;
>> How *Pole's* right king meanes, without leave of hoast,
> To warme with ill-made fire cold *Moscovy;*
> If French can yet three parts in one agree;
>> What now the Dutch in their full diets boast;
>> How *Holland* hearts, now so good townes be lost,
> Trust in the shade of pleasing *Orange* tree;
>> How *Ulster* likes of that same golden bit
> Wherewith my father once made it halfe tame;
> If in the Scottishe Court be weltring yet;
> These questions busie wits to me do frame;
>> I, cumbred with good maners, answer do,
> But know not how, for still I thinke of you.

Sidney leaves us with the puzzle for thirteen and a half lines. The answer to our question, what is it all about? is quite simple, and also surprising, and surprisingly disruptive. It is about the 'real' world, existing outside and independent of the literary world in which sonnets are written. Its material is drawn from the day's current affairs and news bulletins: foreign affairs, politics and diplomacy. Its issues are, I take it, all, in that useful French word, *actualités*. The events mentioned in the sonnet are used by Sidney's editors and biographers to assign a date to the composition of *Astrophil and Stella* – the summer of 1582. We note the ironic wordplay of 'If French can yet three parts in one agree (*Omnia Gallia in tres partes divisa est*) and, crucially, we notice the lines

> How *Ulster* likes of that same golden bit
> Wherewith my father once made it halfe tame.

Whose father? Here Sidney, pushing aside the fictions of Astrophil/Stella, steps out as himself. His father was Lord Deputy of Ireland and we know Sidney accompanied him to Ireland on at least one occasion.

It is possible, of course, to account for what Sidney is doing here in terms of verisimilitude. The problem then identified is how to be convincing in a mode in which personal evasiveness is in fact, despite its formal denial, *de rigeur*. Thus it may be suggested that Sidney is making his fictional characters more lively, more life-like (and following too the example of Petrarch) by giving them real identities – that is, identities in the world outside the enclosures of sonnet-writing. To support this idea we may turn to Sidney's *Defence of Poetry* (printed 1595 but written over ten years earlier) in which Sidney, very sensitive to the merely eloquent and (in Holden Caulfield's word) 'phoney' complains that

> truly many of such writings as come under the banner of unresistible love, if I were a mistress, would never persuade me they were in love: so coldly they apply fiery speeches, as men that had rather read lovers' writings . . . than that in truth they feel those passions.

Sidney, then, is using his device of naming to help persuade with circumstantial detail. After all, he argues elsewhere in the *Defence*, you have to call your fictional characters *something*: just as the generic names John-a-stiles and John-a-nokes are used by lawyers in hypothetical legal cases, so in the hypotheses of fiction: 'Their naming of men is but to make their picture the more lively, and not to build any history: painting men, they cannot leave men nameless'.[9]

In order to pursue the implications of this argument we should stay with Sidney's *Defence*. In his remarks on the inauthenticity of current love lyricists he says that they behave like men who 'had rather read lovers' writings' than men who 'in truth . . . feel those passions'. Although his point seems to be that you need to feel those passions before you can write about them, not merely crib them from other people, Sidney's argument also drives a wedge between *writing* and *feeling* 'in truth' yet implies that the distinction should not exist, neither really nor apparently. In the second quotation he is asserting that the naming of names is not in order to 'build any history' (it is not, then, 'real') but only a necessity of art, of 'painting men', a function of the art of writing convincing fiction, so that it *looks* like real life though it is not.

And yet we all know perfectly well that there is in this context the greatest difference in the world between 'writing' and 'feeling', between 'story' or fiction and 'history' or fact. Sidney knows it too – indeed, his Astrophil complains bitterly of Stella's all too

human propensity for preferring feeling-that-is-written-about to
feeling in reality – preferring in the sense of being moved to tears
at a *story* of unhappy love, while unable (or unwilling) to be
moved by the real unhappy love right under her nose:

> *Stella* oft sees the verie face of wo
>   Painted in my beclowded stormie face:
>   But cannot skill to pitie my disgrace,
> Not though thereof the cause her selfe she know:
> Yet hearing late a fable, which did show
>   Of Lovers never knowne, a grievous case,
>   Pitie thereof gate in her breast such place
> That, from that sea deriv'd, teares' spring did flow.
>   Alas, if Fancy drawne by imag'd things,
> Though false, yet with free scope more grace doth breed
> Then servant's wracke, where new doubt honor brings;
> Then thinke my deare, that you in me do reed
>   Of Lover's ruine some sad Tragedie:
>   I am not I, pitie the tale of me.

(Sonnet 45)

We may easily sympathise with Astrophil's sense of frustration. It
was, after all, a mere 'fable' about 'Lovers never knowne'; the
pictures the imagination drew were 'false' (that is, fictional, not
real). Part of the bafflement too is derived from incompatibility,
as of a torturer operating to the strains of Mozart: how is it possible for Stella not to perceive the inauthenticity, even hypocrisy,
of her response ('Not though thereof the cause her selfe she
know')? Astrophil's final recommendation is not, however, to resist but to enter into the complicity: if stories make you weep,
pretend that you and I are a story; pretend I am not I; 'pitie the
tale of me'. Perhaps if I fictionalise myself I may get somewhere.

Of course, there is more to it than this. Part of Sidney's 'joke'
involves the witty allusion to Aristotle's concept of catharsis, a
joke which has Astrophil begging Stella to turn him into a tale so
that she can be appropriately moved. And exactly what might be
meant here (reductively decoding the Petrarchan language of
'pitie' and 'grace') is outrageously exhibited by the possibility
Sidney makes so conspicuously available of the double sense of
'pitie' and the sexual pun upon 'tale'. Nor should we forget, in
our 'delight' at the complexity of ironies Sidney deploys, that
Sidney himself (that unstable and elusive 'I' of the sequence) is

already fictionalized in the persona of Astrophil (except when he is not). So that, as in series of Chinese boxes, a fictional character complains to a fictional Stella of the peculiar and inconvenient power of fictions, of 'imag'd things, / Though false', to move and breed grace. And yet the 'servant's wracke', and his 'painted' (depicted) 'face of wo', are fictions too; and the tale which he asks to be pitied is itself, already, a tale.

This device of the 'double-take' is perhaps most familiar in drama – as in the playing of women's parts by boys who are playing women being boys; in Fabian's comical 'If this were played upon a stage now, I could condemn it as an improbable fiction' (*Twelfth Night*, III.iv.131–2); in that extraordinary moment when the actor playing Macbeth is fleetingly exposed as merely himself, the 'poor player / That struts and frets his hour upon the stage'; in the device of the play within the play; or in the densely pervasive theatrical self-reference of *Hamlet* where, in an effect curiously like Sidney's Sonnet 45, Hamlet responds to the player's reaction to Hecuba, a player who 'But in a fiction, in a dream of passion' can be so moved to distress, 'and all for nothing! / For Hecuba! / What's Hecuba to him, or he to Hecuba, / That he should weep for her?' (*Hamlet*, II.ii.555–63). The irony of what Hamlet says is dependent on, and reinforces, our sense of the real-life situation in which Hamlet is able to do nothing, so that it is quite possible to say, as Anne Barton says in her subtly perceptive introduction to the play, that it is 'only natural, when he finds himself swept against his will into a real-life revenge action, that he should remember his fictional experience of such situations, and turn to the stage for assistance'.[10] Strictly (and perhaps pedantically) we have to assert that it is not 'natural' that he should do so but 'artificial', an effect of art; nor is it a real-life action but only another, alternative, stage revenge action. Hamlet may be reminded by the player of how thin the dividing line between art and life can be, but Shakespeare registers that recognition on the stage and in the elsewhere and nowhere of a fictional Elsinore.

Sidney's poem, like Shakespeare's play, is offered as *performance*, a poetic performance in which human experience is displayed as if it were real experience but which is also known to be, and advertises itself as, fiction; and the degree to which that fictionality is exposed or referred to by the poet can make very subtle tonal differences. Sidney, we might then say, is constructing, in *Astrophil and Stella*, a fiction which bears enough resemblance to verifiable biographical (or autobiographical) fact to make it convincing while at the same time including various sorts of commentary on its fictional nature. Why Sidney – or anybody else – should want to make fictions at all when the 'truth', that which is not an 'imag'd' thing, is actually available, is, of course, a crucial question. It is a question Spenser volunteers in the Bowre of Bliss, inviting us to contemplate, for instance, the decoration of the fountain:

> And over all, of purest gold was spred,
> A trayle of yvie in his native hew:
> For the rich mettall was so coloured,
> That wight, who did not wel avis'd it view,
> Would surely deeme it to be yvie trew.
> (*The Faerie Queene*, Bk II, Canto XII, 61)

So what is the point? A possible point in favour of 'art' rather than 'nature' has already been rehearsed in Sonnet 45: a story can make Stella weep for pity whereas the (apparent) mere fact cannot. The poems in *Astrophil and Stella* are shot through with moments which highlight the paradoxes of fiction and reality and explore, or make implicit commentary on, the relationship between story-telling and living. And it is, of course, in his *Defence of Poetry* that Sidney addresses himself to precisely this relationship.

However conciliatory and even celebratory the mood of the *Defence* may be, there lurk within it difficult, and sometimes dark, questions. We follow Sidney in his task of defending poetry from the charges that it is immoral, debilitating and lying, and note his adaptation of Aristotle's defence against those same charges. Where Plato had claimed that poets and artists merely imitated what was already second-hand, Aristotle suggested the possibility that the artist, the fabulator, the creative poet might be the one who could more truly indicate the ideal form rather than lead us yet further from it. But what Sidney argues is not so much that the poet can give us, through imitations of universal human beings or human actions, insights into reality (which was what Aristotle seemed to be arguing) but that the poet creates an *alternative* 'reality' which is in every way superior to the real one, and that this golden world of the poet is created for our edification and, specifically, for us to emulate and to imitate. We are invited – stimulated by delight – to imitate not the unsatisfactory real world but the ideal alternative world the poet invents.

Just how unsatisfactory Sidney feels the real world to be appears at times in his text with poignant clarity. The real world is 'brazen', 'the Poets only deliver a golden'. The actual world, unlike the possible worlds of fiction, is not, unfortunately, ruled by 'poetic justice', and Sidney catalogues the injustices of real life with unmistakable bitterness:

> History, being captivated to the truth of a foolish world, is many times a terror from well-doing, and an encouragement to unbridled wickedness. For see we not valiant Miltiades rot in his fetters? The just Phocion and the accomplished Socrates put to death like traitors? The cruel Severus live prosperously? The excellent Severus miserably murdered? Sulla and Marius dying in their beds? (*Defence*, pp. 37–8)

There seems to be every reason for supposing that for Sidney the fabrications of poets and writers of fiction are indeed no more than that. They offer us a fantasy world, a never-never land of the imagination which is constructed as a consolation for the difficulties, injustices and imperfections of real life. His famous idiosyncratic and syncretic definition of poetry contains within it profound contradictions:

> Poesy therefore is an art of imitation, for so Aristotle termeth it in the word *mimesis* – that is to say, a representing, counterfeiting, or figuring forth – to speak metaphorically, a speaking picture – with this end, to teach and delight. (*Defence*, p. 25)

Whatever Aristotle may or may not have meant by *mimesis*, it was clearly not what Sidney intends here by his counterfeiting speaking picture of a *better* world than the real one. The paradoxes of what Sidney is saying here appear quite clearly when he uses (as Plato had done) the sister art of painting as an analogy, leading him to make this curious statement about portrait painting:

> As to a lady that desired to fashion her countenance to the best grace, a painter should more benefit her to portrait a most sweet face, writing Canidia upon it, then to paint Canidia as she was, who, Horace sweareth, was full ill-favoured. (*Defence*, p. 35)

Sidney seems to be inviting us to assent to the notion that it is the function ('a painter should') of portrait painting to help people improve their own faces by imitating their portrait – a task infuriatingly impossible of achievement and reminding us of the maid Foible's words to Lady Wishfort, 'a little art once made your picture like you; and now a little of the same art must make you like your picture. Your picture must sit for you, madam' (Congreve, *The Way of the World*, III, vi). In other words, it is not at all clear why Sidney's notion of transferred imitation from the artist to his public (in which the artist eliminates all the warts) should necessarily enable us to follow that fiction. The true portrait of ourselves may be far from flattering but there is little, beyond cosmetics or plastic surgery, that we can do about it.

Sidney himself is aware of, and clearly sensitive about, this problem too. There is, for instance, that famous, but brief and diffident, paragraph which he slips into the discussion of the relation between art and nature, claiming that the poet shows his likeness to God 'in nothing . . . so much as in poetry, when with the force of a divine breath he bringeth things forth surpassing her [nature's] doings'. It is offered defensively (Sidney hopes it will not 'be deemed too saucy a comparison' and admits 'these arguments will by few be understood and by fewer granted', *Defence*, pp. 24–5) because according to the received Protestant view of man we are fatally flawed by original sin. Why should poetry, with all its good examples, be capable of persuading us to virtue? Only because, Sidney claims, the poet is like God: the recreated, alternative world the poet shows us may give glimpses of the perfect first state of nature that we have lost since 'that first accursed fall of Adam' and help to bridge the gap between the sinful actual state of man and the lost golden world. In this sense the poet is obliged always to 'deliver a golden'. In a sense Sidney is articulating a Renaissance commonplace, since it is on some such assumption that Spenser is able to claim that his invented 'continued Allegory, or dark conceit' of *The Faerie Queene* has as its 'general intention and meaning' 'to fashion a gentleman or noble person in virtuous and gentle discipline' – that is, morally to improve the reader (Spenser, *Letter . . . to Sir Walter Raleigh*). A similar assumption is ambivalently present in Milton's calls for divine aid in the composition of *Paradise Lost* and his didactic 'justification' – ambivalent because the kind of Protestantism to which Sidney and Spenser and Milton were committed also makes it clear that there are before God (which is the only place that matters) no gentlemen or noble persons. Even Sidney's bold assertion of poetry's efficacy is (and hardly unconsciously) warped by its resemblance to and involvement in St Paul's poignant paradox: Sidney's 'our erected wit maketh us know what perfection is, and yet our infected will keepeth us from reaching unto it' (*Defence*, p. 25) is an echo of Paul's 'For the good that I would I do not; but the evil which I would not, that I do . . . O wretched man that I am! Who shall deliver me from the body of this death?' (*Romans* 7:20, 24). Not, it would seem, the poet. The reader, after all, is from that real world which Sidney has characterised as miserable, unjust and anarchic. Sidney lays himself open here to the sort of question that a fellow-humanist, Guillaume Budé, asked about Hythloday's Utopia: 'What sort of holiness did the Utopians possess to merit the heavenly grace of not having avarice and cupidity break or creep into that island alone for so many centuries?' (Budé, Letter to Lupset), where for 'Utopians' we might substitute 'readers of poetry'.

There is a further difficulty which depends upon Sidney's notion of poetry's power to move. To be moved depends on the active co-operation and commitment of the reader (though the provided experience of 'delight' will help get us there): and it also depends, crucially, on the reader's ability to interpret and understand what the poet is offering. The same premise that requires the active reader also provides the possibility of false readings and bad readers. To the first of his many references to Xenophon's depiction of Cyrus – arguing that what true poets deliver 'is not wholly imaginative, as we are wont to say of them that build castles in the air; but so far substantially it worketh, not only to make a Cyrus, which had been but a particular excellency as nature might have done, but to bestow a Cyrus upon the world to make many Cyruses' – Sidney adds the important rider, 'if they will learn aright why and how that maker made him' (*Defence*, p. 24). Clearly, they might not. The poet's success is contingent upon his audience's desire and ability to understand both his intention (why) and his method (how). Equally, there is the other conditional: 'if the poet do his part right' (*Defence*, p. 35). As we shall see, Astrophil's Stella is just such a hostile, recalcitrant and obtuse reader; she frequently frustrates Astrophil with her misconstructions of his meaning. And Astrophil himself, doing his part as best he can is ultimately a failure in his reciprocal role of

poet and lover. The power of poetry, with all its delights, to
move the reader, not to mention the artist himself, in a desired
direction, is shown as doubtful. Whatever the moral lesson the
sequence may seem to embody, it fails to persuade to action.
Stella is not moved to pitying grace. But if we then say that she is
not because such action would be unvirtuous, we have to say also
that Astrophil's loss of virtue in desiring such action from Stella is
not redeemed either.

In Sonnet 44, Astrophil is quite sure he has done his part right:
'My words I know do well set forth my mind'. However, they do
not achieve the desired effect: 'And yet she heares, yet I no pitty
find'. Worse still, what he is saying is totally misunderstood, is
perversely transformed by Stella into its opposite. Admittedly, it
may be accounted for in terms of the transformation of the earthly
and suspect in its contact with the heavenly and virtuous, but that
does not dissipate Astrophil's puzzlement and frustration:

> when the breath of my complaints doth tuch
> Those daintie dores unto the Court of blisse,
> The heav'nly nature of that place is such,
>   That once come there, the sobs of mine annoyes
>   Are metamorphosed straight to tunes of joyes.

The commonplace Petrarchan polarity of the rhyming 'annoyes'
and 'joyes' can lead, in these poems, only to the sterile dead-lock
and exhausted paradox of its last appearance in the lines concluding the final Sonnet 108:

> So strangely (alas) thy works in me prevaile,
>   That in my woes for thee thou art my joy,
>   And in my joyes for thee my only annoy.

Astrophil's poetic intentions are similarly thwarted in Sonnet 57;
Stella again misreads and misconstrues, despite the poet's mar-
shalling of 'The thorowest words, fit for woe's selfe to grone'.
Stella hears his plaints. She also sings them, transposing them
from life to art, so that even the woeful lover is forced to enjoy his
own complaints thus turned into items of performance:

> I hoped her to bring
> To feele my griefes, and she with face and voice
> So sweets my paines, that my paines me rejoyce.

What Sidney is doing here is, in a sense, recognisable in terms of conventional postures. All the sonnet-lovers plead in vain, and their verses are ineffectual:

> So doe I weepe, and wayle, and pleade in vaine,
> Whiles she as steele and flint doth still remayne.
>   (Spenser, *Amoretti*, 19)
> In vaine I seeke and sew to her for grace.
>   (*Amoretti*, 20)

and their songs are incompetent or inadequate:

> But when in hand my tuneless harp I take,
> then doe I more augment my foes despight.
>   (*Amoretti*, 44)

Although Spenser successfully, and unconventionally, marries the woman he woos, during the course of the wooing Elizabeth, in a typical moment of dangerous Petrarchanism, sets light to his poems, 'all carelesse of his griefe'. But in all of these instances the problems are a part of and are resolved within the sonnet-world: his incompetence with the harp (unlike Orpheus's reconciling music) means not that his poems are *useless* as poems – on the contrary, they are so good that they 'griefe renew, and passions do awake / To battaile' – but that they fail to subdue his desire. Poetic meaning is not *misconstrued*; in fact it is co-operated with in the conventional manner: in Sonnet 20 his vain suit for grace is only vain in the sense that 'her foot she in my necke doth place', like a lioness with a lamb – a posture of dominant feminine ferocity which is not without its satisfactions and is, in any case, firmly within conventional expectations. Similarly, the sacrifice of his 'Innocent paper' to the flames only renews the poet's sense of his poems' true value:

> Yet live for ever, though against her will
> And speake her good, though she requite it ill.

But with Sidney the crises of confidence are more subtle, and their implications more subversive. Astrophil's failures are not merely those of a lover but of a poet. They are all the more disappointing since the strategy laid down in the opening sonnet of the sequence seemed fool-proof enough, and the reader's (Stella's) response seemed guaranteed: 'reading might make her know, / Knowledge might pitie winne, and pitie grace obtaine'. The 'reading' is not offered as problematic; the only real problem appears to be finding the right words: 'I sought fit words . . .' But, as the sequence goes on, Astrophil finds even his best shots inadequate to the case and his most fit and energetically wrought words crumble to nonsense. As A. C. Hamilton succinctly put it: 'In his opening program Astrophil has assumed Stella would be an ideal reader . . . Unfortunately, she is not properly programmed.[11]

Astrophil's failure is of course predetermined. As of the answer to our (fruitless) questions, what would have happened had Cordelia *not* said nothing, or if Hamlet *had* killed Claudius praying? (the answer, that is, that the plays would dissolve into thin air), so with Astrophil's suit: it is only the frustration of the poet's love which keeps the poems going. The persuasion to love and the writing of that persuasion are announced in the first sonnet; through those announcements Sidney enters that ethical and aesthetic gymnasium where Petrarchan love-sonneteers work out. Astrophil may have space here to develop novel exercises, but his declared purpose as poet/lover is bound to be frustrated. If Stella were to return his love, everything would stop. The successful termination of the love affair would render further poetry superfluous – though Sidney, as one would expect, makes exactly the opposite point, that the rejection of Astrophil's suit has destroyed both the lover and the poet:

> Therewithall away she went,
> Leaving him so passion rent,
> With what she had done and spoken,
> That therewith my song is broken.
> (*A & S, Eighth Song*)

We may note the difficulty we have in interpreting these lines because of the apparent presence in them of two men, Sidney the song's 'narrator' whose song is (sympathetically) 'broken', and Astrophil the song's subject who is 'so passion rent'. In fact Stella's actions and words do not break the song: they are the vital ingredient for the song's continuation. The increasing, mentally hyperactive and febrile wish-fulfilments, like the repeated 'Thought', 'Thought', 'Thinke', 'Thinke', 'Thinke, thinke' of the *Tenth song*, with its despairing

O my thought my thoughts surcease,
Thy delights my woes increase,
My life melts with too much thinking

can be relieved only by actions beyond poetry. While Astrophil's 'art' depends upon thinking, his 'life' depends upon what is non-mental and non-verbal, not 'the image of thy lover' but himself *as* lover. (At this point, as at others, one might reflect on the un-likelihood, from what we know of the beautiful, vain, witty and politically assertive Penelope Devereux, subsequently divorced from Rich and illegally married to Sir Charles Blount, of a Sidney/ Penelope affair having the same outcome as the Astrophil/Stella affair.)[12]

Despite the increasing intimacy between Astrophil and Stella, leading up to the crucial encounter in the *Eighth Song*, Stella always denies him her body, so that her body or her physical presence conjured up by incantation becomes the only thing As-trophil wants. Eventually the art suffers too: he has increasing difficulty in sustaining an elevated Petrarchan rhetoric; the Pe-trarchan metaphors of inspiration, virtue, beauty, break down un-der pressure from desire, from metonymic kisses, from a literal and poetically sterile absence. The dead-lock of despair and failure which 'closes' the sequence is artistically inevitable, in the sense that any other closure or termination would have to be an extra-poetical event, an event belonging not to the realm of art, but of experience.[13]

Sidney's *Astrophil and Stella*, then, like the *Defence*, raises prob-lems about our ability to interpret correctly what is written; about our ability to write correctly; about the reader's ability to imitate or respond to the *exemplum* or persuasion offered; and it presents the difficulties of reconciling an imitative theory of art and a didactic theory. Some have even detected a more profound and unsettling scepticism in Sidney which asserts that poetry is only a special instance of the fictionality which pervades all our dis-course, whether that of the lawyer and his fictional John-a-nokes, the 'long orations' which historians put into the mouths of their subjects, or even the piece of wood that chess players call a bishop. Even when we abandon books (the 'mouse-eaten records' of the historian or 'others' leaves') and write from nature (" "Foole," said my Muse to me, "looke in thy heart and write" ') we are still liable to find our words coming out like a player's lines and our actions transformed into theatrical shows:

> There is no art delivered to mankind that hath not the
> works of nature for his principal object, without which they
> could not consist, and on which they so depend, as they
> become actors and players, as it were, of what nature will
> have set forth. (*Defence*, p. 23)

Is Sidney suggesting that *all* attempts to make sense of the world
are based on fictions and illusions?[14] He 'rescues' his poet from
this *incertitudo et vanitas scientiarum* only by releasing him from
such 'subjection' and allowing him to 'grow in effect another
nature, in making things either better than nature bringeth forth,
or, quite anew, forms such as never were in nature' (*Defence*, p.
23): in other words, by asserting that the poet's discourses are
fictional like those of everybody else, but that they are superior
and novel fictions.

The kind of view of the nature and function of imaginative
literature that Sidney describes in the *Defence* is, not surprisingly,
very vulnerable to the suspicion – and it can be a dangerously
subversive suspicion – that it is all a sort of sophisticated kidding.
(It is of course a suspicion which is possible about *any* justification
of acts of the human imagination.) The suspicion will register the
possibility that art, rhetoric, imaginative language, symbol, fable,
metaphor, any kind of figuration, may be only a wish-fulfilment at
best and at worst a profound deception. Sidney's theory of art
makes it very clear that poetry *is* fiction, it *is* invention, it *is*
artifice, and although this may be a characteristic Renaissance
view it is also (and paradoxically) a Renaissance characteristic that
artists (*some* artists) should be exceptionally aware of, and wary
about, the artifices of fiction. Much of the actual poetry (and
drama) of the period shows a deep ambivalence towards the figurative nature of language, and any poet who, while immersed in
figuration and fiction, at the same time questions or doubts the
validity of that figuration, is doing something particularly interesting. And this is precisely what Sidney does in *Astrophil and Stella*,
and it is possible to see its relation to the pure theory of the
Defence (particularly since the two works were written close
together in time) as that between the draughtsman's elegant
blueprint and the (deliberately) ramshackle, unconnected, un-
workable and incoherent three-dimensional product. That is to
say, the claims (however eclectic or even playful some of them

may be) of the *Defence* are undermined or contradicted by the practice of the poems. Sidney seeds his poetic narrative with warning signals, reversals, with the sudden opening of chasms between language and life, with material for dialogue between the instabilities of artifice and the recalcitrance of reality.

It has often been pointed out that *Astrophil and Stella* documents (and this is in part its didactic *purpose*, its moral *exemplum*) the psychological disarray and fragmentation of the rejected and hopeless lover; there is a persistent and 'sharply defined concern for the corrosive effects of love upon the heroic life'.[15] There is also concern for the potentially corrosive, or at least delusory, effects of the *arts* of poetic love (and by extension poetic anything else) upon life. Sonnet 19 has Astrophil, the star-gazer, bathetically fall into a ditch, even though his 'erected wit' is doing its best despite himself: 'My verie inke turnes straight to *Stella's* name'. But the whole business is clouded by a despairing scepticism: what is the point of writing anyway?

> And yet my words, as them my pen doth frame,
> Avise themselves that they are vainely spent.

In part this is within the dialectical pattern of the conflict between the heroic mind and corrupting 'affections', between the 'erected wit' and the 'infected will' in which Desire always seems to win and yet always seems to be frustrated. But, above and beyond this artistic dramatization of conflict, is the suspicion that the whole enterprise, both the wooing and the written-about-wooing, is sick, and the poet is only half aware of it; Astrophil's words seem to know more than he does: they 'Avise themselves' that they are all for nothing. But the poet, picking himself up from the ditch, is ready to start juggling words again and continue to follow the blandishments of ' "Scholler," saith *Love*, "bend hitherward your wit" '.

In consequence of Astrophil's persistence in sonnet writing it may appear that the literary point being made by Sidney (as Sonnets 6, 15, 28, 54, 70, or 90 would seem to indicate) is a criticism of the glib fluency of other poet-lovers and an assertion of his own sturdy independence, forthrightness and veracity, arguing (equally fluently) for the virtues of simplicity. Yet this is a pose, as many critics have pointed out, which is both ironic and itself highly conventional. Yet I would suggest that there may be crucial moments in *Astrophil and Stella* when we absorb, or deflect, or even actually emasculate Sidney's primary point by deferring to our own (possibly self-congratulatory) recognition of, and Sidney's implied participation in, the *conventions* of the genre. What I mean may be shown by considering the customary account of, or explanation of – why exactly should it need explaining? – the gesture Sidney's Astrophil makes at the end of the famous opening sonnet of the sequence. The whole sonnet is not without its paradoxes and problems: its multiple writer/audience of Astrophil/Stella and Sidney/ the sonnet-reading public; its deliberate procedural gaff, jumping straight to Elocution before Invention and Disposition; its tone, at once sardonic and self-mocking and yet fully serious; its delicately balanced diagnostic and didactic air. But the crucial line, which we are urged not to misconstrue, is the climactic one: ' "Foole," said my Muse to me, "looke in thy heart and write." '

Ringler calls it 'the most quoted and the least understood line of all Sidney's poetry' (Ringler, *Poems*, p. 459). Sidney's Muse is not, we are assured, telling him to write his autobiography 'but to look for the materials for a love poem in the proper place' – that is, the proper rhetorical place.[16] Sidney is purely objective here and is not, like some Romantic, advocating self-exploration and self-expression as ends in themselves: 'personal' feeling is appealed to only 'for the purpose of rhetorical persuasion'.[17] The final line is not a plea for heartfelt spontaneity or sincerity, for we need to understand what Sidney means here by the 'heart': it is the shrine of the beloved's image, his heart *is* Stella, so that 'the proper source of invention is a conventional Petrarchan conceit'.[18] So too David Kalstone: 'The substance of the line is entirely conventional . . . the poet is advised to look at Stella's image'. Ringler says that 'What the poet will see when he looks into his heart is the image of Stella'; he informs us that ' "Heart" refers to the mind in general, the seat of all the faculties', and it may well mean that in the other examples he cites (for example, Sonnets 4, 12; 5, 5–7; 32, 13–14; 88, 9–14; 105, 4) (Ringler, *Poems*, p. 459). But 'heart' clearly does not mean that in Sonnet 76, 'My heart cries "ah", it burnes'; nor in 91, 'they seeme my hart to move', nor in 107, 'Sweete, for a while give respite to my hart'. As Kalstone suspects, there may be something else going on in Sonnet 1. He notes the 'violence and release of tension' in the line, and that there is something 'quite special' about Sidney's presentation of the conventional.[19] The something quite special may well be identified as that which everyone (I would guess) confronting the poem instinctively recognizes in their experience of reading it: that, despite its conventional attributes and its conformities to the Petrarchan code, the line *does* (whether we like it or not) assert self-expression, self-exploration, personal feeling, subjectivity. But since that seems unlikely, or unacceptable, we consequently (and subsequent to our primary experience of reading the line) gloss it out of existence by reference to Renaissance poetics. Yet it seems to me perfectly possible to argue that Sidney knows that we, his audience, will do precisely that, and that he wishes to register *both* the *a priori*, ante-poetic (and potentially, because anti-fictional, anti-poetic) gesture of desiring to write from the heart, *and* the *post priori*, poetic gesture which reminds us that his heart is, of course, not what one might normally mean by that word in a 'real-life' context but what one means in a context of poetic convention, that is, Stella's image engraven there. The line exposes, in other words, the more compressed conundrum of the sonnet's opening assertion: 'Loving in truth'.

When in jaunty or confident mood, Astrophil repeats the theme of self-proclaimed sincerity and simplicity against the conventions of poetic fashion and the clichés of Petrarchan emotionalism, keeping his eye and his words firmly on his heart where Stella resides: he 'reads' Stella's face and copies 'what in her Nature writes' (Sonnet 3); he advises himself to behold Stella 'and then begin to endite', rejecting 'poore *Petrarch's* long deceased woes' (Sonnet 15); he uses no 'eloquence', '*Love* onely reading unto me this art' (Sonnet 28); the only explanation of his success so far is that his 'lips are sweet, inspired with *Stella's* kisse' (Sonnet 74); and so on. In the process Astrophil sneers at and belittles a whole range of ornate, allegorical or conventional modes of writing which were highly regarded in the sixteenth century and were practised by the most considerable poets, including Sidney himself and also including at moments, Astrophil himself (as he acknowledges in Sonnet 55). Dwelling on Stella to the exclusion of all else ('I thought all words were lost, that were not spent of thee') (*Fift song*), Astrophil seems to declare the procedures of what was universally understood as 'poetry' to be frivolous, decorative artefacts written by 'Pindare's Apes', larded with exotic and irrelevant similes (Sonnet 3), the work of those merely seeking 'brasen fame' (Sonnet 28). Sidney even has Astrophil deny that he wants to be thought of as a poet at all. (Sonnet 90) . In this line

of discourse about poetry it is possible to recognize one of
Sidney's strategies of irony. No one, presumably, would in
Sidney's time seriously propose a deliberately cultivated poetic of
derivativeness and insincerity; yet Astrophil's rejection or scorn of
the traditional methods of poets may be simultaneously admir-
able and ironic. At any rate, the 'debate' broached by Sidney here
is about *method*, the best, most effective way of wooing Stella
when 'faine in verse' his 'love to show'.

But there is also a more serious debate apparent, not about
method (how) but about *why*. Its basic questions are announced in
the second sonnet, disguised, as it were, behind Astrophil's contra-
diction of the conventional method of falling in love at first sight:

> now like slave-borne *Muscovite*,
> I call it praise to suffer Tyrannie;
> And now employ the remnant of my wit,
>   To make my selfe beleeve, that all is well,
> While with a feeling skill I paint my hell.

This, abruptly following the opening declaration of truth, is a
confession not only of debility resulting from forced agreement to
Love's decrees but of outright dishonesty. Its ironic relationship
to Sonnet 1 is apparent, and so too is the irony of its paradoxically
knowing self-deception. His wit (or what is left of it) and his
'feeling skill' are to be employed in an elaborate game of pretence. To parody that poignant opening of Shakespeare's Sonnet
138, it is as though Sidney is saying something like: 'When my
verse swears that it is made of truth, / I do believe it though I
know it lies'. It is as though one unintended consequence of the
rhetoric of persuasion to which the sequence is committed is the
detection or revelation of falsehood and deception just where
honesty and sincerity are most paraded. To return to our original
question (what are the poems for?) we can answer that they are
for Stella; they are for the *cognoscenti* in Sidney's audience; they
are for ourselves, as readers. But that may be to turn the 'what'
into a 'who'. A response to 'what are they for?' will furnish the
answer: they are to win Stella – and in that ambition they signally
fail. Not surprisingly then they also contain their own expressions
of doubt about their status, a doubt mooted in the second sonnet.
For example, Astrophil, wondering where the next sonnet is
going to come from, pauses to interrogate himself: 'Come let me
write'. But why? 'And to what end?'. Well, it is therapeutic: 'To

ease / A burthned hart'. But how can that be possible, 'How can *words* ease' (my italics) since the available words are all reflective of his misery? That misery might be depicted with special brilliance or originality: 'Oft cruell fights well pictured forth do please', so that we forget the actual cruelty and the mayhem and simply admire the picture. Ought not Astrophil be ashamed to publish his disease (a dis-ease which is unresponsive to the therapy of versifying)? Possibly, but he regards his despair as being so spectacular that it may secure his reputation: 'Nay, that may breed my fame, it is so rare'. But anyone with any sense will see that what he is offering for sale is not only worthless but silly and will 'thinke thy words fond ware'. So perhaps it is better to say nothing at all, then no one will be offended. But 'What harder thing then smart, and not to speake?' Sidney has Astrophil run through the gamut of possible motivations, noting the disconcerting way in which wit and writing can have effects quite different from those intended. So Astrophil is trapped in an *impasse*: 'Thus write I while I doubt to write'. Some might suggest that it is Stella who has thus bankrupted him – 'perhaps some find / *Stella's* great powrs, that so confuse my mind' – but it is a limp addendum (hardly a conclusion) which explains nothing; it merely locates the poem, Sonnet 34, in its dramatic locale.

This frame of mind, in which confusion and uncertainty not so much about Stella as about the viability of poetic composition itself, is not one that Astrophil wishes to maintain. He would prefer to get back to more sonneteer-bashing and more plaintive invocations of Stella's name. But the doubting mood spills over into Sonnet 35, with its opening question:

> What may words say, or what may words not say,
> Where truth it selfe must speake like flatterie?

It is a good question, but one that is dispersed in the sonnet through mere witticism and verbal sleight of hand:

> Wit learnes in thee perfection to expresse,
>   Not thou by praise, but praise in thee is raisde:
>   It is a praise to praise, when thou art praisde.

Yet this subterranean alternative perspective surfaces at sometimes unexpected moments. When Astrophil begs kisses from Stella Sidney writes a beautifully poised and amusing poem in which, in Donne-like fashion, Astrophil turns Stella's argument against herself: if you want me to stop writing these embarrassing poems to you, then 'Stop you my mouth with still still kissing me' (Sonnet 81). Yet what Astrophil seems largely concerned with in the poem is not so much kissing Stella as writing about kissing Stella. He begins with a fulsome poetic vocative:

> O Kisse, which doest those ruddie gemmes impart,
> Or gemmes, or frutes of new-found *Paradise*,
> Breathing all blisse and sweetning to the heart.

Pursuing his address, but now with his eye towards the idealistic Stella, he explains how a kiss can tie souls together ('even soules'), and it does so 'By linkes of *Love*'. How much he would like to be able, artistically, to show the world how apt in this respect Stella is:

> How faine would I paint thee to all men's eyes,
> Or of thy gifts at least shade out some part.

Stella, with chilling aloofness, replies that she 'builds her fame on higher seated praise' – higher, that is, than recommendations about her excellence as a kisser. But into this dialogue between artist and model, poet and lover, Sidney infiltrates the phrase 'and only Nature's art' (that is, not mine or the arts of rhetoric):

> O kisse, which soules, even soules together ties
> By linkes of *Love*, and only Nature's art . . .

It is hard to know whether this is at Astrophil's expense or whether Astrophil is wiser than he seems. The 'double-take' here of course is that Astrophil, while engaged in writing a poem about kissing wishes that he could write a poem about kissing; but we are also made aware that writing poems about kissing is not kissing: that is achieved not by poetic art but only by 'Nature's art' and can thus only be an extra-poetical event. Sidney leaves it open to us to read it either as a knowing sonnet of seduction, or as one in which Astrophil's obsession with writing it all down ('I, mad with delight, want wit to cease') is shown to be merely foolish.

Even when Astrophil is in lively, optimistic form, ready to placate his Muse (who, forced 'in sad rimes to creepe', must be thoroughly bored by servicing the catalogué of woes) with a joyful sonnet at last, the poem takes an unexpected turn precipitated by a crisis of confidence. Astrophil prepares to write a happy poem in Sonnet 70 – after all, 'Sonets be not bound prentise to annoy':

> Come then my Muse, shew thou height of delight
> In well raisde notes, my pen the best it may
> Shall paint out joy, though but in blacke and white.

But Astrophil suddenly has second thoughts: 'Cease eager Muse, peace pen, for my sake stay'. Why? The joyful poem never gets written, but not because of doubts about his success with Stella. It is doubt about the capacity of poetry to mediate it: that sense of doubt with which Sidney so subtly comments upon his narrative. Formally sustaining his address to his Muse (and also to his pen) but also, literally, reaching out of the poem towards his audience, the poet renounces his art. And, significantly, he does so in deference to another kind of truth, inviting us to take his proffered hand:

> I give you here my hand for truth of this,
> Wise silence is best musicke unto blisse.

The other may have *seemed* true, or have *pretended* to be true; but he gives us his assurance of the truth of *this*: that it is better, it would seem, not to write at all.

   Nor should Sidney's gesture here be confused with more familiar variations on the *topos* of the artist's inadequacy. It is different in kind from, say, Spenser's

> the lovely pleasance and the lofty pride
> cannot expressed be by any art.
> A greater craftsmans hand thereto doth neede,
> that can expresse the life of things indeed
>   (*Amoretti*, 18)

which, while it draws attention to the relationship between art and life, does so in order to work out a poetic compliment to Elizabeth Boyle.

   Sidney's own variation on this *topos* (Sonnet 91) is a poem uneven in texture but resonant with a peculiar poignancy:

> *Stella*, while now by honour's cruell might,
>   I am from you, light of my life, mis-led,
> And that faire you my Sunne, thus overspred
> With absence' Vaile, I live in Sorowe's night.
> If this darke place yet shew like candle light,
>   Some beautie's peece, as amber colourd hed,
> Milke hands, rose cheeks, or lips more sweet, more red,

Or seeing jets, blacke, but in blacknesse bright.
They please I do confesse, they please mine eyes,
But why? because of you they models be,
Models such be wood-globes of glistring skies.
Deere, therefore be not jealous over me,
    If you heare that they seeme my hart to move,
    Not them, o no, but you in them I love.

He is deprived of 'the life of things indeed' by Stella's absence
and her 'honour's cruell might'; all that remains to him, like the
unreal shadows of Plato's cave, are mental pictures which in 'this
darke place yet shew like candle light'. He catalogues some of
these remembered fragments of 'some beautie's peece', 'as am-
ber colourd hed, / Milke hands, rose cheeks, or lips more sweet,
more red . . .' The syntax is open-ended here, the repeated com-
paratives 'more . . . more' having no explicit 'than'. Perhaps the
lips are only more sweet and red than the 'rose cheeks'; or perhaps they are, like the sweeter smelling flowers and the more
fruitful trees with which the poet in the *Defence* makes 'the too
much loved earth more lovely', 'more sweet, more red' than real,
living lips. These residual, partial and counterfeiting images can
give a kind of delight. 'They please I do confesse, they please
mine eyes'. 'But why?' Astrophil asks. How can he account for
the way 'they seeme my hart to move'? Because they are 'models'
of Stella; in themselves they are valueless and meaningless. The
comparison he offers between the counterfeit representation and
the real thing, between artistic *mimesis*, figuration, picturing forth
and the unfigured, unmediated actuality, is one which diminishes
and exposes, with some pathos, the 'adequacy' of representational forms:

But why? because of you they models be,
Models such be wood-globes of glistring skies.

The point is not primarily the working out of a compliment to
Stella (how much she exceeds the range of art) but that poetic
structures (those crude 'wood-globes' on which are painted the
arrangements of the constellations) are only a consoling fantasy, a
substitute, a toy to comfort us in our confrontations with absence,
darkness and misery:

> Deere, therefore be not jealous over me,
> If you heare that they seem my hart to move,
> Not them, o no, but you in them I love.

Here is a curious inversion of Sidney's scorn, in the *Defence*, for those dullards who 'cannot hear the planet-like music of poetry' and who have 'so earth-creeping a mind that it cannot lift itself to look at the sky of poetry'. For in Sonnet 91 there is no 'sky of poetry': on the contrary, Stella is the 'glistring skies' and poetry only the 'wood-globes'. The desired for traffic is now reversed; it is, as it were, the 'earth-creeping' mind that has perceived the truth that the 'planet-like music' and the 'sky of poetry' are only valuable for what they remind us of in the real world: 'Not them, o no, but you in them I love'. The final irony, it would seem, is that the failed poet / lover is here, ultimately, the victim of Sidney's own curse on the non-poets that closes the *Defence*:

> yet thus much curse I must send you, in the behalf of all poets, that while you live, you live in love, and never get favour for lacking skill of a sonnet. (*Defence*, p. 75)

Yet the irony goes even deeper for, with more than a hundred skilful sonnets to his credit, the poet gets no more favour than the man who never wrote a word.

Sidney's art in *Astrophil and Stella*, when at its most vital and interesting, is working at the problematic interface between the fictions of art and the intractable realities of life. His poetry, both here and in his *Arcadia*, is marked by a sense both of the artificiality of literature's imaginary beings and landscapes and also of the shattering ease with which their ideals of chivalry and virtue, or of pastoral simplicity, or of love, can be dismantled and exposed as *merely* imaginary. This aspect of Sidney's achievement was, it would seem, very apparent to his friend and fellow fiction-maker, Spenser. It is well known, for instance, that Spenser took a very long time to produce an elegy on the death of Sidney. It was not written until several years later than even Spenser thought appropriate, and was not published until 1595, nine years after Sidney's death. Spenser addressed in 1591 an apology to Sidney's sister, the Countess of Pembroke, but failed to explain his apparently ungrateful delay, 'for that I have not shewed any thankful remembrance towards him' (Dedication of *The Ruine of Time*). Possibly Spenser wanted to wait until the outpourings of a nation's grief at Sidney's death had finished before offering his own. Or perhaps he was delayed for technical reasons. Certainly, when it finally appeared, *Astrophel, A Pastorall Elegie upon the death of the most Noble and valorous Knight, Sir Philip Sidney* seemed to conduct a series of experiments in various traditional poetic expressions of loss, as if working through the repertoire of artifices designed to satisfy our needs as mourners. About all of them, as modes of figuration, Spenser seems dissatisfied and sceptical.[20]

As the poem's title indicates, Spenser conflates Astrophel and Sidney, and a figure called Stella plays a large part in the fictions of mourning – 'His lifes desire, his deare loves delight'(54). Yet just as the identity, or the proper signification, of Stella in Sidney's sonnets may be so teasing, so here, for the elegy is dedicated (surprisingly) 'To the most beautifull and vertuous Ladie, the Countesse of Essex', that is, to Frances Walsingham, Lady Frances Sidney, Sir Philip's widow, now married to the Earl of Essex (and later to be the wife of the Earl of Clanrickard). Is Spenser tactlessly celebrating the late husband's infidelity? Or is his account of Stella merely a poetic platonic exercise? Or is he tacitly putting Lady Sidney in the place of Stella (Lady Rich)?[21] Perhaps the problem is part of Spenser's meaning. The confusions, uncertainties and disappointments of real life eddy around the deliberately conventional unrealities of pastoral elegy elegantly structured from Bion, Moschus, Ovid and Ronsard. Early on in the elegist's picture of the young Astrophel are limned ominous signs of what is to come, for Astrophel was not content with a merely verbal wooing and praising of Stella but chose finally, as the only possible closure, the almost suicidal pursuit of violent action:

> Ne her with ydle words alone he wowed,
> And verses vaine (yet verses are not vaine)
> But with brave deeds to her sole service vowed . . .
> For both in deeds and words he nourtred was,
> Both wise and hardie (too hardie alas).
>
> (67–72)

What is the effect of Spenser's first parenthesis here? Verses are vain; but verses are not vain. Are they, or aren't they? Are words alone 'ydle' and only actions meaningful? But Sidney's actions, as Spenser demonstrates, led to his death. Astrophel, Adonis-like, bleeds to death in a line whose parenthesis again pulls in an opposite direction, contrasting pastoral fiction with cruel history: 'They stopt his wound (too late to stop it was)' (145). Like Adonis, Astrophel is mourned by his Venus figure, Stella. Social identity and human 'history' are subsumed, or abandoned, in the poetic death of both Astrophel and Stella, who are transformed, in a figuration of such self-conscious contrivance that it provides a whole page of densely written horticultural and herbal commentary in the *Variorum* edition, 'Into one flowre', a flower including both lovers in a single emblem which changes from red to blue, which resembles '*Stella* in her freshest yeares' and carries a star insignia at its centre, which darts forth beams of light representing her tears, and which is named Penthia ('tearful sorrow'), and Starlight, and Astrophel (182–198). That such a mystifying and insubstantial figuration should give rise to scholarly despair at identifying the precise flower, or to glosses on *Borago officinalis* or *Mertensia virginica*, with notes on their culinary uses, rather than to concern to identify the person of Stella, is perhaps a proper response to Spenser's deliberately dehumanizing and depersonalizing poetic gerry-building. Somewhere in these gestures of dissatisfaction with the adequacy of metaphor is an inner debate in which Sidney's own voice may be heard to participate.

Such gestures, though less sophisticated and more crude, occur elsewhere in the volume of verses in which *Astrophel* was printed. One of the contributors, Spenser's friend and colleague in Ireland, Lodowick Bryskett, author of *The Mourning Muse of Thestylis* in the *Astrophel* collection, was perhaps present too among the distinguished mourners at Spenser's graveside in Westminster Abbey who 'Camden tells us, composed elegies and threw them into the grave together with the pens used in writing them'.[22] The composer of the final 'Epitaph' section of the *Astrophel* volume depicts, with something more than the routine conventionality of this rhetorical device, the elegist-poet's uncertainty and inadequacy to the task: the brute fact – 'Sidney is deed, deed is my friend' – has somehow to be versified; but literary self-consciousness, the whole apparatus of the *ars poetica*, is reduced to confusion: 'Silence augmenteth grief, writing encreaseth rage':

> Enrag'd I write, I know not what: dead, quick,
> I know not how.

We are finally directed, with some bitterness, away from unstable and precarious poetic fictions to seek in Sidney's tomb some more substantial *memento*:

> Now rime, the sonne of rage, which art no kin to skill
> And endles griefe, which deads my life, yet knowes not how to
> kill,
> Go seeke that haples tombe, which if ye hap to finde,
> Salute the stones, that keep the lims, that held so good a minde.

Spenser's own habitual sensitivity about figurative language (as for example in his extraordinary and daring gesture in setting the allegorical, cosmic debate of the last book of *The Faerie Queene*, peopled with Titans and gods, in his own back garden in Ireland – 'who knows not Arlo hill?') must have been all the more acute since he was writing about Sidney: for who more than Sidney had so thoroughly exposed the fictive nature of poetry? 'It is not rhyming and versing that maketh a poet . . . but it is that feigning notable images'. Like an echo the words *feign, image, figure* and *counterfeit* repeat themselves throughout the *Defence*, as Sidney emphasises again and again just how far ideal poetic constructions are *removed* from the flawed nature of the given world. Sidney may mean us to be swept along by his celebration of privileged poetry over mundane reality, but mundane reality is where we live and it provides the basic ontological data with which artists and poets will necessarily have to deal and to which they will have to return. Sidney's theory may at times leave us stranded between the morally obtuse, degraded world of history and nature on the one hand, and an unreal, golden, or star-lit, or candle-lit, world of images on the other. It is not irrelevant, as Spenser perceived, to recognise that Sidney died not of old age constructing ideal fictions for imitation; he died a young man of thirty two as result of one of those frequent skirmishes against Catholic aggression in the Netherlands. It is as though what Sidney chose finally to do was to engage the fallen and imperfect world directly in heroic action, not feign improved and improving versions of it, mediated by art, in the enclosures of his verse.

His last words were, 'Love my memory', and there is a curious and unconscious irony in the no-nonsense tribute to him offered by Arthur Golding, who completed Sidney's unfinished translation of Philip Mornay's *The Trewnesse of the Christian Religion*:

> He died not languishing in idleness, riot, and excess nor as
> overcome with nice pleasures and fond vanities, but of

manly wounds received in service of his Prince, in defence
of persons oppressed, in maintenance of the only true Catholic and Christian religion . . . whereby he hath worthily
won himself immortal fame among the godly and left example worthy of imitation to others of his calling.[23]

Is it possible that Golding means to designate poetry among the
'nice pleasures and fond vanities'? Or that Sidney's 'defence of
persons oppressed' is somehow more manly than the defence of
poetry? Sidney becomes, like Ben Jonson's son, his own best
piece of poetry, for he himself becomes, in the loving of his
memory, the example to be imitated.

Sidney's encounter with what Golding describes as 'manly
wounds', or his own captivation by 'a foolish world . . . many
times a terror from well-doing', was grim and excruciating. He
was struck by a musket ball above his unprotected knee and the
thigh bone shattered. He did not die on the battlefield of
Zutphen but was taken to Arnhem, twenty miles away. He hung
on for more than two weeks, finally succumbing to gangrene,
though his equanimity and apparent detachment impressed all
observers: with characteristic panache and high breeding he composed, amid the gangrenous stench of his wound, a song entitled
La cuisse rompue. The account of his last days written by his close
friend Fulke Greville describes Sidney's exposure to another
kind of human art, for he made himself available to the doctors
that they might (as he said himself, according to Greville) 'freely
use their art, cut, and search to the bottom'.[24] Towards the end
his shoulder bones had worn through his skin, Greville records,
'with constant and obedient posturing of his body to [the doctor's] art'; Sidney, says Greville, 'judiciously observing the pangs
his wound stang him with by fits, together with many other symp-
toms of decay, few or none of recovery', began 'rather to submit
his body to these artists than any farther to believe in them.'[25]

It is difficult, responding to the pain of this account, not to be
reminded both of the scepticism of Sidney's Astrophil and of
Sidney's elevation, in the *Defence*, of the 'feigned Cyrus in
Xenophon' above the 'true Cyrus in Justin' or the 'feigned
Aeneas in Virgil' the poet above the 'right Aeneas in Dares
Phrygius' the historian, and not to reflect on how consoling the
existence of an imaginary Cyrus might be to someone con-
strained and suffering under a real and actual tyrant Cyrus. Are

the doctor's and the poet's arts no different? Spenser's dilemma
in writing of Sidney (and we may remember too Spenser's own
partial recalling of Cyrus's elevation in his letter to Raleigh
regarding *The Faerie Queene*) is well put by Peter Sacks:

> how easily can a poet who mourns a thirty-two-year-old
> victim of a battle at Zutphen in the Low Countries turn for
> consolation to an ideal realm he knows to be inhabited by
> 'forms such as never were in Nature'?[26]

Sidney also mourned for himself: according to one account of
his last days there was a death-bed struggle of conscience over 'a
Vanitie wherein I had taken delight, whereof I had not ridd my
selfe. It was my Ladie Rich'.[27] 'Vanitie' and 'delight' are jux-
taposed almost like critical terms from the *Defence*, and over
them hangs an air of enigma, like that surrounding *Astrophil and
Stella*, about whether he means his verses to Lady Rich, or the
woman herself, or both.

Thomas Nashe mourned Sidney too. (He also made what he
could on the side by prefacing the pirated edition of *Astrophel
and Stella*, and it is to Nashe that we are indebted for the description of that work as 'the tragicomedy of love . . . performed
by starlight'.) Nashe's mourning of Sidney expresses, like
Milton's puzzlement at the 'thankless muse', the injustice of
the sudden death of one who knew 'what pains, what toils, what
travail conduct to perfection . . . But thou art dead in thy
grave'.[28] And it was Nashe too who, in the bleak aftermath of
the plague, expressed the darkest distrust of language and of the
mediating power of fictions, for how do we, in the face of death
or injustice, prove that 'verses are not vaine'? His lines from
Summers Last Will and Testament reflect a scepticism that is not
merely momentary, nor idiosyncratic to Nashe; they embody an
awareness of our dependence on fictions and offer a definitively
pessimistic response:

> Wit with his wantoness
> Tasteth death's bitterness;
> Hell's executioner;
> Hath no ears for to hear
> What vain art can reply.

NOTES

1. *Astrophil and Stella, First Song*. All quotations from *Astrophil and Stella* are from *The Poems of Philip Sidney*, ed. William A. Ringler Jr, Oxford: Clarendon Press, 1962.
2. See Gary Waller, 'Acts of Reading: The Production of Meaning in *Astrophil and Stella*', *Studies in the Literary Imagination*, 15, 1 (1982), pp. 25–35.
3. J. W. Lever, *The Elizabethan Love Sonnet*, London: Methuen, 1956, p. 129.
4. Ringler, *Poems*, p. 447.
5. J. M. Purcell, *Sidney's Stella*, London: Oxford University Press, 1934, p. 42.
6. Richard A. Lanham, '*Astrophil and Stella*: Pure and Impure Persuasion', *English Literary Renaissance*, 2 (1977), pp. 100–15.
7. See Clarke Hulse, 'Stella's Wit: Penelope Rich as Reader of Sidney's Sonnets', in *Rewriting the Renaissance: The Discourses of Sexual Difference in Early Modern Europe*, ed. Margaret W. Ferguson, Maureen Quilligan, Nancy J. Vickers, Chicago: University of Chicago Press, 1986, p. 272–86.
8. Ringler, *Poems*, p. 447.
9. Sidney, *Defence of Poetry*, ed. J. Van Dorsten, Oxford: Oxford University Press, 1966, pp. 53, 69–70.
10. Shakespeare, *Hamlet*, ed. T.J.B. Spencer, introduction by Anne Barton, Harmondsworth: Penguin Books, 1980, p. 29. Dr Barton also points to the resemblance between Hamlet here and Sidney's Sonnet 45.
11. A. C. Hamilton, 'Sidney's *Astrophel and Stella* as a Sonnet Sequence', *English Literary History*, 36 (1969), p. 82.
12. See for instance Roger Howell's biography, *Sir Philip Sidney: The Shepherd Knight*, London: Hutchinson, 1968, pp. 190–2. However, some have claimed that the riddling language of the songs show that Stella/Penelope *does* actually grant Astrophil/Sidney his heart's and body's desire: see Clark Hulse, 'Stella's Wit: Penelope Rich as Reader of Sidney's Sonnets', *loc. cit.*
13. See Marion Campbell, 'Unending Desire: Sidney's Reinvention of Petrarchan Form in *Astrophil and Stella*', in *Sir Philip Sidney and the Interpretation of Renaissance Culture*, ed. Gary E. Waller and Michael D. Moore, London: Croom Helm, 1984, pp. 86, 90.
14. A question asked by Ronald Levao, 'Sidney' Feigned *Apology*', *PMLA*, 94 (March 1979), pp. 223–33.
15. David Kalstone, *Sidney's Poetry: Contexts and Interpretations*, New York: Norton, 1970, p. 106.
16. Maurice Evans, *Elizabethan Sonnets* (anthology), introduction, London: Dent, 1977, p. xviii.
17. Neil Rudenstine, *Sidney's Poetic Development*, Cambridge, Mass.: Harvard University Press, 1967, p. 200.

18. Richard C. McCoy, *Sir Philip Sidney: Rebellion in Arcadia*, Hassocks: Harvester Press, 1979, p. 76.
19. David Kalstone, *Sidney's Poetry*, pp. 126–7.
20. For an acute account of Spenser's *Astrophel*, see Peter M. Sacks, *The English Elegy: Studies in the Genre from Spenser to Yeats*, Baltimore: John Hopkins University Press, 1985, pp. 51–63.
21. For a summary of views on such questions see *The Works of Edmund Spenser: A Variorum Edition*, The Minor Poems, Vol. 1, ed. C. G. Osgood and H. G. Lotspeich, Baltimore: John Hopkins University Press, 1943, pp. 490–5. Quotations from the *Astrophel* volume here are taken from *The Poetical Works of Edmund Spenser*, ed. J. C. Smith and E. De Selincourt, London: Oxford University Press, repr. 1959.
22. *The Life . . . of Lodowick Bryskett*, H. R. Plomer and T. P. Cross, Chicago: Chicago University Press, 1927, p. 61.
23. P. Mornay, *A Worke Concerning the Trewnesse of the Christian Religion*, London, 1587, Dedication.
24. Sir Fulke Greville, *The Life of the Renowned Sir Philip Sidney*, ed. N. Smith, Oxford: Oxford University Press, 1907, p. 130.
25. Greville, *The Life*, p. 133.
26. Peter M. Sacks, *The English Elegy*, p. 40.
27. See Jean Robertson, *Review of English Studies*, n.s. 15 (1964), pp. 296–7.
28. Nashe, quoted in M. W. Wallace, *The Life of Sir Philip Sidney*, Cambridge: Cambridge University Press, 1915, p. 399.

2

CONVENTIONS OF IMITATION
Donne and the metamorphosis of Ovid

Every writer creates his own precursors.
Jorge Luis Borges,
Other Inquisitions, 1952

The exploration of Sidney left us on a falling cadence. His sceptical testing of the limits of art, his sensitivity to the paradoxes of
fictions that may be real and realities that may be fictions, his own
life perceived as a rejection of figuration in favour of purposive,
heroic action: these qualities suggest in him a kind of mourning,
as if, like perhaps the revengers and the melancholics of Elizabethan and Jacobean tragedy 'where words prevail not' (*The
Spanish Tragedy*, II. i. 110), he is something of an elegist manqué.
His celebrations of life and art in the *Arcadia* and *Astrophil and
Stella* are muted by a sense of *humana fragilitas* and the pre-
cariousness of the fiction we devise to sustain us.

We do not, though, generally think of Donne's robust, witty
and often whimsically sardonic tone as one inhibited by a melancholic self-questioning or a disabled querying of the validity of
the forms he is using. He may refer to his poems in no other voice
than one of disparagement – when he sends them to friends he
invariably excuses them as 'light flashes' or 'evaporations' or
'ragges of verses' – but we do not have to believe him, even
though we may note how he did not bother to keep copies of
some of them (knowing perhaps that others would) and how,
more than once, he announed his resolve to give up the 'vanity' of
writing poems.[1] There is rich material in Donne for the critic-
turned-psychiatrist, who will tell us that he 'led a double life, his
poetry supplying a covert outlet for impulses which his public self
refused to recognise'.[2] This may be one way of saying that
Donne, whatever his private or public inhibitions, or calculations,
continued consistently to pour out poems throughout his life,
even turning his 'playes last scene' into a drama, a bracing poetic
exercise, a literary achievement. There was no sense of anything

here too deep for verse or that verses are 'vaine'; on the contrary, confronted with the inconstancies of love, of life, and the final scape of death, his poetic slogan is

> Vaine lunatique, against these scapes I could
> Dispute, and conquer, if I would,
> ('Womans constancy')[3]

and he may even think he has done so in the Holy Sonnet 'Death be not proud'.

It is to the youthful Donne and his experiments with Ovidian elegy that I wish to direct attention here. This is worth doing because his love poems, like the Satires, were circulated among friends (the usual mode of 'publication' for a gentleman-poet) and were singled out later by Donne as writings he did not wish to be copied: 'to my satires there belongs some fear, and to some elegies, and these perhaps shame . . . I am desirous to hide them'.[4] The reason for this desire for suppression had little however to do with Donne's valuation of the works as poems or their adequacy as artistic forms; but, as John Carey tells us, it had everything to do with concern for his public credentials: the government had shown itself 'suspicious of satires and love elegies and, by order of the Bishop of London, the public hangman had recently burned a number of private collections'.[5] The Bishop's action of disapproval seems directed on behalf of public morals, and Donne himself knew very well, at the time of writing his Ovidian elegies, that there was something daring and naughty about them, and that that was half of the fun.

This encounter with Ovid may have been crucial. His contemporaries regarded Donne as an original and matchless poet; even envious traditionalists recognised his revolutionary impulse. And an important part of their tribute focused on his uniqueness: they had never read anything like it before. As Thomas Carew's celebrated *An Elegie upon the Death of the Deane of Pauls, Dr. John Donne* puts it 'The lazie seeds/ Of servile imitation' were 'throwne away, / And fresh invention planted'. Carew constantly reiterates Donne's refusal to follow conventional patterns and norms; Donne has 'redeem'd' our 'Licentious thefts', our 'Mimique fury' posing as true 'poetique rage', our imitations of Anacreon and Pindar. Others had culled 'the prime / Buds of invention many a hundred yeare, / And left the rifled fields' but Donne 'gleaned more / Than all those times, and tongues could reape before'. And he fears that, now Donne is gone, the hacks and imitators will dominate once more:

> They will repeale the goodly exil'd traine
> Of gods and goddesses, which in thy just raigne
> Were banish'd nobler Poems, now, with these
> The silenced tales o'th'Metamorphoses
> Shall stuffe their lines, and swell the windy Page,
> Till Verse refin'd by thee, in this last Age
> Turne ballad rime, or those old Idolls bee
> Ador'd againe, with new apostacie.[6]

Carew's *Elegie* remains one of the best pieces of Donne criticism. Yet there may be a faint unconscious irony about Carew's reference to the return of Ovid. What he gloomily predicts is a return of the Ovid of the edifyingly allegorized *Metamorphoses*, but it was the other, under-the-counter Ovid of the *Amores* that first fired Donne: the sort of stuff that helps get a poet banished (as Ovid was) or his English translator knifed in a Deptford tavern.

There may be many ways of attempting to account for Donne's perceived originality and uniqueness. Some have tried to locate Donne's 'metaphysical' strain in the Petrarchan tradition, accounting for it as an exaggerated and decadent version of some Petrarchan mannerisms; others find the true origins of his stylistic devices in Ramistic logic; others in Euphuism; some cite the literature of emblems and the emblem habit of mind; some draw analogies with baroque architecture, or mannerist painting, or invite us to sample Gongora or Marino. It may therefore be only a glibly useful explanation for the shift from 'Elizabethan' to 'metaphysical' poetry to argue that at least part of what we are witnessing is not so much a change of heart but a change of models: Petrarch is out, and Ovid is in. The success of Marlowe's translation of the *Amores* (c. 1595) in a number of clandestine editions is an indication of the popular interest of the day. I think it can be fairly said that it is difficult to read Donne's amorous poetry without feeling that it is not quite respectable somehow, and we may simply conclude that this is because Donne was a rake. But there may be other possibilities, one of which may be that that sense of the not quite respectable, that determined and sometimes flamboyant social and moral non-conformity, is very evident in Ovid's *Elegia* and is reflected and adapted – *pace* Carew, a calculated, mimetic effect – by Donne. Both the attitudes and the machinery of Petrarchanism are derided: witness Donne's high-spirited anti-Petrarchan horror, 'The Comparison'. It also means that the Petrarchan poet-lover's postures of devotion and dependence, his quasi-liturgical acts of wooing-worship, his suits for 'pitie' and 'grace', give way to apparently more robust amatory and sexual exchanges between equals in which the poet-lover's rhetorical weapons are no longer those of the transcendental compliment or the plaint but vigorous, often cunning and sophistical, argument, verbal fencing, and a confident imperiousness ('Come, Madam') which, for all its evident chauvinism, at least acknowledges the woman as a worthy antagonist or conspirator.

That Donne found much of this in Ovid, and that he subtly both reflected and modified it, is the drift of what follows. One way of explaining Donne's uniqueness may be 'to explore . . . the structure of his imagination', as John Carey undertakes to do in his study of Donne. Lacking confidence in the belief that such an enterprise is in any case possible, I have opted for the more modest ambition of showing an example of Donne's commerce with some literary models.

The mannerisms of suavity, or of pique, or disingenuousness, or of deliberate outrage, or outrageousness, apparent in Ovid are evident too in the Roman love elegists of his circle: repeated editions of Tibullus and Propertius during the sixteenth century indicate the accessibility and currency of these poets among educated people, even though they may not be so frequently translated or echoed in the vernacular.[7]. The similarities between the Roman love elegists themselves may be extended to plot fascinating similarities between them and Donne and the 'metaphysicals'. Catullus, Propertius, Tibullus and Ovid thought of themselves as a group (*sodales*), a friendly yet competitive circle of poets conscious of writing poems which had a certain *nequitia* or naughtiness, which they defended by pointing to the playful (*lusus*) nature of their love elegies. They seem to have read and circulated poems to each other, cultivating a common tradition. They resisted 'poetic' language, disliking archaisms and the non-current, preferring an approximation to the language of everyday conversation, at least as compared with the elevated language of epic and tragic modes of poetry. They were overtly in competition not only with each other but with famous poetic models from Homer up to their present time, and exhibit a highly sophisticated *literary* sense.[8] And many of the things one might say about Ovid's *Amores* can also be said about Donne's erotic poetry. Thus Georg Luck will note how Ovid 'has the ability to experience romantic emotions and, half an hour later, regard them with detachment' ('For by to-morrow, I may thinke so too'); he invites us to wonder 'which is the true Ovid, the faithful lover of Elegy 1.3, or the roué of Elegy 2.4?', just as we might wonder the same about Donne's 'The Anniversarie' and 'Loves Usury' among the *Songs and Sonets*. A possible answer, in each case, might be what Luck suggests of Ovid: 'Neither, it seems; for both his tender devotion and his cynical frankness are literary attitudes'.[9]

And yet, whatever the resemblances and however likely it may be that Donne's attraction to Ovid was because he found there materials useful for mounting an elegant and pungent attack on, or reaction against, Petrarchan idealism, there are too profound and inevitable differences. Not the least among them is the fact that Ovid was a poet of Augustan Rome, whose attitudes towards love and marriage and erotic adventuring can be frankly pagan and *ad hominem*: merely *socially* acceptable or unacceptable. Between Ovid and Donne falls the shadow of guilty love, the temptations of 'the world, the flesh and the devil', the higher demands of Christian or Christian-Platonic transcendentalism, not only the limited anguish of *Odi, nec possum, cupiens, non esse quod odi* ('I hate what I am, and yet, for all my striving, I can only be what I hate') (*Amores*, 2.4) but the ultimate anguish of Sidney's 'Leave me o Love, which reachest but to dust'. Thus there is an added dimension of *nequitia*, more properly designated, in its full theological rigour, as sinfulness. Donne may *imitate* that Ovidian world, the young man's *Playboy* world in which women may be carelessly sampled, enjoyed, discarded and in which faithful love is an unnatural embarrassment; but the nature and the rules of the 'game' Donne plays in his Ovidian versions are complicated by the Christian assumptions and values of the world into which Donne projects his squibs. Neither he nor his readers can forget what the idealistic Petrarchan lovers knew only too well, that the sensual fixation upon an earthly object, even when wrought to a point of the highest spiritual refinement, is a diversion which may imperil not only the heroic life but the immortal soul. We may recall that

Petrarch's *Canzoniere*, which Renaissance poets were to take for a manual of the highest and most ennobling human love, is framed, in its first and last songs, by the severest possible judgement on the thirty one years of devotion it celebrates.

In part what Donne offers is not only a revision of poetic models and practice but a revision of poetic theory. The dominant (and, as we have seen, often precarious) Sidneyan apologetic – that poetry is ultimately morally edifying and teaches by delight – is frankly abandoned in favour of acute and frequently exaggerated analyses not of what people *should* do or be like, but what they actually *are* like. It is difficult, for example, to fathom what moral lesson Donne has in mind in his discussion (delightful or salacious, according to taste) about which end of a woman's body, the face or the feet, is the best point of departure for a journey towards 'the Centrique part' (*Elegie XVIII*, 'Loves Progress').

On the whole, Donne's moments of high-spirited and deliberately outrageous eroticism are clear enough, and clearly offer themselves as such. They also clearly draw much of their stimulus from the examples of the Roman love elegists. The really interesting moments are those such as when Donne implicitly acknowledges the un-Ovidian dimension of so Ovidian a poem as *Elegie XII*, 'His parting from her', with its adulterous lovers 'ambush'd round with household spies, / And over all thy husbands towring eyes'; its 'becks, winks, looks', its nudgings of feet 'under-boards'; for the poem is also shot through with Christian imagery of martyrs broken on the wheel and of Purgatory. *Elegie VIII*, 'The Comparison', can allow the extraordinary intrusion into its verbal and sexual nastiness of the tremblingly delicate analogy, 'So kisse good Turtles, so devoutly nice/ Are Priests in handling reverent sacrifice'. So too in *Elegie XIX*, 'To his Mistress Going to Bed', the whimsically manipulated language of theology (women 'Themselves are mystic books, which only wee / (Whom their imputed grace will dignifie) / Must see reveal'd') reinforces a special kind of *nequitia* unavailable to Ovid.

This is one important aspect of Donne's adaptations of Ovid. When we come to wonder what exactly Donne was doing with his Ovid (or his Marlowe-Ovid) we are too struck by his linguistic imitations. Ovid may have his *plorare* (to cry) instead of the more dignified and high-toned *flere* (to weep), or *lassus* (beat) for *fessus* (weary), and Donne may have his 'snorted' and 'suck'd'.

Stylistically, Ovid may have his racy monologue at a race-course (*Amores*, 3.2) and Donne his clandestine lover betrayed by his own after-shave (*Elegie IV*, 'The Perfume'), both apparently asserting, artfully, the oneness of literature and life. But where Ovid (and Catullus, Propertius and Tibullus) make their mark most significantly perhaps is through the Renaissance poets' discovery of the *dramatic* element in the Roman elegy, and their triumphant imitations of that dramatisation: imitations in which the dramatic representation leaves the speaker in the poem, who is himself dramatized, in an uncertain or ambivalent position. He may alternate between assurance and doubt, be crafty or cunning, jealous or helpless, caught in a drama of shifting involvement.[10] Added to this dramatic vigour is the peculiar (if largely undemonstrable) influence, or correspondence, of the Elizabethan theatre itself, which can be reflected in miniature in poems which are dramatic soliloquies or monologues, single speeches which, like iceberg tops, suggest an implied drama that underlies and surrounds them.

The dramatic disclosures of Ovid can certainly be recognised in Donne's most direct 'imitations':

> *tu, quia tam longa es, veteres heroidas aequas*
> *et potes in toto multa iacere toro;*
> *haec habilis brevitate sua est – corrumpor utraque.*
> *conveniunt voto longa brevisque meo*
> (The tall girl over there comes straight from Homer –
> Andromache on a *chaise longue*.
> Her friend's petite. I find them both irresistible –
> Short or tall they measure up to my dreams)
> (*Amores*, 2.4)[11]

and the speaker who expansively gestures:

> I can love both faire and browne,
> Her whom abundance melts, and her whom want betraies
> ('The Indifferent')

though Donne's poem, unlike the Roman Ovid's merely voluptuary smugness –

> *denique quas tota probat Vrbe puellas*
> *noster in has omnis ambitiosus amor*
> (Put it like this – there's beauty in Rome to please all

tastes, and mine are all-embracing) –

may contain in its final thrust a manoeuvre that shows the speaker himself as subtly disorientated since the joke of heretical and 'dangerous constancie' in love can only be funny if it is serious first:

> But I have told them, since you will be true,
> You shall be true to them, who'are false to you.

Similarly, the overtly Ovidian scenario of

> and at next nine
> Keepe midnights promise; mistake by the way
> The maid, and tell the Lady of that delay,
> ('Loves Usury')

reminding us of that wickedly devious pair of elegies (*Amores*, 2.7, 8) to Corinna and to Cypassis her maid, the incomparable coiffeuse, has its dying fall, suggesting another and inverted world of values altogether, in

> I'll beare it, though she bee
> One that loves mee.

We can of course read so familiar a poem as 'The Sun Rising' without any reference to Ovid at all, though we could hardly say that Donne wrote it without reference to Ovid: *Amores* 1.13, *Ad Auroram ne properet*, a waking-up-in-the-morning poem, catalogues those who are called to work by the sunrise (Ovid's seamen, travellers, soldiers, farm labourers, sleepy schoolboys, Donne's huntsmen, apprentices, 'country ants', sleepy schoolboys), and sustains a similar taunting or conspiratorial badinage with the Sun or Aurora the dawn, including jokes about being senile. Again, where Ovid leaves us with the laconic 'What-did-you-expect?' of

> *scires audisse – rubebat.*
> *nec tamen adsueto tardius orta dies*
> (She must have heard me – she turned pink.
> But the sun came up on time – as usual),

Donne offers by contrast a poem of superficial Ovidian character, exploiting Ovidian tones and devices, but which rises to affirmations quite alien to Ovid's urbane entertainments and carrying an ironic, and diminishing, contrast with their Ovidian counterparts: nobody in Ovid's world is going to say

> She is all States, and all Princes, I,
> Nothing else is.[12]

One of Donne's most sustained, and most theatrically vital, 'dialogues with the convention' is his *Elegy XVI: On His Mistris*, a poem often thought of as anomalous among Donne's *Elegies*, though perhaps for the wrong reasons. For those whose primary interest in the *Elegies* is to demonstrate Donne's imitations and adaptations of Ovidian themes and mannerisms the elegy has usually appeared an intractable oddity.[13] It does not have quite the usual bravura, lacks the self-justifying or cynical or peremptory voice, and is not full of whistling silks, betraying perfumes or haughty expostulations. Although we can point to Propertius (I, 8) or Ovid (2, 11) as models, forbidding the mistress to undertake a dangerous journey, Donne's poem has a quality of passionate tenderness which is quite un-Ovidian. Certainly it has its echoes: Marlowe's version of

> Lo country Gods, and known bed to forsake,
> *Corinna* means, and dangerous ways to take
> (*Elegia, XI, Ad amicam navigantem*)

may suggest

> Thou shalt not love by wayes so dangerous.

Ovid's

> *vade memor nostri, vento reditura secundo*

may hint at 'thirst to come backe' and 'when I am gone . . . ' The question

> *quid tibi, me miserum, Zephyros Eurosque timebo*
> *et gelidum Borean egelidumque Notum?*

is raised and expanded in Donne's poem. And the advice that

> *litora marmoreis pedibus signate, puellae –*
> *hactenus est tutum, cetera caeca via est*
> (Beauty should walk the beach with shining feet;
> beyond the water's edge lies danger)

sounds throughout the elegy. But again, instead of Ovid's frolic-some response (he is really looking forward to this moment) of

> *excipiamque umeris et multa sine ordine carpam*
>   *oscula, pro reditu victima vota cadet,*
> *inque tori formam molles sternentur harenae*
>   *et cumulus mensae quilibet esse potest . . .*
> *haec mihi quam primum caelo nitidissimus alto*
>   *Lucifer admisso tempora portet equo*
> (I'll carry you ashore – smother you with kisses –
> lay the promised victim low.
> We'll make a couch of soft sand
> With a dune for a table . . .
> Oh bring me that day, bright Lucifer!
> Bring it me soon – at full gallop),

the ending of Donne's poem reverberates with the ominous tones of a 'real' separation and a 'real' danger that can hardly be contained by the straightjacket of literary artifice.

For a poet of Donne's technical virtuosity the writing of public display poems wittily adapting Roman elegies is, in terms of literary craftsmanship, a serious business; the poetic exploration of reciprocal and committed love is also a serious business, and in this elegy Donne explores such a relationship. That he does so through a genre and medium whose built-in code is often designed not to sustain but rather to deny, regret or even wriggle out of such passionate seriousness adds a special tension to the poem, and the tension in its formal qualities is a function of the living tension it dramatically depicts within it.

The 'theatrical' effect of *Elegy XVI* is very striking, yet in this elegy, unlike most of Donne's others, we are not listening to a speaker who, half over his shoulder, is calculating his effect upon a public audience; instead we overhear an intimate conversation in which the speaker's whole force is directed to the dramatic occasion and whose eyes never leave the woman's face for an instant. We have a sense of eavesdropping on a living moment – and if such an interpretation of Donne's technique here may seem too Browningesque, that may only mean that Browning had been reading his Donne. The poem is conceived (like so many of the *Songs and Sonets*) as a little piece of theatre, a miniature play in one brief scene, beginning *in medias res* and concluding with a sense of a future that has yet to be unfolded but which will have been modified by this single moment that we, the reader-audience, have just witnessed. Donne's poem is neither monologue nor soliloquy, but a drama of conflict. The man in the poem certainly does all the talking, but his mistress is there, listening, objecting, responding. Her 'lines' are not written in but, as I shall try to show, her reaction is indicated by, and seems to influence throughout, the speaker's oaths, appeals, orders and advice.

The situation is simple enough, though it has too a romantic theatricality: he has to go abroad (we do not know why – it is simply rendered as an unavoidable fact) and she has the idea of going with him dressed as his page. He tries to dissuade her from such a foolhardy adventure, and, after some difficulty, succeeds. He is energetically articulate, at times overbearingly so, but both poet and persona are aware of their own verbal dexterity: 'my words masculine perswasive force'. His mission is likely to bring him into danger – he may be crossing the Alps, certainly the Channel. There are risks, and they both know it. He may even be going to fight. She is full of spirit and devoted to him or she would not have entertained such an extravagant notion. She is relatively young (like Juliet, she has a nurse), and unlike him she has never travelled abroad before. Of their relationship up to this point we know that her parents find it unacceptable ('by thy fathers wrath'), that their affair has been irked by 'spies and rivals' (an Ovidian literary motif transformed into a living situation); their relationship has been conducted in secret and they have at times been forced to lie low ('By our long starving hopes', 'pains, which want and divorcement hath'). They have also sworn mutual oaths to 'seale joynt constancy' in the face of these difficulties. There is a hint that she may even be pregnant, though Donne may only mean to suggest that the man has made love to her and is referring to that first occasion and to

> that remorse
> Which my words masculine perswasive force
> Begot in thee.

The theatricality of the disguise device, so much part of the stock-in-trade of the contemporary drama (Julia and Viola, Portia and Nerissa, Jessica, Rosalind, Imogen) has not prevented the verisimilitude of this 'biographical' information about the *dramatis personae* from registering with authentic conviction. Indeed, so artfully is it accomplished that the Bridgewater MS falls straight into the trap of assuming that the poem is about Donne and Ann More and offers the explanatory (and fanciful) subtitle 'His wife would have gone as his Page'.

> By our first strange and fatall interview,
> By all desires which thereof did ensue,
> By our long starving hopes, by that remorse
> Which my words masculine perswasive force
> Begot in thee, and by the memory
> Of hurts, which spies and rivals threatned me,
> I calmly beg. But by thy fathers wrath,
> By all paines, which want and divorcement hath,
> I conjure thee, and all the oathes which I
> And thou have sworne to seale joynt constancy,
> Here I unsweare, and overswear them thus,
> Thou shalt not love by wayes so dangerous.
> Temper, o faire Love, loves impetuous rage,
> Be my true Mistris still, not my faign'd Page;
> I'll goe, and, by thy kind leave, leave behind
> Thee, onely worthy to nurse in my minde,
> Thirst to come backe; o if thou die before,
> My soule from other lands to thee shall soare.
> Thy (else Almighty) beautie cannot move
> Rage from the Seas, nor thy love teach them love,
> Nor tame wild Boreas harshnesse; Thou hast reade
> How roughly hee in peeces shivered
> Faire Orithea, whom he swore he lov'd.
> Fall ill or good, 'tis madnesse to have prov'd
> Dangers unurg'd; Feed on this flattery,
> That absent Lovers one in th'other be.
> Dissemble nothing, not a boy, nor change
> Thy bodies habite, or mindes; bee not strange
> To thy selfe onely. All will spie in thy face
> A blushing womanly discovering grace;
> Richly cloath'd Apes, are call'd Apes, and as soone
> Ecclips'd as bright we call the Moone the Moone.
> Men of France, changeable Camelions,
> Spittles of diseases, shops of fashions,
> Loves fuellers, and the rightest company

Of Players, which upon the worlds stage be,
Will quickly know thee, and no lesse, alas!
Th'indifferent Italian, as we passe
His warme land, well content to thinke thee Page,
Will hunt thee with such lust, and hideous rage,
As *Lots* faire guests were vext. But none of these
Nor spungy hydroptique Dutch shall thee displease,
If thou stay here. O stay here, for, for thee
England is onely a worthy Gallerie,
To walke in expectation, till from thence
Our greatest King call thee to his presence.
When I am gone, dreame me some happinesse,
Nor let thy lookes our long hid love confesse,
Nor praise, nor dispraise me, nor blesse nor curse
Openly loves force, nor in bed fright thy Nurse
With midnights startings, crying out, oh, oh
Nurse, o my love is slaine, I saw him goe
O'r the white Alpes alone; I saw him I,
Assail'd, fight, taken, stabb'd, bleed, fall, and die.
Augure me better chance, except dread *Jove*
Thinke it enough for me to'have had thy love.

The scene begins with the speaker summoning his full resources to nip this folly in the bud, though Donne creates a long
moment of suspense by not revealing the cause of this lengthy
unswearing and overswearing until we are fourteen lines into the
poem. The atmosphere is highly charged from the opening line:

By our first strange and fatall interview.

'Strange' means extraordinary, unpredicted, out of the normal
course of likely events, and their first 'interview', or literal look-
ing-across at each other, was 'fatall' both because it was an act of
fate and because in some sense their old selves died then. They
received a fatal wound from Cupid's arrow, and Donne suggests a
whole world of Renaissance and medieval love-lore by that single
word. Some readers may already be prepared to think that the
man's motives and desires are not what they seem, and that what
we are about to witness is a truly Ovidian situation: the man has
made up his mind that it is time to move on and this is going to be
his opportunity. The poem thus becomes a drama of clever and

cynical manoeuvring. Such a pre-emptive reading may seem too insensitive to require refutation, but it may also indicate an aspect of the poem's tension. According to this interpretation the opening 'strange' may imply 'odd' and I want to get back to normal; 'fatall' may imply it killed me, or that I have been trapped by fate, but I intend to go on living again, free. Such a situation at the beginning of an Ovidian elegy is perfectly familiar. But any possibility of over-subtle ambiguity or of Freudian slips in the opening line is rapdily swept away by what follows and its true import becomes clear. It is six lines before the tension is relieved by the appearance of the main verb, and the effect of 'I calmly beg' is not unlike that of a man who when told he is shouting asserts *fortissimo* that he is not. The alleged calmness is belied by the rapid accumulation of instances, and the syntactical crescendo.

Nor has he done, for he begins again with another catalogue of energetic conjurings which conclude in the male assertiveness of

> Thou shalt not love by wayes so dangerous.

As far as the speaker is concerned the matter is now closed, the 'poem' over. There is a moment's pause. He then tries, more gently, to explain himself, to justify this *fiat*:

> Temper, o faire Love, loves impetuous rage,
> Be my true Mistris still, not my faign'd Page.

In a courtly, punning phrase, 'I'll goe, and, by thy kinde leave, leave behind / Thee', he seeks her consent and capitulation, but the syntax quickly breaks down from that opening flourish and he offers the tenderly elliptical

> Thee, onely worthy to nurse in my minde,
> Thirst to come back.

Again there is a pause, as though his persuasion has ended in her agreement. But there follows the extraordinary

> O if thou die before,
> My soule from other lands to thee shall soare.

What has provoked this sudden flight of rhetoric, this new departure? It can only be her response, the unwritten but clearly implied question, psychologically inevitable at such a tremulous moment: 'Suppose I die while you are away, before you come back?' In retrospect the 'O' is perhaps significantly mimetic, for towards the end of the elegy he gently mocks her speech patterns: 'oh, oh / Nurse, O my love is slaine'. His own exclamations are more subdued, merely explanatory or persuasive: 'O faire Love', 'O stay here'. And the comfort he offers to this nervous question takes the form of a poetic flourish, of his soul soaring to her from distant lands. Combining a neat compliment with pragmatic common sense, he tells her not to behave like King Canute:

> Thy (else Almighty) beautie cannot move
> Rage from the Seas, or thy love teach them love,
> Nor tame wilde Boreas harshnesse.

The appeal here is to what she has read in Ovid's *Metamorphoses* about Boreas, 'How roughly hee in peeces shivered / Faire Orithea, whom he swore he lov'd'. He seems to be telling her that the apparent favour of the North Wind himself is no guarantee of safety: remember Orithea. But, as Helen Gardner's bald note to the lines in her anthology *The Metaphysical Poets* assures us, 'In all known versions of the myth Boreas . . . carried the maiden undamaged to the mountains, where she bore him many children'. Is Donne simply getting it wrong? Or is Donne's persona only? Or is Donne's persona craftily adapting the story to his own ends, hoping she may not have the details clear enough to argue with him? Is the reader supposed to notice the error? Whether we do so or not, the impression given is of a man thinking on his feet, grasping at tactical arguments as they come to hand; if we see that he is twisting them to his own advantage, so much greater is the impression of a man under pressure to find authority and instance for his urging of caution, even to the point of a trifling deception.

And then, for a second time, the speaker asserts his conclusion and lays down the law. The whole scheme is folly, whether it were to succeed or not, and the risks may be avoided entirely by staying at home:'Fall ill or good, 'tis madnesse to have prov'd / Dangers unurg'd.' Our life together, it is implied, is full enough of dangers already; don't invent new ones. Again, the poem should end, but again he feels the need to justify or mollify this rejection of her. In doing so he finds a curious turn of phrase: 'Feed on this flattery, / That absent Lovers one in th' other be.' It is 'flattery' because he wants to pre-empt her anticipated response to the otherwise pat and routine consolation that absent lovers are in each other – her response of 'I *knew* you would say that' – by conceding in advance that it *may* be only lovers' self-flattery. Nevertheless he urges her to 'feed' on it, implying that it is no more than the truth. 'Nurse', 'thirst', 'feed' – these are the verbs that carry the tenderness of nurturing and sustenance which will keep them alive while they are apart.

She is still not convinced and won over. In trying still further tactics, the speaker must get down to specific detail. He brings to bear on her the weight of his superior experience and judgement, arguing that she will never get away with it, and then (inconsistently) that even if she does it will not help her. Her disguise will fail because 'All will spie in thy face / A blushing womanly discovering grace'. The beautiful and tenderly admiring cadence of the lines culminates in 'grace', that quality which he uniquely finds in her but which all the world will see. To prove his point that disguise is impossible he offers a witty analogy: 'Richly cloath'd Apes, are call'd Apes', sensing too late the inaptness (and ineptness) of the comparison and retrieving it with 'and as soone / Ecclips'd as bright we call the Moone the Moone.' This is the thought process of a living moment, imitated by Donne with the most artful effects of spontaneity and drama.

The section on the French, the Italians and the Dutch which follows has proved a stumbling-block for some readers. Wilbur Sanders, for example, expresses the unease which this passage can generate:

> It's very disconcerting, as one gets further into the poem, to find Donne permitting himself – or is it another creature escaped from his menagerie of personae? – a xenophobic diatribe against the diseased French, the spongy Dutch, and other deviant national groups who can't quite manage to be English.

It is disconcerting and disappointing because the poem 'seemed to promise much more'. For Sanders the outburst effectively destroys the poem, for Donne's wit is here pushed 'too far in the direction of display for any wholly tactful handling of the reality to be possible'.[14] But 'reality' of a kind could be said to be asserting itself, for according to theatrical convention, disguise as a page is invariably held to be impenetrable: nobody 'sees through' Caesario or Fidele. The speaker's implication is that such theatrical stunts may succeed in the theatre, but they do not in life – and here is what life will do to it. Moreover, the French – 'the rightest company / Of Players, which upon the worlds stage be' – know all the tricks. And despite the length of the diatribe, the reality of the dramatic situation remains clear and unimpaired. It is another tactical deception, like the story of Orithea. The pure verbal energy and display of the passage is perfectly consistent with the persona's characterization as it has already been revealed. The poem's opening (which Sanders curiously describes as having 'an intent stillness') is a similar accumulative catalogue rising to its climax, 'Thou shalt not'. Here the climax, the whole point of the grisly narration, lies in 'If thou stay here', asserted with the now familiar thump of monosyllables. It is part of the power of his persuasion, and its intention is obviously to scare her out of the proposed adventure.

John Carey's explanation of the poem's tone and the speaker's motives depends upon a larger sense of Donne's fascination with power, and his urge to impose it. This elegy, while not quite reaching the 'almost pathological imperiousness' of 'To his Mistress Going to Bed', nevertheless 'aggrandizingly establishes Donne's power over the girl's thoughts and actions' (Donne of course being always *in propria persona* in his poems). For Carey the poem is not about love at all but about power and authority, evidenced by the fact that it is 'composed, throughout, of instructions'. It would be difficult to argue that trying to scare somebody into submission is not an exercise of power, and Carey justifiably points to Donne's (or Donne's persona's?) dictatorial attitudes, in this poem as in many others. However, the poem is not ' composed, throughout, of instructions', as I have shown; nor does this view adequately account for those momentary tender inflexions which, in a context of orders and vetoes, register like punctures of gentle collapse. It can also become an explanation *ad absurdum* when Carey adds to his evidence the observation that even the 'effort of the dramatic imagination' in the poem is only another version of Donne's lust for power, the satisfaction derived from entering 'the subconscious mind of another being'.[15] Leaving aside the obvious fact that the so-called subconscious mind of the other being which is entered into is itself a construct of the poet's imagination (unless we are back with the Bridgewater MS), it would appear that no maker of fiction can then be free from the suspicion of tyranny over those who inhabit his creations – and a maker who deliberately exhibits 'masculine perswasive force' diagnoses his pathological condition infallibly. Perhaps the explanation only begins to make sense when we pretend that nobody but Donne had ever written poems on such subjects, and even better sense when we abandon the idea that Donne is making fictions, or poems, at all.

The device has its Ovidian counterpart in *Amores* 2.11, where Ovid too attempts to dissuade Corinna from her sea journey:

> *sero respicitur tellus ubi fune soluto*
> *currit in immensum panda carina salum,*
> *navita sollicitus cum ventos horret iniquos*
> *et prope tam letum quam prope cernit aquam.*
> *quod si concussas Triton exasperet undas,*
> *quam tibi sit toto nullus in ore color!*
> *tum generosa voces fecundae sidera Ledae*
> *et 'felix' dicas 'quem sua terra tenet!'*
> (Too late to look back when the rope's cast off
> and your freighter heads for the far horizon,
> when the captain scans the sky for squalls
> and sees death as near as the water.
> How pale you'll turn
> if Triton sets the waves tossing!
> How hard you'll pray to Leda's twins,
> and how you'll envy people ashore!)

For Ovid's merely *gemütlich*

> *tutius est fovisse torum, legisse libellos,*
> *Threiciam digitis increpuisse lyram*
> (It's far safer to put your feet up
> and read a book or strum a guitar),

Donne has

> O stay here, for, for thee
> England is onely a worthy Gallerie . . .

And instead of Ovid's shoulder-shrug

> *at si vana ferunt volucres mea dicta procellae,*
> *aequa tamen puppi sit Galatea tuae*
> *vestrum crimen erit talis iactura puellae,*
> *Nereidesque deae Nereidumque pater*
> (Still, if I'm wasting words on the winds
> may Galatea do her level best for you.

> On your heads be it, Nereids and father Nereus,
> if such a girl is lost for ever),

Donne's persona actually succeeds, through the sheer force of his scabrous hyperbole. He assaults the listener with superior knowledge, with a vision of a world of predatory sexuality and drunkenness in which she will be like a lamb to the slaughter. His last card, played with all the exaggerated verve he can muster, works. From that point on in the elegy the lovers speak only of what she will do, how she should behave, while he is away. She has at last capitulated.

To take with the wrong sort of seriousness the apparently self-contained 'xenophobic diatribe' is another form of the kind of uncontextual reading which can isolate, and attribute the wrong sort of seriousness to, the later exclamation

> Nurse, o my love is slaine, I saw him goe
> O'r the white Alpes alone,

and offer it (as in Auden and Garrett's anthology *The Poet's Tongue*) as if it were a fragment of Romantic *angst*. In its context it is nothing of the kind. Similarly, take out of their dramatic context the bisexual Italians, lusty French and drunken Dutch may remind us of the world of the *Satires* or of other elegies, but here the hint of over-indulgence need not be Donne's but the authentic voice of the strenuously protective persona producing his clinching argument. Taken in context the final movement of the elegy conveys an unaffected tenderness now that the skirmish is over.

England and home is the only 'Gallerie' worthy of her, where she may 'walke in expectation' of his return in safety. Not only would he protect her from such dangers now, but always: 'till from thence / Our greatest King call thee to his presence' (perhaps harking back to 'o if thou die before'). 'When I am gone' is an accomplished tense, and he will go alone – not 'I'll goe, and, by thy kinde leave . . .' – but an achieved, negotiated and imminent fact. What remains is for her to wish him well, and for him to give her some practical advice: 'When I am gone, dreame me some happinesse'. The mood for the moment is of the 'Song', 'Sweetest love, I do not goe':

> Let not thy divining heart
> Forethinke me any ill,

> Destiny may take thy part,
> And may thy feares fulfill;

and the elegy's line has the same lyric cadence. Moreover she
must not give the game away at home:

> Nor let thy lookes our long hid love confesse,
> Nor praise, nor dispraise me, nor blesse nor curse
> Openly loves force.

This might appear for an instant as a merely literary Ovidian
motif and remind us of *Elegy IV: The Perfume* where the girl is
warned of her mother who 'fearing lest thou'art swoln, doth thee
embrace'. But the contrast of tone, situation and feeling is much
more apparent than the likeness – it is Ovid unmasked and
brought to face and do service to the reality of a love that is
depicted in its full and mysterious seriousness.

The tension and the fear that lies between the two lovers is
relieved, as such moments often are, by a joke, an exaggeration, a
tenderly mocking piece of mimicry which defuses the situation
by jesting about the very thing they fear most:

> nor in bed fright thy Nurse
> With midnights startings, crying out, oh, oh
> Nurse, o my love is slaine, I saw him goe
> O'r the white Alpes alone; I saw him I,
> Assail'd, fight, taken, stabb'd, bleed, fall, and die.

One can see the man, always ready to warm to his verbal work,
miming the action for the woman until she is forced to smile at
such virtuosity, and this laughter-through-tears is confirmed by
his 'Augure me better chance'.[16] His final words, perhaps *sotto
voce*, are addressed almost to fate or to Jove himself:

> except dread *Jove*
> Thinke it enough for me to have had thy love.

It may be impious to expect more happiness than I have already
been given. The lines point to what lies ahead and acknowledge
his sober recognition that should he die there is little he could
complain of – a recognition that both affirms the nature of his
love for her and the danger of what is to be undertaken. The last
lines do not exactly, I think, 'supply the calm after the storm';[17]

rather they leave an ominous reminder that the jest 'bleed, fall, and die' may be in truth what destiny has in store.

Elegy XVI is an example of Donne's dramatic writing at its finest – the accuracy of ear, the sureness of touch, the depiction of shifting tones and shifting involvement, the captured record of a living moment. Donne catches this elusive quality at times in *Songs and Sonets*, but nowhere is it so sustained nor handled with more deftness and tact. What is all the more remarkable is that in such a poem of tender and difficult parting Donne can also offer a sophisticated comment on the elegiac mode itself, almost challenging us to read it in the wrong way. The reader is teased with the usual ingredients and expectations of an Ovidian form – tones of self-justification or self-abasement, grandiose or ironic gesturing, bravura expostulations, a finely discriminating sensuality, a world of jealousies, secrecies and frustrated desires – dramatically transformed and superseded by a voice of unaffected and authentic candour. *Elegy XVI* shows a poet capable of effecting that metamorphosis not merely by brazenly 'witty' sleight-of-hand but by the subtle and simultaneous exhibition and suppression of that very 'literariness' which his genre implies.

NOTES

1. See Edmund Gosse, *The Life and Letters of John Donne*, 2 vols, London: Heinemann, 1899, 1, pp. 171, 197.
2. John Carey, *John Donne: Life, Mind and Art*, London: Faber, 1981, p. 70.
3. Text of Donne's poems from *The Complete English Poems of John Donne*, ed. C.A. Patrides, London: Dent, 1985.
4. E. M. Simpson, *A Study of the Prose Works of John Donne*, 2nd edn, Oxford: Oxford University Press, 1948, p. 316.
5. Carey, *John Donne*, p. 70.
6. Thomas Carew, *An Elegie*, printed in the posthumous first edition of Donne's *Poems*, 1633.
7. For example, the first and second Aldine editions, 1502; 1515. See A. J. Peacock, 'Donne's Elegies and the Roman Love Elegy', *Hermathena*, 119 (1975), pp. 20–9.
8. See J-P. Boucher, *Etudes sur Properce*, Paris, 1965, chap. 1, 'La génération elégiaque'; Georg Luck, *The Latin Love Elegy*, London; Methuen, 1959.
9. Luck, *The Latin Love Elegy*, pp. 157, 160–1.
10. See A. LaBranche, '*Blanda Elegia*: the Background of Donne's Elegies', *Modern Language Review*, 61 (1966), pp. 357–68.
11. Text and translation from *Ovid's Amores*, by Guy Lee, London: Murray, 1968.

12. See J. B. Leishman's perspicuous comments on the relationship between the two poems in *The Monarch of Wit*, London: Hutchinson, 1951, pp. 190–1.

13. Leishman discusses only the 'biographical' questions behind the poem and merely says: 'Whether, though, the experience behind this elegy was real or imaginary, it is a superb piece of drama'. Donne appears to be 'writing tenderly rather than merely wittily, cynically and impudently' – a remark which is absorbed in the general judgement on the *Elegies* that in them 'Donne's attitude . . . is almost wholly unserious, is never more, one might almost say, than a kind of serious trifling' (*The Monarch of Wit*, pp. 70–1, 90).

14. Wilbur Sanders, *John Donne's Poetry*, Cambridge: Cambridge University Press, 1971, p. 42.

15. John Carey, *John Donne*, pp. 116–17.

16. John Carey's account of Donne's effect here seems hampered by his discovery of a resemblance between 'the simplified, surreal landscape, void except for one looming feature' in Donne's *Satyre III* ('On a huge hill . . .') and its reappearance in these lines (the 'White Alpes'). Since I cannot see the connection it is difficult to comment. What is more approachable is the inaccuracy of 'that weirdly lit nightmare which the waking girl describes to her nurse' (*John Donne*, pp. 11–12). Such a way of describing the situation (and thus of reading it) fails to register the fact that there *is* no nightmare, no 'waking' or 'frightened' or 'nightmare-shocked' girl, no description to her nurse; there is only the man-in-the-poem's tactically imagined depiction of it. In a later comment on the lines (pp. 116–17) Carey concedes that there is 'an effort of the dramatic imagination' about it all, but only then to accuse Donne of Svengali-like obsessions.

17. Roma Gill, '*Musa Iocosa Mea*: Thoughts on the *Elegies*', in *John Donne: Essays in Celebration*, ed. A. J. Smith, London: Methuen, 1972, p. 71.

3

CONVENTIONS OF DEVOTION I
Vented wit and crossed brains

You may know a new utterance by the element of danger in it.
D. H. Lawrence, review of 'A Second Contemporary Verse
Anthology', 1923

The questions posed in Chapters 3 and 4 are designed to expose
the implications of some of the antitheses, or colliding conventions, that lie at the heart of the activity of devotional writing.
The first concerns the relationship between the almost obligatory
(in the earlier seventeenth century) fashionable poetic mannerisms of wit, paradox, and conceited quasi-logical argument, and
the conventional subject-matter and the conventional posture of
the practitioner implied in a form of discourse – Christian prayer
and meditation – with more than a thousand years of tradition
behind it. What is the nature of the relationship between wit and
devotion? Seventeenth-century devotional poets writing in the
current 'metaphysical' style could be particularly vulnerable to,
and also show themselves to be acutely sensitive about, the kind
of charge made by Dr Johnson in his famous remark (in the *Life of
Waller*) that 'The ideas of Christian Theology are too simple for
eloquence, too sacred for fiction, and too majestic for ornament;
to recommend them by tropes and figures, is to magnify by a
concave mirror the sidereal hemisphere'. We may notice in passing that even this apparently clear statement is not without a
wrinkle, for Johnson lapses, quite naturally, into a metaphorical
trope to illustrate his point: unless, of course, his figure is not
meant as metaphor at all but as literal, and carries with it a vision
of the absurd Laputa-like apparatus necessary for such an attempted magnification. Nevertheless, a poet with a heavy invest-
ment in eloquence, fiction, ornament, tropes and figures is, it
would seem, on treacherous ground when he turns his skills to
make addresses to God, risking that sort of tactlessness and
fundamental *irrelevance* that one can readily detect (to take an
example from the approximate human analogy of the elegy) in

comparing Milton's pastoral 'Lycidas' with some other contributors to the anthology *Justa Eduardo King*, such as Cleveland's up-to-the-minute, flashily hyperbolic but inconsequential witticisms:

> When we have fill'd the rundlets of our eyes,
> We'll issue 't forth, and vent such elegies,
> As that our tears shall seem the *Irish* Seas,
> We floating Islands, living *Hebrides*.

His opening gambit of

> I like not tears in tune, nor will I prize
> His artificial grief that scans his eyes

is certainly not going to prevent his own artificial expression of grief, though his declamatory flourish of

> I am no Poet here; my pen's the spout,
> Where the rain water of my eyes run out

may, in its first part, readily elicit agreement.

The sort of disabling doubt that even a Cleveland may have been privately exercised over – awareness of the opportunistically self-advertizing character of his proffered study of grief – is one that a writer committed to a poetic of witty metaphor encounters with even greater force in devotional discourse. It may be very well for a Sidney to speak of poetic wit as a reflection of God's creativity, or for later theorists of wit, like Baltasar Gracián or Emanuele Tesauro, to argue that conceited, tropological, allegorical and analogical wit is both a discovery and an imitation of God's wit already fully written in the book of nature.[1] The 'theory of correspondence' justifying conceited writing may be easily recognized and easily documented in the familiar 'Elizabethan world picture'. And this apparently secure Elizabethan analogy between poetic and divine creation, which regards human wit as a quasi-divine aptitude or faculty apprehending and manipulating relationships either expressed or existing potentially in nature through the wit of the Creator, may produce an orderly, yet also clever and surprising, perceptiveness in its imitative poetic artefacts. But what if (as Bacon among others had darkly suspected) it was all nonsense?[2] And weren't there anyway (as St Paul and Calvin among others had explained) very good theological reasons for supposing that it *was* all nonsense?

Bulky questions of cultural history loom up here. I want therefore to direct attention to smaller matters of human anatomy and physiology. Dr Helkiah Crooke (a sort of early seventeenth-century Dr Jonathan Miller) offers in his book *A Description of the Body of Man* (1615) a prospectus of the prodigious fund of analogical imagery opened up even by our belches, coughs and sneezes; in his second chapter 'Of the dignitie and wonderfull Frame of Man's Body' he writes:

The rumbling of the guts, their croaking murmurs, the rapping escapes and the hudled and redoubled belchings of the stomach, doe represent the fashion and manner of all kinds of thunders. The violent and gathering rage of blustering winds, tempestuous stormes and gusts, are not onely exhibited, but also fore-shewed by exhaled crudities and by the hissing, singing and ringing noyses of the eares. The humor and moistnesse that fals like a current or streame into the empty spaces of the throat, the throtle and the chest, resembleth raine and showres.[3]

Such physiological analogies can of course be modulated into Lear's

Blow, winds, and crack your cheeks! rage! blow! . . .
Rumble thy bellyful! Spit, fire! spout, rain!

and the secular poet need have no inhibitions about exploring, for wittily explicative purposes, even the most fundamental of human functions. Donne's lovers may suck and snort and be bitten by fleas, but others might go further. If one were (by some eccentric chance) to look up the word *fart* in Dr Johnson's *Dictionary* (1755), one would find 'FART n.f. wind from behind' mischievously illustrated by Johnson with a perfectly crafted and theoretically impeccable urbane enthymeme, or metaphysical conceit, from Sir John Suckling:

Love is the *fart*
Of every heart:
It pains a man when 'tis kept close;
And others doth offend, when 'tis let loose.

Johnson also relishes the inclusion, under 'To FART v.a. to break wind behind', of Swift's comically reductive

> As when we a gun discharge,
> Although the bore be ne'er so large,
> Before the flame from muzzle burst,
> Just at the breech it flashes first;
> So from my lord his passion broke,
> He farted first, and then he spoke.

Yet, despite the sacred writing inscribed within our bodies, this is a range of allusion hardly available (for good reasons of taste, decorum, tone) to the devotional poet or writer, though the relentless anatomical details of Donne's *Devotions*, or some of the engraved 'devices' of emblem writers (like John Hall's *Emblems with Elegant Figures*, 1658, one of which is of an inoffensive-looking old man exposing his anatomically dissected chest cavity to illustrate the epigram. 'See how these poisonous passions gnaw and feed'), may sometimes seem to get close to it.

The nature of the doubt at issue here, however, is not really a question of taste or decorum. It is a more profound scepticism which distrusts that very mental agility and excited perceptiveness which is so characteristically celebrated by Renaissance poets, artists, playwrights, organisers of pageants and processions, emblem writers, or compilers of medical handbooks. In rhapsodic mood, Donne can write about (and thus underwrite) the theory of correspondence with breathless excitement:

> Consider the immensitie of the creatures this world produces; our *creatures* are our *thoughts, creatures* that are borne of *Gyants*; that reach from *East* to *West*, from *Earth* to *Heaven*, that doe not onely bestride all the *Sea*, and *Land*, but span the *Sunn* and *Firmament* at once; My thoughts reach all, comprehend all. (*Devotions upon Emergent Occasions*, IV)

But in moments of doubt, or of a more ponderous sense of what the doctrine of the Fall, of mankind's depravity, and of what sheer human craziness might mean, Donne has a very different view of the capabilities of these creatures of the mind. He is aware, like Fulke Greville, that

> when each of us in his own heart lookes,
> He finds the God there, farre unlike his Bookes.
> (*Chorus Sacerdotum, Mustapha*, 1633)

In the same *Devotions* Donne can conjure up the *frisson* of those thundering Protestant rhetorics of man's inadequacy:

> When God made this *Earth* of *nothing*, it was but a little helpe, that he had, to make other things of this *Earth*: nothing can be nearer nothing, than this *Earth*; yet how little of this *Earth* is the *greatest Man*! Hee thinkes hee treads upon the *Earth*, that all is under his feete, and the *Braine* that thinkes so, is but *earth*. (*Devotions*, XI)

But it is this brain, the generator which sparks the metaphysical flicker from world to world, that is the active centre of the poet's creativity. Thus Herbert's 'The Forerunners' asks:

> The harbingers are come. See, see their mark;
> White is their colour, and behold my head.
> But must they have my brain? must they dispark
> Those sparkling motions, which therein were bred?
> Must dulnesse turn me to a clod?

Paradoxically but characteristically, the brain's imminent extinction is rendered with the sublest kind of wit, Herbert punning on 'dispark' and 'spark'. His usage is singled out by the *OED* to illustrate 'dispark' as 'disimpark, as of deer', 'to throw open parkland, or to convert it to other uses'. (In 'The Church Militant' Herbert speaks of 'our Saviour . . . Disparking oracles'.) The proximate 'sparkling', with its associated 'disparkle', meaning both to disperse or scatter, and to sparkle forth, like the 'towering . . . disparkling' desires of the amorous bridegroom in Herrick's 'Nuptiall Song iv', defines the brain as the breeding place ('therein were bred') of poetic wit, analogously and synonymically.

'The Forerunners' reviews the poet's past attempts to baptize the products of that brain: 'invention . . . possessing heart and brain' ('Love I'); 'then shall our brain / All her invention on thine Altar lay' ('Love II'); 'The propositions of hot blood and brains' ('The Pearl'); 'Thousands of notions in my brain did runne' ('Jordan II'):

> My God must have my best, ev'n all I had.

But he concludes with a note of resigned indifference to what was probably no more than otiose 'embellishment' anyway:

> Yet if you go, I passe not; take your way.

It is not difficult to suspect a certain kind of double-think here, a poetically fruitful tension between commitment to two incompatible ideals that gives so much seventeenth-century devotional verse its peculiar poignancy.

The notions, propositions and inventions of the brain are ambiguous not only because of the suspicion that our wit may not be quite as 'erected' as Sidney seemed to believe, but also because of their inevitable (however unintended) concomitant of 'Decking the sense, as if it were to sell' ('Jordan II'), and to sell not only the poem, but the poet too. Donne's *A Litanie* glances at the problem in

> Those heavenly Poets which did see
> Thy will, and it express
> In rhythmique feet, in common pray for mee,
> That I by them excuse not my excesse
> In seeking secrets, or Poetiquenesse,
>
> (VIII)

and confronts it head-on in the pungently laconic:

> When wee are mov'd to seeme religious
> Only to vent wit, Lord deliver us.
>
> (XXI)

Every devotional poet must excuse his 'excesse', devise some strategy, apologetic, or justification of his enterprise. Herbert may practise witty writing and say that he does not care if that facility (his *raison d'être* as a poet) is ultimately withdrawn. He may write witty verses deploring wit,

> Wit fancies beautie, beautie raiseth wit:
>   The world is theirs; they two play out the game,
>   Thou standing by –
>
> ('Love I')

where it may not be enough to say he simply means secular wit – and convince us that 'Dust blown by wit' ('Love II') is just as much dust as that blown by the wind. The edge of wit may 'cut and carve' while 'faith lies by' ('Divinitie'). In 'Assurance' he claims,

> When wit contrives to meet with thee,
> No such rank poyson can there be,

(meaning there can be none more rank), and in 'The Posie' the arts of poetry are waved aside with

> Invention rest,
> Comparisons go play, wit use thy will.

The poems themselves can be protected from the scouring effects of this constant, self-deprecating and art-deprecating undercurrent only by the claim that, at their best, they were only half written by the poet, that they are fortunate, though not quite serendipitous, collaborations, as *The Dedication* to *The Temple* suggests:

> *Lord, my first fruits present themselves to thee;*
> *Yet not mine neither: for from thee they came.*

So many of Herbert's poems find their resolution in a shift of responsibility for them: a voice from outside the poem, revaluing it or rescuing it; a running refrain, implied or expressed, of *'But thou shalt answer, Lord, for me'* ('The Quip'); a resigned abrogation of poetry in the act of making it – 'Farewell sweet phrases, lovely metaphors' ('The Forerunners') – or an incontestable authenticating device, like that of 'Assurance':

> Thou didst at once thy self indite,
> And hold my hand, while I did write.

Much of the interim may be full of 'long pretence' that goes wide of the mark ('Jordan II'), 'false embroyderies' ('Vanitie II'), and 'poore paper' ('Deniall'), 'lost in flesh' and 'sugred lyes' ('Dulnesse'), a mere 'brittle crazie glasse' ('The Windows'). Without miraculous divine intervention the poems merely deconstruct, like Marvell's shattered 'curious frame' of both the poem and the poet himself in 'The Coronet'. Donne (though we don't have to believe him) may sometimes think it is better not to write at all: in his extraordinary poem *Metempsycosis: The Progresse of the Soule*, he has the lines:

Except my legend be free from the letts
Of steepe ambition . . .
O let me not launch out, but let mee save
Th'expense of braine and spirit; that my grave
    His right and due, a whole unwasted man may have,
                    (43–50)

with a final phrasing that so oddly recalls Shakespeare's 'Th'
expense of spirit in a waste of shame'.

Donne's own solution to this devotional paradox is (again paradoxically and characteristically) one of his most witty and resonant conceited figures. *The Crosse* is a poem which exhibits *par
excellence* that intoxicated leaping from correspondence to correspondence, which plunders all the figures or likenesses of the
cross to be found in art and nature, and which shares in that sort
of Renaissance mental habit which produced Lipsius's compendium of analogies, *De Cruce* (Antwerp, 1595):

> Who can deny mee power, and liberty
> To stretch mine armes, and mine owne Crosse to be?
> Swimme, and at every stroake, thou art thy Crosse,
> The Mast and yard make one, where seas do tosse.
> Looke downe, thou spiest out Crosses in small things;
> Looke up, thou seest birds rais'd on crossed wings.
>
> (17–22)

J. A. W. Bennett pointed out that all the likenesses Donne indicates here were collected by early Christian writers; the most
concise commentary is ascribed to Jerome (Migne, *Patrologia Latina*, XXX, 638). Bennett also noted that editions of Lipsius's work
include an illustration showing a swimmer, a bird, a man praying,
a sail furled cross-wise, and similar figures.[4] Donne's flourish concludes with an impossible mathematical feat Hobbes would have
appreciated (though it comes again from this tradition), the imaginative squaring of the circle:

> All the Globes frame, and spheares, is nothing else
> But the Meridians crossing Parallels,
>
> (23–24)

though Donne might have recalled his own opening to *Upon the
translation of the Psalmes by Sir Philip Sydney, and the Countesse of
Pembroke his Sister*, where he precisely endorses Dr Johnson's
point:

> Eternall God, (for whom who ever dare
> Seeke new expressions, doe the Circle square,
> And thrust into strait corners of poore wit
> Thee, who art cornerlesse and infinite).

But Donne has yet more devices, this time sematic ones. He puns his way through *cross* as check or restrain ('therefore cross/ Your joy in crosses') and *cross* as making the sign of the cross ('And cross thy heart'). Meanings tumble over one another: cross as 'check', cross as 'cross out', cross as 'cross over', cross as 'counter to'. This same collection of puns is, of course, conspicuously available to other devotional poets too: Herbert's actual and poetic sinner who finds

> quarries of pil'd vanities,
> But shreds of holinesse, that dare not venture
> To shew their face, since crosse to thy decrees;
> ('The Sinner')

his prayer 'Let suppling grace, to cross his [sin's] art, / Drop from above' ('Grace'); or his question

> And art thou grieved, sweet and sacred Dove,
> When I am sowre
> And crosse thy love?
> ('Ephes.' 4.30)

Similarly, Henry Vaughan has 'Crosses are but curbs / To check the mule, unruly man' ('Affliction', *Silex Scintillans, or Sacred Poems*), and in 'Love, and Discipline' Vaughan gives thanks

> Blest be thy Dew, and blest thy frost,
> And happy I to be so crost,
> And cur'd by Crosses at thy cost.

But Donne's *tour de force* is reserved for the poem's conclusion, and takes us back to the imaginative anatomy of a Dr Helkiah Crooke – though this time it is not a conceit which trails behind it copious previous analogues, but seems, in its concise clarity, to be entirely original to Donne:

> And as thy braine through bony walls doth vent
> By sutures, which a Crosses forme present,
> So when thy braine workes, ere thou utter it,
> Crosse and correct concupiscence of witt.
> (55–58)

It is a remarkable image, and one which asserts the Creator's wit in organizing the cranial structure so that the frontal suture continues the line of the sagittal, across the coronal, making the front of the skull at our birth present 'a Crosses forme'. (*Gray's Anatomy* notes that the frontal bone 'consists of two pieces separated by the frontal suture, but union begins in the second year, and the frontal suture is usually obliterated, except at its lower part, by the eighth year', though in some adults it may persist.)[5] At the same time the image impresses a warning that what issues from that brain, thus enclosed and crossed in infancy, must be a crossed and corrected wit. Of course, the claim which diminishes that human wit, which checks poetic 'concupiscence' or exuberance, and seeks to cow us with the fact that the Creator's wit is in any case far superior to and infinitely more witty than our own, is itself a witty 'discovery', a brilliant *aperçu*, an imaginative construction, like Donne's repeated conundrum of East and West, or the magical trick of

> We thinke that *Paradise* and *Calvarie*,
>   *Christs* Crosse, and *Adams* tree, stood in one place.
>   ('Hymne to God my God, in my sicknesse')

In this cranial seat of activity there are ventilation flues. According to Aristotle (*De Partibus Animalium*, ii, 7, 653[b]) the size of the human brain (though Dr Helkiah Crooke disagrees scornfully with him) is due to the excessive heat generated by the heart and lungs which requires, as counterpoise, the superabundant fluidity and coldness of the brain: 'the cranial bone, which some call the Bregma, is the last to become solidified; so long does evaporation continue to occur through it under the influence of heat . . . Man, again, has more sutures in his skull than any other animal . . . The reason is again found in the greater size of the brain, which demands ventilation, proportionate to its bulk'.[6] It is as though a warm weather front were meeting a cold one. But for Donne this venting is not a merely physiological feature, or a function of our internal meteorology. It is metaphorically and iconographically significant. What is vented is *wit*:

> When wee are mov'd to seeme religious
> Only to vent wit, Lord deliver us,

and the verb *vent* has connotations, like the issuing of steam under pressure, of literal and metaphorical hot air.

Venting implies some kind of evacuation of superfluities: they may be passions – as in Donne's 'Then our land waters (teares of passion) vent' in the *Elegie on the Lady Markham* (elegists perpetually *vent* grief), or in Jonson's 'To vent that poore desire', or the passion of jealousy (*The Under-wood*, X); it may be mischief, as in 'To vent their Libels, and to issue rimes' (Jonson, *The Under-Wood*, XLVII) – a usage which draws attention to that 'very common from c1600 to c1750, now somewhat rare' (*OED*) sense of *vent* as to give out publicly, to *publish* (a crucial meaning for the poet); or it may be language itself, as Herbert rehearses it in 'Sinnes round', where the further potential pun on *vent* and *vend*, to sell (for which the normal spelling up to c1670 was *vent*), is made explicit:

> My words take fire from my inflamed thoughts,
> Which spit it forth like the Sicilian Hill.
> They vent the wares, and passe them with their faults,
> And by their breathing ventilate the ill.

The shoddy goods are passed for sale by a lax quality control, and the abrupt transition of metaphor, from the incandescent words belched out by a Mount Etna, is made possible by the pun. Returning to the passionate lord of Swift's lines quoted earlier, we are reminded by the *OED* that 'the hole or channel in the breech of a canon or firearm through which fire is communicated to the charge' is known as a *vent*, and its mechanism a *vent-piece*. We should not need reminding that *vent* is also 'the anus, anal, or excretory opening of persons or animals' (*OED*).

But the deeper paradox, the human dilemma in which not only the teachers in the synagogue but also the artists or poets at work with their creations are implicated, is made clear in Donne's *La Corona* 4, Temple, where the Christ child 'doth sit'

> Blowing, yea blowing out those sparks of wit,
> Which himselfe on those Doctors did bestow.

The first 'blowing' allows the eye, travelling the line in anticipation of 'sparks of wit', momentarily to register the possibility of the sparks being blown into radiant life; but the iteration 'yea blowing *out*' withdraws all possibility of divine co-operation and makes instead a judgement on that frivolous and pretentious human wit.

One might suppose Donne's 'speaking picture' of the human skull marked with the sutured sign of the cross to be a figurative commonplace, but this seems not to be the case. It is not among Jerome's or Lipsius's examples (though a cruciform was detected in the human face). Dr Helkiah Crooke's vast *Description*, which is continually drawing parallels and correspondences between the body of man and God's art in creation, discusses, and illustrates, the bones and sutures of the skull, but nowhere recognizes a significant cruciform pattern.[7] Charles Estienne's *De dissectione partium corporis humani* (Paris, 1545), with figures cut by Estienne de la Rivière, shows, by shading the areas in the neighbourhood of the sutures, preparatory to dissection, a clear cruciform configuration, but neither he nor Vesalius, who followed him into the cranium, seem inclined to draw any conclusions from this.[8] Nor have I been able to find it offered as a 'device' in the emblem books where, because of its strong visual effect, one might expect to find it pictured. There are skulls in abundance in, for instance, Whitney or Wither: a skull or skulls at the foot of the Cross (Golgotha), and skulls as *memento mori* in various states of decomposition, but none with their frontal bones marked with the cross. It seems that Donne had 'discovered' the correspondence, just as he could say '*We thinke* that *Paradise* and *Calvarie*. . . stood in one place' when 'Nobody has, so far, produced any authority for such an idea'.[9]

The question of the conceit's originality is not merely one of complete scholarly annotation. If a devotional poet is deploying a traditional trope, already baptized by generations of Christian commentators and used by 'Those heavenly Poets which did see / Thy will', his conceit, his child of wit, draws attention to itself only as a gesture of consensus, of human solidarity on the point, a version of 'mine auctor says'. It is a notorious critical pitfall that what *we* may think is an original conceit turns out to be a recognized (by contemporary practitioners if not by us) typological or iconographical device. But is Donne's device of 'We thinke . . .' meant, possibly even disingenuously, to absolve the conceit of its daring, or at least to disguise it?

> Not a word or look
> I affect to own,
>   But by book,

And thy book alone.
(Herbert, 'Discipline')

Is the devotional poet permitted only the versified advice column: 'Who cannot live on twentie pound a yeare, / Cannot on fourtie' (Herbert, 'The Church-Porch'); must he accept the 'losse of rime' implied in the unpoetic plain-speaking of *'My God, My King'* ('Jordan I'); are his thoughts likely only to hatch 'their cockatrice' and his words create another Babel ('Sinnes round')? The children of Donne's wit, with their saining virtue, issue furtively through the cranium's 'bony walls' (can we say of them, as of pride, 'tis no child, but monster'? *The Crosse*, 41), and are to be crossed and corrected by the emblematic cross their own wit has perceived and identified. The witty devotional poet seems ultimately obliged to plead guilty to Herbert's question, and to abide by the consequences:

Woulds't thou both eat thy cake, and have it?
('The Size')

NOTES

1. See Sidney, *A Defence of Poetry*, ed. J. Van Dorsten, Oxford: Oxford University Press, 1966, pp. 23–5; Gracián, *Agudeza y Arte de Ingenio*, 1642; Tesauro, *Il Cannocchiale Aristotelico*, 1645: cited by S. L. Bethell, 'The Nature of Metaphysical Wit', *Northern Miscellany of Literary Criticism*, 1 (1953).
2. For example, Bacon, *Novum Organum*, XLI–XLVII.
3. Helkiah Crooke, Μικροκοσμογραφία: *A Description of the Body of Man*, etc. 2nd rev. edn, London, 1631, p. 7.
4. J. A. W. Bennett; *Review of English Studies*, V (1954), pp. 168–9; see also Helen Gardner, *John Donne: The Divine Poems*, 2nd edn, Oxford: Clarendon Press, 1978, Supplementary Notes, p. 155.
5. *Gray's Anatomy*, 30th edn, London: Longmans, Green, 1949, p. 318. Helen Gardner, *Divine Poems*, p. 94, refers to J. E. Frazer, *The Anatomy of the Human Skeleton*, 4th edn (1940) for similar information.
6. Cited by Gardner, *Divine Poems*, p. 94.
7. See Helkiah Crooke, *A Description*, 1631, *VII. Booke*, 'Of the third & uppermost *Venter*, called the Head', and *XIII. Booke*, 'Of Bones'.
8. See *Vesalius on the Human Brain*, trans. with Introd. by Charles Singer, London: Oxford University Press, 1952, p. 135.
9. See Gardner, *Divine Poems*, Appendix F, p. 135.

4

CONVENTIONS OF DEVOTION II
The artifice of spontaneity

An artist is a person who has invented an artist.
Harold Rosenberg, *Discovering the Present*, 1973

The question to be raised here concerns not so much the matter
of figures and ornaments but what might be called, somewhat
tendentiously, the hermeneutics of *tone* – though it is also true
that our interpretation of tone may (as turns out here) ultimately
be dependent on our understanding of the figures and ornaments.
What are we to make, for instance, of the extraordinary, and to
many readers puzzling, amalgam in Donne of the conventional
dramatically urgent voice of supplication, in which the poet
creates the effect of spontaneous spiritual anguish, and another,
and apparently antithetical, convention which relies upon meditative, decently ordered and biblically researched exegeses?

A convenient, but unsatisfactory, way of dealing with the question may be to locate the meditative exegeses in the *La Corona*
sequence and set pieces such as *Good Friday, 1613. Riding Westward*, and allow Donne his exhibitionist head in the 'Holy Sonnets'. Louis Martz and Helen Gardner emphasised Donne's use
of Ignatian meditative techniques in the 'Holy Sonnets',[1] and
Helen Gardner warned that although 'we have not accounted for
the "Holy Sonnets" if we say that he wanted to write a set of
meditations in sonnet form, any more than we have accounted for
Paradise Lost if we say that Milton wished to write a classical epic
on a Christian subject', nevertheless the recognition of the way a
poet's conscious intentions are implemented 'can save us from
too simple a correlation between the experience of the poet and
his translation of it into poetry'.[2] Yet despite these qualifiers,
there are still those for whom it is open season for psychological,
psycho-sexual analyses of Donne's anxiety states as revealed in
those apparently spontaneously anguished sonnets.

The Holy Sonnet 'Batter my heart' is one of the best known,

most quoted and most frequently anthologised of Donne's devotional poems. I would guess that a large element contributing to
its success, in this sense, is its sheer uninhibited aggression, its
surplus, as it were, of tone over exegesis. Important too in this
respect is its final air of naughtiness, as though Donne is bringing
off (as he appears to have done too in the Holy Sonnet 'Show me
deare Christ, thy spouse') that impossible hybrid, an Ovidian
devotional poem. A further reason for looking at it again is that it
can represent a case-history of a kind of problem recurrent in our
reading of Renaissance poetry. The broad outlines of the problem
have been exhaustively argued out by a previous generation in
the disputes between 'historical critics' and 'new critics'. Its
ramifications can be clearly seen in, for example, the notorious
exchanges between William Empson and Rosemond Tuve over
the 'way of reading' (and hence the 'meaning') of the apparently
innocent line in George Herbert's 'The Sacrifice':

> Man stole the fruit, but I must climbe the tree.

In the debate, typological and biblical meanings did battle with
myth, psychology, incest, and the story of Jack-and-the-
beanstalk.[3] The problem is not resolved by saying that Tuve was
right and Empson wrong (though we might want to venture that
Tuve was more right than Empson). To each reader the other's
response was either blinkered or perverse; at any rate, incomplete. But we may properly retain a sneaking admiration for
Empson's reading and what it represents. However, our sympathetic response to the ingenious or the ambiguous or the *ad hoc*,
whether deft or whether daft, can itself be ambiguous: for it both
asserts the ultimate value of ourselves as readers, and generates
doubt about the accuracy or adequacy of our reading.

This point can be illustrated by indulging in a little critical
autobiography. Once asked to review the second, revised edition
of Helen Gardner's *The Divine Poems of John Donne*, I noted the
striking parallel by Ronsard to Donne's 'Batter my heart' sonnet
which is printed in the Supplementary Notes; I also made a
casual remark about the absence of any comment on the image of
God the potter in this sonnet – a remark which, due to a composi-
tor's error, came out in print as 'God the otter'. It made me think.
No one (not even William Empson) would want to argue that
God was there depicted, ambiguously, as an otter; but nor perhaps was anyone willing either to concede that God was there as a

potter. Why had I supposed that he was, and how had I arrived at this instinctive and unexamined reading? The printer's creative error sent me back to the sonnet to find out what people had thought was going on in it.

Some twenty-five years ago there was an extraordinary flurry of critical activity around the poem, and particularly its opening lines:

> Batter my heart, three person'd God; for, you
> As yet but knocke, breathe, shine, and seeke to mend;
> That I may rise, and stand, o'erthrow mee, 'and bend
> Your force, to breake, blowe, burn and make me new.
> I, like a usurpt towne, to'another due,
> Labour to'admit you, but Oh, to no end,
> Reason your viceroy in mee, mee should defend,
> But is captiv'd, and proves weake or untrue,
> Yet dearely 'I love you, 'and would be lov'd faine,
> But am betroth'd unto your enemie,
> Divorce mee, 'untie, or breake that knot againe,
> Take mee to you, imprison mee, for I
> Except you'enthrall mee, never shall be free,
> Nor ever chast, except you ravish mee.[4]

The discussions, which were never adequately resolved, seem to have been sparked off by J. C. Levenson's confession that he had read the first quatrain for years without feeling 'any discomfort at insufficient comprehension'. And yet there was clearly a problem about the lines. Whereas the conceit, or metaphor, of the second quatrain (the usurped town) and of the sestet (the divorce and ravishment) are obvious enough, the opening lines seem to show Donne writing 'as though no single metaphor could be adequate'.[5] The sonnet *as a whole* was rigorously explored[6], but uncertainty, hesitancy and a sense of either insufficient comprehension on the reader's part or, more likely, an insufficient control on Donne's part, still shrouds the opening in mystery. Most readers are pretty clear about the general drift, the kind of gesture that is being made, but as to what *exactly* Donne is talking about in those verbal triplets circling an apparently unspecific image, one guess seems as good as another.

In the absence of a finally satisfying metaphor to hold those explosives together, attention has subsequently been directed to the mannerism rather than the meaning. For some it is merely a more highly coloured version of 'Therfore that he may raise the Lord throws down' (*Hymne to God my God, in my sicknesse*); a violently emphatic expression of the paradox of the grain of wheat falling into the ground (to live, we must be destroyed); an enactment of the retribution and destruction which is the prerequisite for atonement. The *way* in which Donne here expresses this Christian commonplace has led to severe censure: Donne's penchant for drama can lead him, it is suggested, into 'the forced sensationalism of melodrama, especially when he gets his hands on an erotic conceit'.[7] So for some the opening quatrain of battering, rising and standing, being broken and blown, is an erotic conceit, a view developed by Wilbur Sanders who reads the end of the sonnet into its beginning and concludes that the 'vulgarity' in this poem 'springs from a dangerously uncontrolled sensationalism'. Sanders wonders how the end of the poem, the 'sweet female passivity' (and one might wonder where he gets *that* from), is related to 'this invocation of violence at the beginning, to the desire to be battered and hammered, overthrown and bent, hurled about with exciting brutality . . . a hankering for *sexual* violence'. It is hardly surprising that such a reading of the poem should find that 'there's something hysterically out of control'.[8] It may appear to be out of control just because we can't find a stabilizing conceit to which those words can be attached and in terms of which they may be decoded. Uncertainty about what it might be, or the assumption that there isn't one, or aren't any, seems to have led Sanders to the extraordinary view that Donne is doing little more than hysterically exhibiting his masochistic sexual predilections.

One way of coping with this sort of conclusion about the nature of Donne's activity here is to point to the ubiquity of the *ecce sto* theme, where the 'Kyng of love, strengest of all' stands at the door and is invited to break in by violence, and to demonstrate how characteristic violence, even metaphorically sexual violence, is of the mystical and ecstatic conception of love.[9] But it is an 'explanation' that evades the *particularities* of Donne's depiction of that violence.

A principle of control in terms of the *organisation* of the quatrain is not hard to find, and has been much discussed. The 'three person'd God' works through three-fold verbs, the triplet sequence corresponding, in the view of some, 'to the respective members of the Trinity', God crushing the spirit as a prelude to

the inspiration of the Holy Ghost and the warming benevolence
of the Son / Sun.[10] Others had argued, notably A. L. Clement,[11]
that the verbs knock, breathe, shine cannot be assigned ex-
clusively to one each of the parts of the Trinity but imply all
three in each verb, as do their counterparts, break, blow, burn.
Whatever the subtleties of interpretation, the mechanics of
Donne's organisation are fairly clear: a Trinity working through
trinities of verbs, and reflected in the sonnet as a whole in a trinity
of metaphors. According to this mechanism (and it is still only a
mechanism, still without any concrete metaphor around which its
opening flourish centres) Donne appears to suggest that the normal biblical activities of three-personed God are going to be inadequate in his particular case. The door is open not only for
accusations of sexual deviancy but also of a flamboyant egoism: as
though Donne, in an ecstasy of guilt, is claiming that 'there can
bee / None of that kinde, of which he is, but hee', and God must
adopt a novel approach.

The search for the implied conceit has thrown up an impressive
array of suggestions. Some see no conceit at all, apart from the
generalised one of the hardened human heart.[12] Many see it as an
implied anticipation of the military image of the besieged town,
and in it the heart is already being compared to a city wrongfully
appropriated and helplessly possessed by God's enemy. The
force of the verbs can thus become apparent only retrospectively.
John E. Parish offered to tidy up the difficulties by interpreting
the opening entirely in military terms. The conceit here is of a
walled town, and Satan is inside. The King (God) knocks at the
gate. But the King must burst the gates with a battering ram.
'The town must be destroyed and a new one *rise* in its place to
stand for ever'. 'The verbs . . . suggest storming a citadel, and
even "blowe" may be intended to suggest the use of gunpowder
to blow up the fortress or blow it into smithereens.'[13] Such a
reading may be confirmed by others: 'bend / Your force' may have
siege connotations that suggest the bending of bows and cata-
pults.[14] At all events we are asked to read the opening in terms of
what follows, and not to worry too much if the whole sonnet
appears to be articulated as a triplet, with three conceits, not two.

Other suggestions have involved allusion to Jacob wrestling
with the angel, 'stand' and 'o'erthrow' being interpreted as wrestling terms: 'God is to overthrow the cowed wrestler, in order that
the latter may raise [*sic*] and stand on his own feet'.[15] The

technical wrestling argot which will accommodate 'breathe, and shine' and 'blowe, burn' is yet to be unearthed.

The curious thing about all these attempts to account for Donne's extraordinary language in the first quatrain is that the tentative observation made by Levenson that 'the various metaphors coherently suggest a single situation' was followed by the equally tentative suggestion that 'God is a tinker, Donne a pewter vessel in the hands of God the artisan'.[16] It seems to me by far the most useful suggestion, though it was promptly ruled out of court in the ensuing debate, George Herman even facetiously asking what the point was of shining pewter anyway. (Louthan, some two years before, had considered that Donne may have been 'a defective utensil', but the thought was not developed.) Levenson stoutly resisted criticism and asserted again that the stylistic obstacles to seeing any conceit at all in the first quatrain were overcome 'by the discovery of a single implied metaphor': 'the argument that Donne's neologism for the potter-clay metaphor makes God here a worker in metals seems to me to hold.' However Levenson withdraws his use of the word 'tinker' since Donne's point is that tinkering is not enough.

Why God as metal-worker should be thought of as a 'neologism' or 'a modern version of the potter-clay image' is difficult to understand, since the image is biblical ('And I will turn my head upon thee, and purely purge away thy dross, and take away all thy tin', Isaiah 1:25) and lovers of Handel will know all about the refiner's fire. God as a goldsmith, or as a smith, occurs too in Ezekiel 22:20–21, and Jeremiah 6:29, and was developed by Alanus de Insulis and Deguileville.[17] It is also of course used by Donne: 'Burne off my rusts, and my deformity, / Restore thine Image' (*Good Friday, 1613. Riding Westward*). Such a conceit certainly brings those otherwise unattached verbs more sharply into focus: the tinkering which knocks (hammers), breathes (polishes) and shines (buffs up), and the remaking which breaks up, blows (in the furnace), burns, and 'makes new'.

Yet it seems unnecessary so readily to abandon the potter-clay image. Donne may well be suggesting both at once, and the crucial line, which underlines the dominant conceit here, is 'That I may rise, and stand, o'erthrow mee'. Unless we are happy enough to let Donne metamorphose his metal pot into a wrestler pro tem and then return to it, there is for the metalwork image little *specific* sense in these particular and equally precise verbs, beyond the general sense of regeneration alluded to earlier. God as potter is of course a recurring image of God's creativity, 'But now, O Lord, thou art our father; we are the clay, and thou our potter; and we all are the work of thy hand' (Isaiah 64:8), or as an image of God's vengeance, 'And he shall break it as the breaking of the potter's vessel that is broken in pieces' (Isaiah 30:14). Donne uses the image, or plays variations on it, in his poetry (e.g. *Epitaph on Himselfe*, or *La Corona* 7, *Ascention*, in which 'this Sunne and Sonne' has 'burnt your drossie clay'), and he employs it in *A Litanie* in a petitionary and verbal context which is very similar to the opening of the Holy Sonnet:

> come
> And re-create mee, now growne ruinous:
> My heart is by dejection, clay,
> And by self-murder, red.
> From this red earth, O father, purge away
> All vicious tinctures, that new fashioned
> I may rise up from death, before I'm dead.

What is usually glossed at this point is Donne's punning on the Hebrew *adom* (Adam) meaning 'red earth'; but what is relevant here is the prayer 'recreate mee', the earth-clay that must be 'new fashioned' ('make me new') so that 'I may rise up' ('that I may rise'). Donne does not *need* to mention clay specifically in the sonnet because it is already there, as it were, in this particular concatenation of words.

What difference might such a perception make to our comprehension of Donne's language? God the Father, Son and Holy Ghost knocks, breathes on, shines the defective clay pot – taps it to test its strength, breathes on it and shines it up to make it look all right superficially. But this is not enough: the pot must be broken, the bellows worked, the kiln fired again. Between these activities referring to technical processes are equally technical and punning verbs: 'That I may rise, and stand' certainly implies rising from eternal death, but more immediately it suggests the clay rising on the potter's wheel to 'stand'. 'O'erthrow' certainly implies being crushed and humbled, but again more immediately it suggests the punning over-throw or throwing over again of the vessel. The potter's wheel was sometimes known as the 'throwing wheel' and *OED* certainly confirms such usage at this period, citing an account of 1604 'To the disshe-thrower, ix days throwing disshes and bassenes, iiis'.

It may be objected that in this reading of the lines Donne appears to be asking for the pot (himself), which has already been thrown and fired, to be broken up, rethrown and fired again – a process which is not possible for reconstituted rubble. Donne of course knows this perfectly well, and may have chosen to ignore it, just as he knows perfectly well how porcelain is made but offers a quainter and more poetically useful version of it in his *Elegie on the Lady Markham* . . . '(As men of China, after an ages stay, / Do take up Porcelane, where they buried Clay)'. It is more likely however that Donne is thinking of two incompatible ideas at the same time (which is, after all, the rhetorical mode of the sonnet as a whole). One is the image of the vessel which, in the words of Jeremiah, 'he made of clay' and which was 'marred in the hands of the potter; so he made it again another vessel, as seemed good to the potter to make it' (Jeremiah 18:4). The other is that the marring of the vessel is the result both of original sin and active individual sin ('Wilt thou forgive that sinne where I begunne, / Which was my sin, though it were done before', *A Hymne to God the Father*), and that for true regeneration he must become a new man in Christ and hence analogically a new pot, the re-throwing representing the motion of grace. There is certainly no evidence in Jeremiah that the pot was marred in the firing or after: Jeremiah's lump of clay could be made again because things had gone wrong in the shaping 'upon the wheels'. There is an obvious theological difficulty in the passage from Jeremiah and the simile there is a loose one: God cannot logically be conceived of as having marred anything in the making; the marring must be symbolic of man's original sin. When God makes it 'again another vessel, as seemed good to the potter to make it' this can only be interpreted as the grace which regenerates marred and fallen men. In either case, whether marred in the making or marred after the firing, the basic material is nothing more than clay in God's hands. Donne's prayer is to be made in a similar way, and it is quite consistent with the hyperbole and paradox of the sonnet that he should ask God to perform a physically impossible feat. 'O'erthrow mee' out of rubble need be no more difficult to swallow than 'Nor ever chast, except you ravish mee'.

A further interest lies in this particular passage from Jeremiah (which naturally Donne knew) because it may be a clue to the creative process of the poet's mind as he forges a new image to follow the opening one. The prophet declares an analogy between the potter's vessel and the House of Israel: 'as the clay is in the potter's hand, so are ye in my hand'. Similarly a nation, or a kingdom, may be plucked up, pulled down, and destroyed. The following chapter pursues the same image of the 'potter's earthen bottle' which is to be shown to the people: 'And thou shalt say unto them, Thus saith the Lord of hosts; Even so will I break this people, and this city, as one breaketh a potter's vessel, that cannot be made again' (Jeremiah 19: 10–11). Thus the connection is already made between the opening image of the poem and the 'usurpt towne', this city 'to another due' that follows.

The suggestion is, then, that the opening quatrain of this sonnet can be seen in another way than as a gesture of disorganized and uncontrolled sensationalism. I say 'can be seen', rather than a prescriptive 'should be seen', deliberately. If we do not agree that there is an implied conceit in those lines, weighing in with considerable specificity and a good deal of intellectual poetic muscle (that is, if my analysis has nothing to recommend it), we may, I suppose, respond to the lines in any way we please. But if we think we have seen something there, we cannot reasonably pretend that we have not. The opening quatrain then initiates the trio of metaphors which may be thought of as assigned to the Father (the potter), the Holy Ghost (whose inspiration releases captive reason) and the Son (whose Bride Donne prays to become). It is no longer an outburst of whirling words, nor simply a verbal arithmetic of only vaguely focused triplets; and though its imagery is rendered entirely through its verbal activity it is as clear and as internally consistent as the two subsequent extended metaphors.

The sonnet seems a perfect example of Puttenham's commendation: 'Therefore shall our Poet receave prayse . . . more for his artificiall well desembled, then for the same overmuch affected'.[18] Indeed, so well dissembled is Donne's artifice that some have seriously wondered whether it is there at all. That Donne should have brought off this feat of compressed allusiveness and the tight interconnectedness of ideas in a voice pitched in a tone of emotional distress, marked by all the outward effects of immediate anguish and dramatic urgency, is so remarkable that, even when we acknowledge its structured exegeses, we still blink at this Neckar-cube of a poem as it flexes alternately between its 'spontaneous' and its 'artificial' dimensions.

NOTES

1. See Louis L. Martz, *The Poetry of Meditation*, New Haven: Yale University Press, 1954, 2nd rev. edn, 1962; Helen Gardner, *The Divine Poems of John Donne*, Introduction, Oxford: Clarendon Press, 2nd edn revised, 1978.

2. Helen Gardner, *The Divine Poems*, p. lv.

3. The debate may be followed in William Empson's explication of 'The Sacrifice' in *Seven Types of Ambiguity*, London: Chatto & Windus, 1930, and in Rosemond Tuve's 1950 essay on 'The Sacrifice' in the *Kenyon Review* and later, in an expanded form in *A Reading of George Herbert*, Chicago: University of Chicago Press, 1952.

4. Text from *The Complete English Poems of John Donne*, ed. C. A. Patrides, London: Dent, 1985.

5. J. C. Levenson, 'Donne's *Holy Sonnets*, XIV', *The Explicator*, 11, item 31, March 1953.

6. George Herman, 'Donne's *Holy Sonnets*, XIV', *The Explicator*, 12, December 1953, item 18; J. C. Levenson, 'Donne's *Holy Sonnets*, XIV', *The Explicator*, 12, April 1954, item 36; George Knox, 'Donne's *Holy Sonnets*, XIV' *The Explicator*, 15 October 1956, item 2; A. L. Clements, 'Donne's Holy Sonnet XIV', *Modern Language Notes*, 76, June 1961, pp. 484–9; John E. Parish, 'No. 14 of Donne's *Holy Sonnets*', *College English*, January 1963. The sequence may be followed in *John Donne's Poetry*, selected and edited by A. L. Clements, New York: Norton, 1966.

7. Clay Hunt, *Donne's Poetry*, New Haven: Yale University Press, 1954, p. 136.

8. Wilbur Sanders, *John Donne's Poetry*, Cambridge: Cambridge University Press, 1971, pp. 129–30.

9. Quotation from the translation of the twelfth-century Latin poem 'Philomena' by John of Howden, in Rosemary Woolf, *The English Religious Lyric in the Middle Ages*, Oxford: Clarendon Press, 1968, p. 161. Helen Gardner's *The Divine Poems*, cites John of Howden and refers us to 'other medieval poems on the reluctance of the soul to respond to gentleness' in *The Oxford Book of Medieval Verse*, e.g. nos. 20 and 21.

10. Murray Roston, *The Soul of Wit*, Oxford: Oxford University Press, 1974, pp. 172–3.

11. A. L. Clements, *supra*; see also Lucio P. Ruotalo, 'The Trinitarian Framework of Donne's Holy Sonnet XIV' *Journal of the History of Ideas*, 27, 1966, p. 445.

12. George Knox, *supra*.

13. John E. Parish, *supra*.

14. Doniphan Louthan, *The Poetry of John Donne*, New York: Bookman, 1951, p. 124.

15. Louthan, *ibid.*

16. J. C. Levenson, *The Explicator*, 11 March 1953, item 31.
17. Alanus de Insulis, s. xiii; Deguileville, *Deus . . . tanquam mundi elegans architectus, tanquam aureae fabricae fater aurarius . . . etc. Patrologia latina*, CCX, 453.
18. Puttenham, *The Arte of English Poesie*, ed. G.D. Willcock and A. Walker, Cambridge: Cambridge University Press, 1936, III, xxv.

5

CONVENTIONS OF REFORM
Right spelling in Milton's *A Masque* and *Il Penseroso*

> Thy word is all, if we could spell.
> George Herbert, 'The Flower'

On 10 September, 1802, from Greta Hall, Keswick, Coleridge wrote to W. Sotheby wishing Sotheby were there, 'even in this howling Rain Storm that dashes itself against my windows – on the other side of my blazing Fire, in that great Arm Chair there'. Were he there, Coleridge guessed they 'should encroach on the morning before we parted'. What Coleridge wanted specifically to discuss (besides the great subjects of 'the Hebrew & Christian Theology, & the Theology of Plato') were some few lines from Milton's *Comus* – 'Do look at the passage':[1]

> Care and utmost shifts
> How to secure the Lady from surprisal,
> Brought to my mind a certain Shepherd Lad
> Of small regard to see to, yet well skill'd
> In every vertuous plant and healing herb
> That spreds her verdant leaf to th'morning ray,
> He lov'd me well, and oft would beg me sing,
> Which when I did, he on the tender grass
> Would sit, and hearken even to extasie,
> And in requitall ope his leather'n scrip,
> And shew me simples of a thousand names
> Telling their strange and vigorous faculties;
> Amongst the rest a small unsightly root,
> But of divine effect, he cull'd me out;
> The leaf was darkish, and had prickles on it,
> But in another Countrey, as he said,
> Bore a bright golden flowre, but not in this soyl:
> Unknown, and like esteem'd, and the dull swayn
> Treads on it daily with his clouted shoon,
> And yet more med'cinal is it then that *Moly*

> That *Hermes* once to wise *Ulysses* gave;
> He call'd it *Haemony*, and gave it me,
> And bad me keep it as of soveran use
> 'Gainst all inchantments.
>
> (618–40)[2]

'All the puzzle is to find out what Plant Haemony is – which they discover to be the English Spleenwort – & decked out, as a mere play & licence of poetic Fancy, with all the strange properties suited to the purpose of the Drama.' But what, asks Coleridge, about 'Milton's platonizing Spirit'? Lifting a line from *Il Penseroso*, 'Where more is meant then meets the ear', Coleridge asserts that, of all poets, Milton 'wrote nothing without an interior meaning' (866). And he proceeds to elucidate the interior meaning of these lines, aware that he is by no means the first to go hunting for verbal parallelisms in this wood (nor, as we know, would he be the last).

Lifting another line from *Il Penseroso* (from the climax this time), and taking Coleridge's hint, we may be able to expose some Miltonic strategies. The line 'Where I may sit and rightly spell' (does it really echo George Herbert's 'Thy word is all, if we could spell'?) is vibrant with interior interrogatives and suggestions. Its major activity, spelling – major, that is, as long as we assume it is not coequal with the activity of sitting – is itself ambiguously concerned, passively, with getting the words, as definitions or significations, right, and actively with getting the words, as spells or charms, right. It is concerned with appropriate *location*, 'where': a place wished for, or dreamed of? Or achieved, reached, described? It is subjunctively concerned with appropriate *posture*: sitting, not running or jumping. It is concerned with appropriate *mental activity*: right spelling, not wrong spelling, drawing attention to what it means to spell – is it to find out about, to interpret, to decipher? Or is it to have interpreted, deciphered, discovered? Or is it, more magus-like, a question of a Ficinean control over what is being denoted? Finally it is concerned implicitly with questions about its appropriate *mode*: is to 'rightly spell' suggestive of struggling simplicity, or of suave virtuousity?

These may appear elusive questions, but the burden Milton puts upon his reader or audience to interpret (let alone rightly) the drift of his poetic discourses is a notoriously demanding one.

For example, how do we read Milton's *A Masque*? There is recognisable in it a tension between virtue (virtuosity) and innocence (simplicity) whose struggles can only be relieved by supernatural intervention; and this may be true both on the level of its dramatic and moral action and on the level of its authorial poetic feats, for which Milton more and more called, by invocations, upon a source of divine inspiration.[3] It may be said that *L'Allegro* and *Il Penseroso* are partly concerned to show, respectively, ambitions towards a certain sort of simplicity and a certain sort of virtuosity. In lieu of a map, an exploration might begin from two basic assumptions: first, that Milton is a Christian poet addressing a Christian society, and second, that he is chronically, and masterfully, cryptographic.

The delicacy and tact required of the young Milton in offering Christian, reforming instruction to the noble household which made up the audience, and some of the participants, of his masque is of course obvious. This aspect of Milton's text has recently been admirably dealt with, together with the fertile question of what Milton, the puritan-republican poet-prophet, thought he was doing writing a Caroline masque in celebration of the aristocracy.[4] It is clear that his compliment and celebration is often muted by moral realism, sometimes astringent, always zealously defining to the nobility the roles of nobility. It may have been a reforming lesson that took some time to mature, for there is no sense yet, in the 1630s, of the gulf that was to open up – such that, some fifteen years after the performance of *A Masque*, the Elder Brother, embittered by political developments and the burdens of debt, could endorse one of Milton's books which came into the Bridgewater library, the *Defensio*: 'the book deserves the flames, the author the gallows'.[5] In this moral entertainment Milton undoubtedly exploits the conventions of the masque form to make it examine the bases of its own rituals and the rituals of the aristocratic society he is addressing. What I want to focus on here, however, is not so much Milton's dialogue with masque conventions but rather to explore an aspect of the spiritual instruction he conveys and the means (which are often not those of masque) he uses. The Haemony allegory is an example of an art, peculiarly cryptographic, whose actual effect in performance is, as many commentators have pondered, difficult to fathom. Part of this worry may actually be redundant, since much of the allegory was probably omitted from the performance anyway. But that

Milton wanted subsequent readers of his work to pay close attention to it is evident from his revisions and reworkings of the
passage, as I shall point out later.

Coleridge was quite sure he could spell his way through
Milton's *Comus* passage:

> apply it as an Allegory of Christianity, or, to speak more
> precisely of the Redemption by the Cross – every syllable is
> full of Light! – ['] a small unsightly Root ['] – to the Greeks
> Folly, to the Jews a stumbling Block – ['] the leaf was
> darkish & had prickles on it ['] – If in this Life only we have
> hope, we are of all men the most miserable / & [a] score of
> other Texts – ['] But in another country, as he said, Bore a
> bright golden Flower ['] – the exceeding weight of Glory
> prepared for us hereafter / ['] but [not] in this soil, unknown
> & and like esteem'd & the dull Swain treads on it daily with
> his clouted shoon ['] / The Promises of Redemption offered
> daily & hourly & to all, but accepted scarcely by any – [']
> He called it Haemony ['] – Now what is Haemony? Αιμα
> οινοζ – Blood-wine. – And he took the wine & blessed it, &
> said, This is my Blood – / the great Symbol of the Death on
> the Cross.

And if this appears to be farfetched Coleridge tells us to 'read
Milton's prose works, & observe whether he was one of those'
who joined in the 'general Ridicule cast on all allegorizing of
poets' (866–7).

Coleridge's (it seems to me sensible) basic assumption about
Milton's 'platonizing' (by which he means here 'allegorizing') is
that what is being 'allegorized' is Christian doctrine and Christian
truth, however pastoral Milton's allusion and however Procrus-
tean Coleridge's etymologies may be. In other words, the passage, taking its *raison d'être* and its dramatic occasion from within
the whole masque of which it is part, draws attention to those
Greek (Platonist and Aristotelian) elements (the self-sufficiency
of virtue and the ideal of transcendence) and to those British, or
Welsh, elements (the landscape, folklore and fairy lore), but only
ultimately to divert our attention from them and to focus our
thoughts not on them but on something else. Before seeing
whether we think Coleridge's excitement at having cracked the
code may be justified, we might review what has been said about

the lines in terms of the 'play and licence of poetic fancy' and 'the strange properties . . . suited to the drama'.

To Coleridge's question, 'Now what is Haemony?' a multiplicity of answers have been given, most of them pointing either to Greek or to Celtic significances. It may be derived from *Haemonia*, Thessaly, the land of magic and magical herbs (as in Milton's *Elegia secunda* 7–8, or as used by Spenser, *Astrophel* 3). Hence it has been suggested that in *A Masque* it may represent pastoral poetry as opposed to epic poetry.[6] Or it may derive from αιμωνιοζ (blood-red) and be connected with the account of the moly given by Eustathius in his commentary on the *Odyssey*, the moly that sprang from the blood of Pikolous, who was killed by the sun when trying to ravish Circe.[7] It may mean the 'rhamnus' plant mentioned in Fletcher's *The Faithful Shepherdess* (II. ii. 15–18) as an antidote against enchantment. It may be similar to Virgil's *amellus (Georgics* 4, 271–78).[8] As if in response to Coleridge's testy observation, 'What an unthinking & ignorant man we must have supposed Milton to be, if, without any hidden meaning, he had described it as growing in such abundance that the dull Swain treads on it daily – & yet as never *flowering*' (866), it has been argued that it may stand, wholesale, for 'the Christian and Platonic doctrine of virtue', while the reference to 'another country' draws a contrast between the creative mind of England and Northern Europe (where presumably it is too cold for it to flower) and that of Greece and Italy.[9]

Cedric Brown argues, in his subtle and comprehensive account of the Haemony allegory, that 'Haemony figures the word of God', and its 'divine effect' echoes the usual Protestant description of the ministry of the word as efficacious. Certainly the parable of the sower and the seed fallen by the wayside where it was 'trodden down' (Luke 8:5) (and in Matthew's version including perhaps the 'dull swayn': 'for this people's heart is waxed gross, and their ears are dull of hearing, and their eyes have closed', Matthew 13:13–15), may provide an important way of understanding Haemony.[10] But it cannot be the whole story, since it leaves out of account both the Celtic resonances and the clear association with *blood*. A judgement on the dull swain might be that of the author of the Epistle to the Hebrews: 'Of how much sorer punishment . . . shall he be thought worthy, who hath trodden under foot the Son of God' (Hebrews 10:29) – a passage Brown cites to illustrate the Word of God 'trodden down' as in the pastoral parable. But the association in Hebrews is not primarily with Christ as the Word of God but with the blood of Christ's offering, for it continues: 'and hath counted the blood of the covenant, wherewith he was sanctified, an unholy thing'.

Stories in the Welsh tradition depend heavily on magical objects, some of the most common of which Milton uses in his masque: magic dust, a magic wand, magic potions, an enchanter's glass, a protective herb. The druids recommend *Selago*, an evergreen, as a charm against evil;[11] hyssop, elder tree, snapdragon, something the Welsh call *Meipen Fair*, may all be candidates.[12] But the herb singled out especially is St John's Wort, or *Hypericum*, 'one of the most beneficent of the magic herbs, protecting equally against Faeries and the Devil'.[13] The plant was ubiquitous in Welsh lore, and was sought by young women on St John's Eve since it has some connection with marriage.[14] Charlotte F. Otten, after reviewing the plant's physical properties and researching written accounts of its alleged effectiveness against sickness and ghosts in England, asserts that St John's Wort is actually Milton's haemony.[15] The Welsh, moreover, did not carry the actual plant about but only the powdered root worn in a sachet on the chest,[16] just as the Attendant Spirit explains how, when he obtained haemony, 'he purs't it up' in some small container that could be worn rather than carried.[17]

What status, we may wonder, can we assign to all such information about Milton's haemony? Closer to the spirit of Coleridge's analysis are the suggestions that haemony may be interpreted as 'grace', and that one type of the 'rhamnus' plant is mentioned in Gerard's *Herbal* as the material of the Crown of Thorns.[18] But on the whole such annotations serve to fuel a Coleridgean impatience, not calm it.

There may be an important key to Milton's method here in the way he himself has already deflected us from these sorts of scholarly culs-de-sacs through a method characteristic (or that was to become characteristic) of him, the device of the dismissive simile. We are expressly told of haemony that 'yet more med'cinal is it then that *Moly*/ That *Hermes* once to wise *Ulysses* gave'. We are quite free to expand our glosses on moly: a plant with a black root and white flower given to Ulysses (*Odyssey* 10.302–6) to make him proof against the charms of Circe (to complicate our response, Pliny suggested that 'some Greek authorities have painted its blossom yellow' [Pliny 25. 27]). We can compile moly's allegorical associations with prudence and temperance.[19] We can pursue Mercury or Hermes to their lairs of significance. But whatever our pursuits reveal, we have actually been told that they are in any case irrelevant because this was *not* 'that *Moly*', just as we are warned in *Paradise Lost* that Eden is 'not that faire field / Of *Enna*' which 'not nice Art' (even Milton's) but something else created (*PL* 4.268–69, 241). The lines invite us simultaneously to think about moly and to stop thinking about it. And, plotting our path towards this climax of dismissal (all we are told is that the shepherd lad 'call'd it *Haemony*', which lexically may have something to do with blood), Milton involves us in an elaborate syntactical game of 'not that but this'.

Three times he nudges us rhetorically in the ribs. The first concerns 'a certain Shepherd Lad / Of small regard to see to'. Milton is asserting the insignificance of the lad who, like Wordsworth's Lucy perhaps, dwelt among the untrodden ways and whom nobody noticed. At the same time he is also setting off a diversionary hare, for this shepherd lad has been variously 'identified' with Diodati, Nathaniel Weld, or Milton himself.[20] The lad's insignificance is then promptly withdrawn by the 'yet well skill'd / In every vertuous plant and healing herb'. Things are not always what they seem. Coleridge does not quote them, but clustered around this trope concerning the child-pastor are echoes of New Testament descriptions of Christ that have a precisely similar rhetorical form. For instance, St Paul in Philippians 2:2–11: 'But he made himself of no reputation, and took upon him the form of a servant, and was made in the likeness of men. And being found in fashion as a man, he humbled himself'. St Paul then produces the triumphant 'Wherefore God also hath highly exalted him . . . at the name of Jesus every knee should bow, of things in heaven, and things in earth, and things [like Comus's 'greisly legions that troop / Under the sooty flag of *Acheron*' (603–4)] under the earth'. Or again, the resonant opening of St John's Gospel: 'He was in the world, and the world was made by him, and the world knew him not. He came unto his own, and his own received him not' (1:10–11). Like Milton's haemony, Christ appears 'Unknown and like esteem'd', followed immediately in John's account, however, by the *but* of power and glory and the fullness of 'grace and truth' (1:12–15).

A second nudge occurs in line 629: 'Amongst the rest a small unsightly root, / But of divine effect', making, with 'But in another

Countrey' and 'but not in this soyl', a trio of *buts*. The leaf of this root (Christ as the root and stem of Jesse is familiar iconography, as is the analogy of Christ as a plant) is 'darkish, and had prickles on it' – the darkness of the sixth hour to the ninth hour, and the thorns of suffering. The same rhetorical device occurs a third time: 'the dull swayn / Treads on it daily with his clouted shoon, / And yet . . . '

The association of 'another Countrey' with Hebrews 11:15–16 – 'the better country, that is, an heavenly' – apparently eluded the compiler of the Bridgewater MS of *A Masque* (a presentation copy to the family and possibly the performance version itself), for it omits this reference, and the reference to the dull swain. A censor appears to have cheerfully dismembered Milton's religious allegory, presumably so that 'another Countrey' could not possibly be construed as a tactless criticism of Welsh religion or of the whole church in Britain, and has deleted too the dull swain in case it might seem a comment on the yokel-like qualities of the local residents of Ludlow.[21] The Bridgewater MS – a poor copy made without Milton's supervision – omits lines 631–37 altogether. It has been demonstrated that the uncorrected Trinity MS, in Milton's hand, preceded the Bridgewater MS, and that various changes were made in the Trinity MS after Bridgewater had been copied (the 1637 printed text was probably based on the Trinity MS at an early stage of correction).[22] The Trinity MS shows Milton resetting and expanding this passage, and his alterations and insertions have at least two important effects. One is to introduce a method for *evaluating* the information. Between the previously run-on lines, 'treads on it dayly with his clouted shoone / he call'd it Haemony & gave it me', Milton inserts in the margin the simile of unlikeness, '& yet more med'cinall is it than that ancient [crossed out] Moly, that [crossed out] wch Mercury [crossed out] Hermes once to wise Ulysses gave'. A second is to sustain and reinforce the pattern of 'not that but this', apparently *x* but actually *y*, which directs the whole passage.[23]

We might note (speculatively) in passing how frequently the triads and tricolons appear in Celtic, and particularly Welsh, oral traditions.[24] It has been noted that Milton's masque contains six speaking characters, three mortals, three immortals; that the action is divided into three scenes; that concrete images of triads are numerous throughout the work (not least among them Bridgewater's three children), climaxing in Sabrina's touching of the

Lady 'Thrice upon thy fingers tip, / Thrice upon thy rubied lip' (914–15) to break Comus's spell. A Coleridge would have spotted the 'allegorizing' here without a moment's hesitation. And coincidentally as it were, Milton deliberately employs in this crucial and microcosmic passage a syntactical triad of the shepherd lad, the root / flower, the moly.

Endemic also in Welsh traditions is the imagery of life as a constant struggle between darkness and light. Without rehearsing yet again the imagery of light and darkness in Milton's masque, we might note the sudden luminosities in the movements of the passage from dark to light: the obscure and umbrageous shepherd lad who knew 'every vertuous plant and healing herb / That spreds her verdant leaf to th'morning ray', and the unsightly root and dark leaf that 'in another Countrey . . . Bore a bright golden flowre.'

Milton's poetic dialogue here is not perhaps with masque, nor with folkloric conventions, but with the conventions of Platonism and Platonic instruction. For example, the previous debate between the two boys (who are, it should be remembered, aged only eleven and nine) is precociously concluded by the Elder Brother who, like an academic disputant, cites the wisdom of religion and the ancients, finishing with a close reference to the *Phaedo* (81 B-D) and its details of 'earthy' souls (that is, those who have not managed the Platonic ascent) haunting tombs and sepulchres (463–75). The Younger Brother exclaims, 'How charming is divine Philosophy!', just as earlier humanists in the Renaissance had been charmed by the Platonic metaphors, for Plato was generally regarded as the most 'divine' of philosophers despite, or even because of, his idealizing fictions. The Younger Brother's response (though he is unaware of it) is exactly and significantly right: 'charming' is both delightful and suggestive of a magical charm, a way of spelling. It is the affectation of an ardent, innocent and premature idealism which does not fully comprehend the 'real', earthy world of moral evil that lies around it.

An awkward question might now arise. If this passage, rightly spelled, asserts, over and above the Platonic celebrations of human virtue and the local colouring of a primitive and Celtic evil, the primacy of the Christian motif of redemption, how is it that the gift of haemony fails to rescue the Lady? For what frees the Lady from her trance is the rising of Sabrina fair from the water.

Was Milton quite unaware that somewhere circling, at some distance perhaps, his description of the prophylactic plant were the words of Christ's commission in Luke 10:3–4? 'Behold, I send you forth as lambs among wolves' – appropriate enough for the brothers venturing into Comus's territory. But such disciples are enjoined to 'carry neither purse, nor scrip, nor shoes' (a triad oddly echoed in 'purs't it up'; 'leather'n scrip'; 'clouted shoon'). In terms of the drama, the haemony certainly appears merely as an alternative magic to Comus's, almost a pastoral-narrative device, permitting the boys, the Attendant Spirit says, to 'Boldly assault the necromancers hall' and 'with dauntless hardihood, / And brandish't blade rush on him' (649–51). But the redemptive emblems of the eucharist are not simply talismanic; they are more profoundly prophylactic: 'preserve thy body and soul unto everlasting life'. So what goes wrong? Perhaps beyond, and even within, the aristocratic confines of the closet drama, there are only dull swain with clouted shoon. The brothers rout Comus, but they clumsily let him escape, suffering the Attendant Spirit's rebuke, 'O ye mistook, ye should have snatcht his wand' (815), while their sister remains still 'In stony fetters fixt, and motionless' (819). At this point the Attendant Spirit flatly says, 'We cannot free the Lady'. It would seem that, despite the possession of haemony, simple human error, or forgetfulness ('For still they knew, and ought to have still remembered' [*PL* 10.12]) is very possible. The brothers had been warned, first of all, not to rely on shows of strength. The Elder Brother's impassioned speech of youthful muscle-flexing (584–608) is quickly deflated by the Spirit's warning that Comus 'with his bare wand can unthred thy joynts / And crumble all thy sinews' (613–14). Although they are armed with haemony and may now effectively whirl their swords at the enchanter, such activity may be very gratifying but will be useless (as it is proved) unless they 'sease his wand'. The stage direction reads: *The Brothers rush in with Swords drawn*; and in the excitement they forget (again not unlike Milton's Adam and Eve, armed with innocence and Raphael's complete dossier on Satan) the very thing they are supposed to be doing.

The two brothers and their sister are shown in the masque to be self-consciously meritorious, believing virtue to be impregnable. The Elder Brother optimistically asserts his sister's strength (it would be impossible for Milton to say anything less of Lady Alice Egerton), but the exchange between the boys that follows

shows them stumbling over the proper origin and attribution of
that 'hidden strength':

Eld. Bro.   My sister is not so defenceless left
              As you imagine, she has a hidden strength
              Which you remember not.
2. Bro.   What hidden strength,
              Unless the strength of Heav'n, if you mean that?
Eld Bro.   I mean that too, but yet a hidden strength
              Which if Heav'n gave it, may be term'd her own.
                                              (414–19)

The disquisition on the magical, almost talismanic powers of
chastity (420–63) to compel evil and exact the support of the gods
may be read not as Milton's own conviction but as an ironized
resumé of the *Symposium*'s transcendence of sexuality. The moral
thrust of the masque is not towards the praise of youthful idealism, not the celebration of the conquest of a Platonic / Pauline
English lady and her *Boys' Own Paper* brothers over barbaric ani-
mism and paganism, but the more sober recognition that ambitious reasoning, self-confident rectitude and self-sufficient
goodness can achieve no more than a stalemate with evil. And
even with their superstitiously pursed up haemony they still
manage to fudge the victory over Comus at the end. The Attendant Spirit must now resort to Plan B, the summoning of Sabrina,
permitting Milton another piece of complex 'allegorizing' to
which it is hard to imagine Coleridge not responding.

Milton weaves here a very subtle net of implications that are
partly dependent on the circumstantial details of the masque's
original performance. Sabrina is the river Severn, verging on the
traditional boundary between England and Wales and sharing in,
or adumbrating, the Earl of Bridgewater's new conciliatory role as
President of the Council of Wales and Lord of the Marches. She
is also, as the Lady of the Lake, a pagan deity encrusted with
both Greek and Celtic allusions: she is the illegitimate daughter
of Locrine, son of Brutus, the Trojan founder of Britain. What
does Milton do with the Sabrina story? The story (an obviously
popular one – it forms the matter of a colourful sixteenth-century
tragedy, appears in the *Mirror for Magistrates*, was narrated by
Geoffrey of Monmouth, Michael Drayton, Spenser in *The Faerie
Queene* 2.10, and by Milton elsewhere in his *History of Britain*)
could have several twists and variations. Milton's Attendant Spirit

tells her pathetic mortal story briefly, as though it were already known, for Sabrina was born of the adulterous union of Locrine and his beloved Astrild, pursued by Locrine's vengeful wife Guendolen, who had both Astrild and her daughter drowned. Milton here says that Guendolen was Sabrina's 'stepdam' and he suggests that Sabrina threw herself into the river rather than being thrown, thus tempering perhaps for his youthful participants the savagery of the story.

This may be one sort of commentary on one sort of tale-telling. But, as in the case of the Orpheus stories of *L'Allegro* and *Il Penseroso*, there may be different ways of telling a story, different ways of spelling. Another kind of commentary, like that on Milton's haemony, avoiding the temporalities of local and mythological details and going to the heart of the allegory, may be possible with Sabrina's story. For she too is a deity who has been superseded by a counterpart from a higher realm, for she is a version (*fons pietatis*) of the Christian Virgin Mother ('Listen and save') and, as water, she symbolizes (as in the consolation of *Lycidas*) baptism and the resolving of sins and the restoration of spirit – a symbolism unmistakable to Milton's Christian audience. The perfunctory narrative does not disguise the *significatio* of the tale as one about an innocent murdered bastard, a pathetic victim who rises (things are not always what they seem) even from the muddy Severn tributary alongside Ludlow Castle to bestow grace upon the aristocratic performers and deliverance from the powers of evil.

The lesson was clearly not an easy one. At this point in the masque's actual performance there seems to have been some uneasy shuffling. Milton's text clearly shows that it is Sabrina's alternative charm and not the Lady's chastity nor the brothers' heroic enthusiasm which finally frees the Lady from Comus's enchantment, and for some this may not have been tactful enough. The Bridgewater MS cannot allow the children to be merely passively silent spectators, but has the boys join in the adjuring verses, and Lord Brackley not Henry Lawes, the Attendant Spirit, invites his sister to rise from the chair. That Milton wanted their symbolically eloquent silence and passivity is evident both from the Trinity MS and from his printed text of 1637.[25]

H. M. Richmond commented that 'If we wish to be doctrinaire, we may christen [has it not already been precisely christened?]

this unpredictable and spontaneously acquired [is she not summoned by prayer?] resource grace, but its name hardly matters and Milton does not stress this terminology'.[26] On the contrary, there is the urgent 'Com Lady while Heaven lends us grace / Let us fly this cursed place' (938–39), and it has been all too evident that without such intervention of grace they could do nothing. It is Richmond's view that 'Milton allows the masque to relapse into naive ideology at its conclusion, an ideology reduced to facile confidence by the Attendant Spirit's dogmatic assertion'[27]:

> Mortals that would follow me,
> Love vertue, she alone is free,
> She can teach ye how to clime
> Higher then the Spheary chime;
> Or if Vertue feeble were,
> Heav'n it self would stoop to her.
>   (1018–23)

It is evidently quite possible, then, to miss the way in which these final lines pull in opposite directions, exhibiting not facile confidence but an enduring paradox (and enduring specifically for Milton as a poet). The masque has demonstrated how love of virtue may teach us how to climb but that does not mean that we can do it; for virtue has been shown to be feeble indeed. The Spirit's generous presentation of the children to their parents with the song,

> *Heav'n hath timely tri'd their youth,*
> *Their faith, their patience, and their truth,*
> *And sent them here through hard assays*
> *With a crown of deathless Praise,*
>   *To triumph in victorious dance*
> *O'er sensual Folly, and Intemperance*
>   (970–75)

is both complimentary and ironical since they all know, or ought to know, that they had more than a little help from elsewhere. It is as if the participants need to understand the Christian dimensions of the classical / Celtic mythology they are enacting. Far from affirming the 'idea that virtue is self-sufficient for salvation'[28] these lines turn upon the 'Or if' that has been shown to be actually the case. Its ironic potential, rightly spelled, remains, though we may concede that Milton strained to the limit the tact required in so addressing the household of a royal official and magistrate.

Milton's ideal pensive man prefers, as Coleridge reminds us, 'sage and solemn' works whose trappings of tourneys and trophies, forests and drear enchantments, like Spenser's (Milton's Meliboeus, from whom Thyrsis learned of Sabrina), shadow more meaning 'then meets the ear'. With no intention of offering yet further interpretations of the relation between *L'Allegro* and *Il Penseroso*, I want to point to some poetic strategies that are similar to the sort observable in *A Masque*, particularly in their dependence upon close attention to Milton's muscular syntax, and in their trick (if that is the right word) of offering perspectives and tableaux that, once affirmed, are dissolved into mere *trompes d'oeil*.

A recent account of the companion pieces has suggested that a key to understanding them aright may be found in Milton's familiarity with the Hermetic tradition, and it plots correspondences in the two poems with hermetic motifs.[29] One of these motifs is of course the hermetic mode of composition, whereby the sacred mysteries are both revealed and remain hidden, a simultaneous alluding to and concealing of, 'Where more is meant then meets the ear'. Another is the formula to which so many Renaissance hermetists were addicted, the paradoxical *harmonia est discordia concors*,[30] by means of which device it may be possible to bring the different impulses of the two poems into a concord expressive of Ficino's Platonic conclusion that man's highest good lies 'in the mixture of wisdom and pleasure'.[31]

All this is well and good. But when we begin to hunt down the sources of a Miltonic flourish in the *Asclepius*, or the *Anthologium* of Stobaeus, the *libelli* of the *Corpus Hermeticum*, or even Ficino's or Pico's hermetic rhapsodisings, we should remember that Milton's relation to such materials was acutely problematic. Milton was perfectly well aware that Isaac Casaubon, in a stunning scholarly coup, had demonstrated that the Hermetic writings, far from predating Moses and Plato, were a ragbag of late forgeries.[32] Jesus's rejection of the wisdom of Greece and Rome in *Paradise Regained* ('little else but dreams') was, for Milton, yet to come, but its implications are subtly evident, as we have seen, even in the youthful poems. We could take an obtuse stance, for instance, like the one the student Milton adopted in his Cambridge *De Idea Platonica quemadmodum Aristoteles intellexit* ('Of the Platonic Ideal

Form as understood by Aristotle'), in which Latin verses he bur-
lesques Plato's doctrine of forms and speaks as a literal-minded
Aristotelian wondering where the ideal or archetypal form of man
is to be found. Nobody knows, Milton jocularly says, not even
that seer who glories in a triple name, Hermes Trismegistus,
although he was a pretty erudite fellow (*ut sic arcani sciens*), and
certainly not Plato, the greatest fictional writer of them all (*ipse
fabulator maximus*). Is it possible that the celebration in those
celebrated lines of *Il Penseroso*, so graphically lit by Samuel
Palmer, is equally obtuse?

> Or let my Lamp at midnight hour,
> Be seen in som high lonely Towr,
> Where I may oft out-watch the *Bear*,
> With thrice great *Hermes*, or unsphear
> The spirit of *Plato* to unfold
> What Worlds, or what vast Regions hold
> The immortal mind that hath forsook
> Her mansion in this fleshly nook.
>
> (85–92)

It is customary (with various caveats and complications) to regard the companion pieces as loosely representing Mirth and
Melancholy, *L'Allegro* exorcising the clinical Galenic disease, *Il
Penseroso* celebrating the Aristotelian (and Ficinean) melancholic
temperament;[33] or perhaps *L'Allegro* simply celebrates the joys of
'common experience', *Il Penseroso* the higher pleasures of 'intellectual experience'.[34] The direction of *movement* (even though
the two may be held in a concord of opposites) is generally agreed
to be one of ascent, the poet graduating by rising steps from lesser
(though wholesome) to greater. Yet if we follow through the lines
just quoted, we find ourselves forced into an unexpected nose
dive from the vast and giddy regions of hermetic contemplation:

> And of those *Daemons* that are found
> In fire, air, flood, or under ground.
>
> (93–94)

We have climbed the lonely tower, the ambitious Platonic ladder
to heaven, but we end our journey underground. However we
interpret the subsequent gloss on the demons, 'Whose power
hath a true consent / With Planet, or with Element' (95–96),

invoking the aid of the *Corpus Hermeticum*, we cannot resist the sudden, almost brutal, change of direction downwards. In a similar fashion the earlier, archetypal description of the Platonic ascent, figured in the 'pensive Nun' (not a member of a Catholic closed order but a pagan priestess) (31), also takes a sudden downward plunge:

> With eev'n step, and musing gate,
> And looks commercing with the skies,
> Thy rapt soul sitting in thine eyes:
> There held in holy passion still,
> Forget thy selfe to Marble, till
> With a sad Leaden downward cast,
> Thou fix them on the earth as fast.
>
> (38–44)

The revelatory skyward-looking trance stubs its toe inevitably ('till'), pulled down by the heavy spondees to fix its gaze with equal intensity ('as fast') on the earth under its feet.[35] It is as though the surge of aspiration toward the ideal in the poem (a certain sort of ideal) is continually frustrated by some magnetic, gravitational force.

There may be, incidentally, another sort of unexpectedness, or an incomplete if not actually wrong spelling, in the allusions to Orpheus in each of the poems. It all depends how you tell the story. In *L'Allegro* the Poet Orpheus imagines achieving verse of such 'lincked sweetnes' and 'giddy cunning' that it will untwist 'all the chains that ty/ The hidden soul of harmony' (140, 141, 143–44),

> Such streins as would have won the ear
> Of *Pluto*, to have quit set free
> His half regain'd *Eurydice*.
>
> (148–50)

As it was, he did not. What Milton's verse actually demonstrates is ineffectiveness: 'would have won' Pluto's ear – Orpheus's strains achieved that – but the syntax spills over to mean would have persuaded him 'to have quite set free' Eurydice, unconditionally. But that even Orpheus couldn't do, and the euphemistic 'half regain'd' really means not just 'and half lost' but totally lost – and through his own all too human error: a situation of frustration capped by the pat irony of

These delights, if thou canst give,
Mirth with thee, I mean to live.
(151–2)

In *Il Penseroso* Orpheus appears again, verbally dressed in stoically dignified accents worthy of an Arnoldian touchstone:

Or bid the soul of *Orpheus* sing
Such notes as warbled to the string,
Drew Iron tears down *Pluto's* cheek,
And made Hell grant what Love did seek.
(105–8)

Orpheus is the masterful poet, deploying his art to save and restore, but its resonance is fatally cracked because this version of the story is only a half-truth: hell granted him his Eurydice, but *Penseroso*, too, lost her.

Throughout *Il Penseroso* is the impulse to forsake 'this fleshly nook' (even though it is also described – routinely or with creative complexity? – as a 'mansion'). Its persona is continually bent on withdrawal, fending off, hiding or retreating from: 'Hence', 'forget thy self to Marble', 'I walk unseen', 'Som still removed place','Far from', 'lonely Towr', 'Where the rude Ax with heaved stroke, / Was never heard', 'in close covert', 'Where no profaner eye may look', 'Hide me' (1, 42, 65, 78, 80, 86, 136–7, 139, 140, 141). As with the triads in *A Masque*, there are three attempts at retirement from the light of day, first in the 'removed place' where light is taught to counterfeit gloom; later in twilit groves sought to escape the sun's flaring beams (131–8); and finally in the 'Cloysters pale' (156). Three times, as the sounds and concerns of earth are evaded, there are moments of postured stillness – sitting high up in the lonely tower, lying prostrate and asleep, and finally standing motionless before the pealing organ and the choir. It would be easy to complete the symmetry by adding that he withdraws from the body three times: first his spirit soars in the company of Plato (89); then he is lost in the *vacatio* of sleep in which 'som strange mysterious dream' (147) signals his initiation into hermetic mysteries (Ficino asserting that sleep makes the soul accessible to divine influence),[36] and finally he is dissolved into that *ek-stasis*, the disuniting of soul from body, so described and striven for by all gnostics, neoplatonists and hermetists. But we may feel that there are some very odd things going on here.

As I suggested, the aspirations towards contemplation of the heavens are dragged back to earth. The revelatory dreaming –

> Entice the dewy-feather'd Sleep;
> And let som strange mysterious dream,
> Wave at his Wings in Airy stream,
> Of lively portrature display'd,
> Softly on my eye-lids laid.
> And as I wake, sweet musick breath
> Above, about, or underneath,
> Sent by som spirit to mortals good,
> Or th'unseen Genius of the Wood
>
> (146–54)

– concludes with a hint at the magical music of *The Tempest* ('Where should this music be? I'the air or th'earth?' [I.ii.390]) sent here by God knows what agency, but, it is hoped, 'to mortals good'. The vagueness ('*som* strange mysterious', '*som* spirit', '*Or*') and the hopefulness concerning the status and outcome of such a self-surrender is rendered by verbal tentativeness. Like that of Orpheus, it is an inadequate sort of music. Another (the third of the triad) promptly succeeds it: 'cleer', 'high', equally sweet, and whose provenance and meaning is precisely known and recognized, the music of Christian liturgy, to be heard not in a secret retreat but in a celebratory, specifically and communally functional building, with its 'high embowed roof', its 'antick Pillars massy proof', its 'storied Windows' ornamented instructionally with scenes from biblical history.

Accounting for just how Milton arrives at this climactic point in the poem has proved a puzzle. It is usually accommodated by a formula such as 'lest this form of prophecy [the hermetic reverie] seem pagan rather than Christian, the desire for an initiation by dream is followed by the desire for an explicitly Christian ecstasy'.[37] The forms of prophecy described earlier do not seem but *are* pagan rather than Christian; the desire for initiation by dream is not 'followed by' (as though it were a slightly different version of the same thing, included as a Christian-humanist afterthought) but is superseded by (as Christ supersedes Orpheus) Christian ecstasy, a specific kind of ecstasy that implicitly rejects those earlier aspirations of the furtively withdrawing persona (oddly and inconsistently concerned, in 'Or if the Ayr will not permit' [77], about the weather) and revalues them.

The crucial syntax here is Milton's resounding 'But':

> But let my due feet never fail,
> To walk the studious Cloysters pale.
>
> (155–6)

Is it casual, or causal? His uses of *but* in the poem are instructive. 'But hail thou Goddes' in line 11 means 'not that but this'. The invitation to the nun to 'Com, but keep thy wonted state' (37) says 'not like that but like this'. 'But first, and chiefest' (51) selects, out of all the possible candidates, the cherub Contemplation – again, 'bring not those but him'. Morn should not be 'trickt and frounc't', 'But kercheft' (125). The *but* of line 155 is of similar force: 'not that but this' – not evasion and hiding, but active seeking; its verbal mood is not the adjuring or summoning 'hence' or 'come', but is expressive of personal activity and volition: 'let my due feet' (dutiful, subject to a higher discipline) 'never fail, / To walk . . . And love'. What brings to ecstasy and dissolving is not a music of unknown provenance but that of the service and the anthems, from which *Penseroso* will be instructed in the authentic biblical analogies between the mansion 'in this fleshly nook' and the heavens, and between earthly and heavenly buildings: 'For we know that if our earthly house of this tabernacle were dissolved, we have a building of God, an house not made with hands, eternal in the heavens' (2 Corinthians 5:1). Its prepositions, adverbs and adjectives, unlike the Ariel sinuosities of 'Above, about, or underneath', are energetically deployed, running together spatial and spiritual categories forcing us to respond to the various significations of 'dimm' and 'light' (a light that is 'religious' now in a very precise sense, 'a light to lighten the Gentiles'), 'dimm' and 'cleer', 'below', and 'high'.[38]

As in the ode *On the Morning of Christ's Nativity*, it is 'Such Musick (as 'tis said) / Before was never made' (117–18), and such harmony that 'alone / Could hold all Heav'n and Earth in happier union' (107–8). Neither the Orphic music of *Il Penseroso* nor the magic music of dream can induce ecstasy: each falters into ineffectiveness or puzzlement. Only the Christian liturgical music of 'the full voic'd Quire' can 'Dissolve me into extasies, / And bring all Heav'n before mine eyes' (162, 165–6).

When the climactic revelatory experience has been achieved,

the persona must descend from this peak of contemplation and project the knowledge gained into the future. His posture is seated, his location a 'peacefull hermitage', his activity that of rightly spelling.

> And may at last my weary age
> Find out the peacefull hermitage,
> The Hairy Gown and Mossy Cell,
> Where I may sit and rightly spell,
> Of every Star that Heav'n doth shew,
> And every Herb that sips the dew.
>
> (167–72)

His eye travels (with no sense now of anticlimax or paradox) from 'every Star that Heav'n doth shew' to 'every Herb that sips the dew', accommodating and reverencing, not rejecting, the facts observed while tied to earth. The movement is from up to down: the properly serious mind is capable of lowering its sight from heaven to earth and of rightly valuing what, in the course of the poem, it has been seeking so assiduously to avoid. One implication of 'rightly spell' is that things have been, and may be still, wrongly spelled. What are the appropriate spells or charms? What is the true God-spell? Sidney had pointed to the etymology of spells and their relationship to song and poetry, calling it 'a very vain and godless superstition' to think that 'spirits were commanded by such verses – whereupon this word charms, derived of *carmina*, cometh'.[39] Milton's *carmina* are not designed to endorse 'vain and godless superstition', nor to rest in a stubbornly transcendent Platonism, but to allegorize and anatomize them.

NOTES

1. Samuel Taylor Coleridge, *Letters*, ed. E. L. Griggs, Oxford University Press, 1956, 2, p. 866.
2. Quotations from Milton's poetry are from Helen Darbishire's *The Poems of John Milton*, London: Oxford University Press, 1958.
3. See Walter L. Schindler, *Voice and Crisis: Invocation in Milton's Poetry*, Hampden, Conn.: Archon Books, 1984.
4. Cedric C. Brown, *John Milton's Aristocratic Entertainments*, Cambridge: Cambridge University Press, 1985.
5. *Liber igni, Author furca, dignissimi*, on the title page of the Bridgewater copy of the *Defensio* (1651), now in the Huntington Library. See

William Ingoldsby, 'Intramuralia' *Huntington Library Quarterly*, 37 (1973), pp. 89–90.

6. S. R. Watson, 'An Interpretation of Milton's Haemony', *Notes & Queries*, 178 (1940), p. 260–1.

7. E. S. Le Comte, 'New Light on the 'Haemony' Passage in *Comus*', *Philological Quarterly*, 21 (1942), p. 283–98.

8. J. Arthos, 'Milton's Haemony and Virgil's Amellus', *Notes & Queries*, 206 (1961), p. 172.

9. J. H. Hanford, 'Haemony', *Times Literary Supplement*, November 3, 1932, 815. Controversy over the meanings of 'haemony' is summarized in *A Variorum Commentary on the Poems of John Milton*, ed. A. S. P. Woodhouse and D. Bush, London: Routledge, 1972, pp. 931–8; and J. M. Steadman's austerely rigorous but inconclusive 'Milton's *Haemony*: Etymology and Allegory', *PMLA*, 77 (1962), pp. 200–7.

10. Cedric C. Brown, 'The Shepherd, the Musician, and the Word in Milton's Masque', *Journal of English and Germanic Philology*, 68 (1979), p. 522–44. A revised form of this essay appears in his *John Milton's Aristocratic Entertainments*, chap. 5.

11. Lewis Spence, *The Mysteries of Britain: Secret Rites and Traditions of Ancient Britain Restored*, London: Rider, 1928, p. 196.

12. Elias Owen, *Welsh Folklore: A Collection of Folk Tales and Legends of North Wales*, 1896; reprint, Norwood, Pa.: Norwood Editions, 1973, p. 249.

13. Katharine Briggs, *A Dictionary of Fairies, Hobgoblins, Brownies, Bogies, and Other Supernatural Creatures*, London: Allen Lane, 1976, p. 346.

14. Elias Owen, p. 280.

15. C. F. Otten, 'Milton's Haemony', *English Literary Renaissance*, 5 (1975), pp. 81–95.

16. T. Gwynn Jones, *Welsh Folklore and Folk Customs*, London: Methuen, 1930, p. 21.

17. On the Celtic material see Violet O'Valle, 'Milton's *Comus* and the Welsh Oral Tradition', *Milton Studies*, 18 (1983), pp. 25–44.

18. Le Comte, p. 293, though Le Comte's reasoning was described by T. P. Harrison ('The 'Haemony' Passage in *Comus* Again', *Philological Quarterly*, 22 [1943], pp. 251–4) as tenuous.

19. R. M. Adams, 'Reading *Comus*', *Modern Philology*, 51 (1953), p. 24.

20. See, respectively, David Masson (ed.), *The Poetical Works of John Milton*, London: Macmillan, 1890, 3. p. 229; B. G. Hall, '*Comus*', *Times Literary Supplement*, 12 October 1933, 691; Hanford, 815.

21. See Cedric C. Brown, *Aristocratic Entertainments*, pp. 113, 173.

22. See C. S. Lewis, 'A Note on *Comus*', *Review of English Studies*, 8 (1932), pp. 170–6; J. S. Diekhoff, 'The Text of *Comus*, 1634 to 1645', *PMLA*, 52 (1937), pp. 705–27; 'Critical Activity of the Poetic Mind: John Milton', *PMLA*, 55 (1940), pp 748–72.

23. Douglas Brooks-Davies (*The Mercurian Monarch: Magical Politics from Spenser to Pope*, Manchester: Manchester University Press, 1983, pp. 139–37) entirely misses Milton's syntax here and consequently expands on 'his comparison of haemony to "that moly" ' without a blink. Cedric Brown detects signs of strain in Milton's syntactical

structures in the Haemony allegory and suggests they are simply the result of the effort at cerebral definition. Brown, 'The Shepherd, the Musician, and the Word.'.

24. Vincent Hopper (*Medieval Number Symbolism: Its Sources, Meaning, and Influence on Thought and Expression*, Columbia University Studies in English and Comparative Literature, no. 132, New York: Columbia University Press, 1932, p. 203) explains that 'among the Welsh triads were extraordinarily popular, both narrator and audience apparently delighting in 'the 3 costly pillages', 'the 3 ill resolutions', 'the 3 frivolous bards', 'the 3 inventors', and so on'. It might also be noted how Milton manipulates the triple impersonation of Henry Lawes the tutor playing the Attendant Spirit who is playing the part of Thyrsis the shepherd.

25. See Cedric Brown, *Aristocratic Entertainments*, p. 116 and Appendix.

26. H. M. Richmond, *The Christian Revolutionary: John Milton*, Berkeley: University of California Press, 1974, pp. 73–6.

27. Richmond, p. 77.

28. Richmond, p. 77.

29. Gerard H. Cox, 'Unbinding The Hidden Soul of Harmony: *L'Allegro, Il Penseroso*, and the Hermetic Tradition', *Milton Studies*, 18 (1983), pp. 45–62.

30. See Edgar Wind, *Pagan Mysteries in the Renaissance*, London: Faber, 1958, 'Virtue Reconciled with Pleasure', pp. 78–88.

31. Quoted by Cox from *Marsilio Ficino: The Philebus Commentary*, ed. and trans. M. J. B. Allen, Berkeley: University of California Press, 1975, Appendix 3.

32. Isaac Casaubon, *De rebus sacris et ecclesiasticis exercitationes XVI. Ad Cardinalis Baronii Prolegomena in Annales*, London: 1614, p. 70ff.

33. L. Babb, 'The Background of "Il Penseroso" ', *Studies in Philology*, 37 (1940), pp. 257–75.

34. Don Cameron Allen, *The Harmonious Vision: Studies in Milton's Poetry*, Baltimore: The John Hopkins University Press, 1954, pp. 3–23.

35. See Richmond's provocative comments on these lines, pp. 62–3.

36. See P. O. Kristeller, *The Philosophy of Marsilio Ficino*, New York: Columbia University Press, 1943, p. 313.

37. Cox, p. 56.

38. See Stanley E. Fish 'What It's Like to Read *L'Allegro* and *Il Penseroso*', *Milton Studies*, 7 (1975), pp. 77–99.

39. Sir Philip Sidney, *A Defence of Poetry*, ed. J. Van Dorsten, Oxford: Oxford University Press, 1966, p. 21.

6

A CONVENTION OF EPIC
Similes of unlikeness, or
the uses of nostalgia

Every man ought to be a judge of pictures, and
every man is so who has not been connoisseured
out of his senses.
William Blake, letter 1806

Milton's extended similes in *Paradise Lost* are an epic obligation,
a requirement of the genre. When confronted with this convention, the poet's option is not whether to insert some or not, but
whether those he writes up are to have, either in any particular
context or throughout, a function and status which is morally
illustrative, historically amplifying, or merely decorative and ornamental, or whatever. William Empson's well known essay on
Milton and the eminent eighteenth-century classicist Dr Richard
Bentley showed us how Bentley, in his annotated and 'corrected'
edition of *Paradise Lost* (1732), ruthlessly excised whole lines and
even paragraphs of Miltonic simile: any 'decoration' not immediately perceptible as either relevant or felicitous was dismissed
as a 'spurious Interpolation' and classed as 'romantic and inserted
by the Editor'. (Bentley's mythical 'Editor' was some 'suppos'd
Friend' whom Bentley imagined must have seen the book
through the press, constantly tampering with and 'improving' the
blind Milton's text on the way.)

Zachary Pearce presented in the following year 'A Review of
the Text of the Twelve Books Of Milton's *Paradise Lost*' which
addressed Bentley's emendations, Pearce sometimes giving in to
them, and sometimes objecting. On the question of long-tailed
similes, Pearce defends Milton largely by appeal to classical authority and to poetic 'Imagination':

For Milton in his Similitudes (as is the practice of Homer
and Virgil too) after he has shown the common resemblance, often takes the liberty of wandering into some

unresembling Circumstances: which have no other relation
to the Comparisons, than that it gave him the Hint, and (as
it were) set fire to the Train of his Imagination.

But, as Empson rightly pointed out, Pearce's defence, although it
is intended to justify Milton, can equally well defend, by its
appeal to poetic licence, the merest distraction and the most total
irrelevance.[1]

Lurking in Pearce's defence, however, are dark matters, the
full relevance of which have perhaps only recently come to light.
Was Pearce really seeing surpluses of signifiers over signified? He
seems to characterize his poet as a free spirit, 'wandering' at large
through the half-constructed building of his poem, open to Hints,
and hoping for something to 'set fire to the Train of His Imagination'. There is no suggestion that the hints and imaginative ex-
cursions have to be related to some 'Grand Design' or explicative
process, or be part of some overall moral or artistic impulse of the
work. 'Authorial intention' is thus difficult to maintain in such a
serendipitous world; and the reader is in the grasp not of authorial
control but authorial whim. His text is therefore a candidly 'open'
one: it may be hacked about and altered at editorial or reader will.
But without going as far as Bentley or Pearce, we may still wonder
about those 'inserted', generically conventional and ornamental
similes, and respond to them as irresponsibly fathered and therefore free to be read just as irresponsibly.

Milton may indeed at times seem to offer us a paradigm for our
own readerly activity. His similitudes amplifying Satan's shield,
for example,

> his ponderous shield
> Ethereal temper, massy, large and round,
> Behind him cast; the broad circumference
> Hung on his shoulders like the Moon, whose Orb
> Through Optic Glass the *Tuscan* Artist views
> At Ev'ning from the top of *Fesole*,
> Or in *Valdarno*, to descry new Lands,
> Rivers or Mountains in her spotty Globe,
>
> (I, 284–91)[2]

may seem to wander, in precisely Pearce's fashion, into memories
of his tour of Italy and his meeting with Galileo, the memory
momentarily illumined with a Claudian evening light, a fleeting

glimpse of a Tuscan landscape, and a village hill-top just outside Florence: than which few things could apparently be more irrelevant to the matter in hand.

The analogy available to the reader may seem to be that we too are not bound to pay deference to authorial intention or even to generic or historical plausibility. Our responses do not have to be documented in such a way as to make them appear the consciously desired effects of a seventeenth-century poet. Since that poet is himself unsure of what he is about and can so easily lapse into imaginative autobiography, it may seem a proper critical activity merely imaginatively to recreate and offer our own reading experience. And, of course, it may seem equally proper without any such *exemplum* from the author.[3]

Milton himself would no doubt call such imaginations 'fancies built on nothing firm'. They might too be called the products of a text wilfully only half-read. Implicit in what follows is the argument (admittedly traditional and conservative) that Milton engages his reader in the task of sorting out relevance from irrelevance, both in what he writes and in how we read what he has written. There is a small moment, already noted, in that simile directing our view of (or is it merely consequent upon?) Satan's shield: the abrupt shift, without warning or explanatory preamble, to a terrestrial scene, a figure in a landscape. The figure is Galileo; the landscape Tuscany. This sort of modulation, or sometimes jolting, is very characteristic of Milton's deployment of simile and comparison – which may indeed have been one reason why they so incensed Dr Bentley. Whenever his credulity is strained by such transitions, Bentley either nit-picks at the landscape –

> Sedge floated because the Winds had vex'd the *Coast*. why the *Coast*? when the Sedge could only be torn up and float by the *Winds* vexing the *Water*, where the sedge grew (on I, 306) –

or scratches them out altogether: 'I suspect the following five verses to be spurious' (on I, 351ff.); 'Here's another Intrusion of Four spurious Lines; unworthy of admittance' (on I, 763ff.). At times he seems prostrate with righteous incomprehension:

> surely he [Milton] had more Judgment in his old Age, than

to clog and sully his Poem with such Romantic Trash. (on I, 580–87)

There is a kind of bluff utilitarianism here which seems to antici-pate Dr Johnson's explosive response to 'the sight of those dif-ferent dispositions of wood and water, hill and valley' while walking with the Thrales in France: 'whenever Mr Thrale wished to point them out to his companion [Dr Johnson], "Never heard such nonsense", would be the reply: "a blade of grass is always a blade of grass, whether in one country or another" '.[4] The dif-ference here of course is that there may well be something very special about a blade of grass when you happen to be located in Pandemonium. Apparently irrelevant or 'romantic' 'dispositions of wood and water, hill and valley' can take on a heavy freight of iconographical and theological significance when they appear in a 'grand consult' dedicated to obliterating them for ever.

The ornamental epic simile is closely associated with land-scapes. Milton had already shown, in 'L'Allegro', his familiarity with that relatively new, technical word 'landscape' or 'lantskip' (the earliest English use of the word recorded in the *OED* is in 1598), and he employs the term on three separate occasions in *Paradise Lost*: the 'dark'nd lantskip' of II, 491; 'so lovely seemed / That lantskip', IV, 152–3; and 'Discovering in wide Lantskip', V, 142. It has been argued that the emergence of an aesthetics of landscape painting (and of gardening) was intimately related to literature. Just as the writing of pastoral poems went hand in hand with depictions of pastoral scenes and their imitation in other media, so the writing of epic poems cross-fertilized with the pro-duction of paintings or actual, imitative landscapes on the ground: gardens, parklands, prospects. For example, in the Court of Fer-rara in the sixteenth century Boiardo, Bernardo Tasso and Ariosto were officials and Torquato Tasso was court poet, all of them vigorously engaged in reviving epic. And with this revival went the generic accompaniment of frequent extended landscape de-scriptions, usually by way of the simile – descriptions that were reflected in specifically landscape art.[5]

How one regards 'landscape' when one is writing a poem about the Fall of man and of nature can be a crucial issue. And Milton's poem is full of landscapes. They are not, however, like a Monet or a Cezanne; nor are they quite like Turner's 'Morning among Coniston Fells' (R. A. 1798), to which independent and free-standing subject Turner nonetheless felt moved to append a quotation from *Paradise Lost*: 'Ye mists and exhalations now arise'. Milton's verbal landscapes are either iconographical, or, in sound Aristotelian terms of a *poesis* imitative of 'men in action', they are landscapes with figures. For example, there is the moment of simile in Book III when the scout

> at last by break of chearful dawne
> Obtains the brow of some high-climbing Hill,
> Which to his eye discovers unaware
> The goodly prospect of some forren land
> First-seen, or some renownd Metropolis
> With glistering Spires and Pinnacles adornd,
> Which now the Rising Sun guilds with his beams.
>
>   (III, 545–51)

This set piece reads uncannily like a programme for a Claude Lorraine or a Gaspar Poussin painting: a vista, dependent on a high point of perspective, an extensive plain, rolling distances seen in the level half-light of sunrise. The observer seems almost like a painter himself who, having reached his vantage point, is about to get out his palette or his Claude-glass. It is however a *moral* landscape: the observer is a military scout, analogy for Satan contemplating the Earth. The imagery of reconnaissance and the implied reporting back for reinforcements to destroy that 'goodly prospect' and those 'glistering Spires' is built into the picture too, darkening the moment with a poignant sense of the landscape's vulnerability. It is not exactly allegory, though there is an implied *Psychomachia* as Envy confronts Nature and *Bellona* confronts *Civilitas*. There is too that ominously unattached adjective 'chearful': whom does the dawn cheer, the scout, or the inhabitants of the plain? But despite the threat offered, there is the unmistakable protective benediction of the 'Rising Sun' (*Ecce vir, Oriens nomen eius*, Zechariah, 6:12) suffusing the scene.

But Milton is not always so helpful in pointing or annotating his scenes. The central landscape of the poem, the prospect of the Garden of Eden – 'So little knows / Any, but God alone, to value right / The good before him' (IV, 201–3) – is assembled for our inspection with remarkable authorial diffidence. The important words in his description – 'if Art could tell' – follow a device of *occupatio* ('whereof here needs no account'):

> But rather to tell how, if Art could tell,
> How from that Saphire Fount the crisped Brooks,
> Rowling on Orient Pearl and sands of Gold,
> With mazie error under pendant shades
> Ran Nectar, visiting each plant, and fed
> Flours worthy of Paradise, which not nice Art
> In Beds and curious Knots, but Nature boon
> Powrd forth profuse on Hill and Dale and Plaine.
>
> (IV, 234–43)

'If Art could tell' (with its repeated 'how', 'How'), and 'which not nice Art', suggest that the depiction is highly conjectural, a possible discursive method, a product of art whose adequacy is by no means necessarily endorsed by Milton.[6] He is merely saying that if you tried (like me) to use art, a description might go something like this, with its 'crisped Brooks' and 'Orient Pearl'. But it would be wrong, or inadequate, since human art has no place here: this particular Garden was by God 'in the East / Of *Eden* planted' (IV, 209–10), and its pre-artful character prepares us for the unartful human figures in that landscape, most notably of course an Eve whose 'unadorned gold'n tresses', like the Garden's vegetation, are 'Dissheveld, but in wanton ringlets wav'd' (IV, 305–6).

It is well known that what later readers responded to was the aesthetic option Milton had taken up and his ratification of a certain *style* of gardening. Thus Horace Walpole, in his *Essay of Gardening* (1771) fixes eagerly on the lines in which Milton appears to disparage formal gardens:

> Flours worthy of Paradise, which not nice Art
> In Beds and curious Knots, but Nature boon
> Powrd forth profuse on Hill and Dale and Plaine.

Joseph Warton, William Collins and many others add their approval of Milton's good sense and his seminal 'picturesque' hint. Walpole's essay commends 'the depiction of Eden' as 'a warmer and more just picture of the present style [of gardening] than Claude Lorraine could have painted from Hagley or Stourhead'. (The way Walpole puts this is actually very odd: he seems to be saying that if Claude had painted a picture of Stourhead – even though Stourhead was itself conceived as an imitation of a Claude picture – it wouldn't be as close to the ideal as Milton's description of Eden.)

Such readers, looking to their own tastes and concerns, found that the impressive thing about Milton's Eden was its character as a natural wilderness. His Garden was emphatically *not* laid out with formal taste like a seventeenth-century palace garden and, better still, it seemed to bring together and reflect the two most fashionable painting styles of Claude and of Salvator Rosa: his Eden could be surrounded by precipices, cavernous glooms and shaggy mountains; and it could be like a Claudian vista:

> about me round I saw
> Hill, dale, and shady woods, and sunny plains,
> And liquid lapse of murmuring streams.
> (VIII, 261ff.)

And, most gratifying of all, his Eden of Book IV –

> Thus was this place,
> A happy rural seat of various view –

sounded exactly like a description of an eighteenth-century English gentleman's country estate.

That it actually *was* meant to suggest English rural landscape may strike some as funny. John Broadbent says that 'happy rural seat' 'is almost laughably the England of Penshurst, Coopers Hill and Appleton House'.[7] Alastair Fowler quite properly slaps him down:

> Milton mingles glimpses of preserved or recovered beauty seen in many different directions: why should it be more laughable to see them in the countryside than in books?[8]

It is a good question. Milton's inspiration for his Eden landscape comes only partly from books, and he tells us what some of those booke are: 'Hesperian fables' from Ovid's *Metamorphoses*, Diodorus Siculus's *Arabia felix*, Spenser's *Faerie Queene*, Ariosto, Tasso, the Garden of Alcinous in the *Odyssey*, and so on, as well as the most important and pervasive bookish source, the book of Genesis. But he is also looking at real life. He knows the English landscape. And during his Italian tour he would have seen and responded to the beauty of the Italian landscape in general and Italian gardens in particular, both of which made profound impressions on many English travellers. Though Milton rejects as models the formal and geometric design of many of these gardens, his Eden is full of walks, a variety of view-points, full of bowers and arbours, plantations ('stateliest covert, cedar, pine or palm'), and it possesses that standard feature of the Italian garden, fountains.[9] This blend of biblical sources, literary Arcadianism, and actual observation is worked together in the service of an idyllic, idealized world of the imagination, no longer accessible but which may be intermittently caught and reproduced on earth as a retreat, a solace or an encouragement. For the important thing about Milton's Paradise is that it is Paradise lost. We should never forget what happens, with sickening finality, to Milton's elaborately and lovingly depicted Garden: it is drowned, and becomes a guano-covered rock somewhere in the Persian Gulf:

> then shall this Mount
> Of Paradise by might of Waves be moovd
> Out of his place, pusht by the horned floud,
> With all his verdure spoild, and Trees adrift
> Down the great River to the op'ning Gulf,
> And there take root an Iland salt and bare,
> The haunt of seales and Orcs, and Sea-mews clang.
>   (XI, 829–35)

Michael's words to Adam poignantly convey the absolute inaccessibility of that Paradise. But if Paradise is lost, is Eden, or a glimpse of what Eden represented, lost too? If it is, then what function – other than of dreadful warning or of rubbing our noses in what we have forfeited – can Milton's similes, his landscapes-with-figures copied from the world that we know, have in a poem infallibly diagnosing our condition as fallen?

The question is pertinent when so many of the epic similes of the poem are peopled by men – in seventeenth-century terms, modern, contemporary men – going about their business. We would expect there to be plenty of obviously 'heroic' personnel: soldiers, sappers, kings and khans, with their paraphernalia of shields, spears, ordonnance and arms-drill; but there are also merchants, sailors, navigators, astronomers, shepherds, peasants, ploughmen, and logically of course poets too. The division of sheep and goats, pastoral man and epic man, is made at the earliest possible stage: the first of the six scenes shown to Adam after the Fall is Cain's murder of Abel. Cain enacts, as it were, the first human epic deed, and Milton makes it clear that God's preference for Abel's sacrifice is not arbitrary: Cain gathers his offering in an unselective, nonchalant fashion,'the greene Eare, and the yellow Sheafe, / Unculld, as came to hand' (XI, 435–36), as if already thinking (Milton's phrase is 'not sincere') that there must be easier ways to make a living. Adam's reaction to the tragedy of Abel's murder is to distrust God's justice – 'Is Pietie thus and pure devotion paid?' – and the inexplicability of God's justice is not unknown response to Milton's poem. Michael, however, deflects that question with an even more unpalatable explanation: it is a function of purely human envy (IX, 456), of men who 'live in hatred, enmitie and strife / Among themselves, and levie cruel warres, / Wasting the Earth, each other to destroy' (II, 500–3).

The ambivalence of that perception of our inheritance and what we have made of it is captured in an interesting passage in Milton's *Brief History of Moscovia*:[10]

> The discovery of *Russia* by the northern Ocean, made first, of any nation we know, by *English* men, might have seem'd an enterprise almost heroick; if any higher end then the excessive love of Gaine and Traffic, had animated the design. Nevertheless that in regard that many things not unprofitable to the knowledge of Nature, and other Observations are hereby come to light, as good events ofttimes arise from evil occasions, it will not be the worst labour to relate briefly the beginning, and prosecution of this adventurous Voiage; untill it became at last a familiar Passage.

This comment might well stand as an epigraph to *Paradise Lost*. It is suggestive of the broader implications of the 'adventurous Voiage' of mankind, the now 'familiar Passage' of a compromising, fallen world, and the affirmation (rather grudging in this context) that 'good events ofttimes arise from evil occasions'. Milton's customary patriotism is here elbowed from prominence by a kind of moral discomfort, a clearly ambivalent valuation of 'heroick' enterprise; there is an almost apologetic admission that, motives of 'Gaine and Traffic' notwithstanding, some good has come of it all, chiefly an extension of our 'knowledge of Nature'.

Yet Milton admits that the enterprise was not, in the event, heroic at all, though it might have been if it had not been so muddied with self-interest. It is not surprising that so many of the similes in *Paradise Lost* which amplify Satan's exploits – like the

scout of III, 545, the spice-traders of II, 636, the industrial tech-
nologists of I, 670ff., the 'weather-beat'n' vessel of II, 1043 –
draw on images of exploration and commercial expansion. At the
same time, however resonant and useful such images may be in
furnishing descriptions of the epic journey from Pandemonium to
Eden, the moral discomfort in Milton's practical view of such
human journeys is made more acute and complicated by the
injunction in Genesis 1:28 to 'subdue' the earth. The injunction
might well sound like a justification of such enterprises, an incentive to found not a new Eden but a New Atlantis. All that needs
subduing in the original Eden is its enormous fertility; but after
the Fall and the curse of the labourer the command becomes an
axiom which seems basic to survival, and the ethical issue is not
whether one should subdue the earth, but how.

It may be true enough that Satan is the epic hero of *Paradise
Lost*, though not perhaps for the reasons advanced by Blake or
Empson.[11] Satan's problem is that he is the epic hero of a profoundly anti-epic heroic poem: that kind of subduing of the earth
which involves subduing one's neighbour (whether human or
angelic) by force or guile represents in *Paradise Lost* all that is
most distasteful to Milton about heroic pretension. Nor does it
matter that exponents of this attitude appear to be on the 'right'
side: 'Baptiz'd or Infidel' share the same odium, and 'Charlemain
with all his Peerage' are syntactically and morally gathered up
into the bee simile at the end of Book I and share in the devils'
embarrassing metamorphoses. Some of Milton's most spikily in-
sistent lines dismiss 'Warres, hitherto the only Argument / Heroic
deem'd' (IX, 28–9). As Milton makes clear in many places in his
writings, the beginning of true prosperity and 'the true florishing
of a Land' (that is, the proper subduing of the earth) lies in
godliness, as in the opening section of the second book *Of
Reformation*:

> To govern well is train up a Nation in true wisdom and
> vertue, and that which springs from thence magnanimity,
> (take heed of that) and that which is our beginning, re-
> generation, and happiest end, likeness to *God*, which in one
> word we call *godlines*, & that this is the true florishing of a
> Land, other things follow as the shadow does the
> substance.[12]

If this is Milton's view of the post-lapsarian world we inhabit and of our efforts to subdue it and make it yield up its reluctant harvest, it must mean that Abel, the industrious and pious sheep-farmer, and those peasants and ploughmen and even perhaps merchants, together with the activities they represent, are not indistinguishably fallen along with the burglar and the sultan and the murderer Cain. All are not equally and indiscriminately wrapped in some total and blanketing Calvinist depravity. In other words, some of those human figures-in-a-landscape who emerge briefly in narrative-suspending moments of simile may be seen as embodying, in their implied 'godlines', alternatives to, or comments upon, Satan's activities.

This point has been made, for instance, about the Tuscan artist in I, 288, where Galileo may be seen to represent 'a culture quite different from, and implicitly superior to, the military heroism' of Satan.[13] Galileo, under house-arrest in Valdarno by the Inquisition of the Roman Anti-Christ, oppressed by Satanic forces of evil, impartially observes the moon of Satan's heroic shield 'at Ev'ning from the top of *Fesole*' through a telescope. As if this were not debilitating enough (for Satan), Galileo describes what he sees in a scientific paper, *Siderius nuncius* (Venice, 1610). It is instructive to note Dr Bentley's reaction to Galileo's irrelevant presence in the simile. He begins by griping about the 'Optick glass', claiming that the Author omits to say that the moon is actually being *magnified*; he goes on to complain that Galileo could not possibly have seen 'Rivers or Mountains' on the moon, 'nor can They be descried through the best Glasses Now improv'd: much less Then by the *Tuscan Artist*'; and he finally consigns the whole section to the Editor rather than the Author, largely because the poem 'has *Galileo* and his *Glass* again, Book V. 261.' Oddly enough, Bentley seemed to miss that moment in Book III when Satan appears to infect the Sun itself:

> There lands the Fiend, a spot like which perhaps
> Astronomer in the suns lucent Orbe
> Through his glaz'd Optic Tube yet never saw.
>
> (III, 588–90)

No doubt he would have thrown that out too, thus missing once more Milton's subdued but telling little simile. Satan's original sunspot is not of course from our point of view observable ('yet never saw'); what we see are, presumably, infinitely smaller manifestations of Satan's first visit. And these manifestations are observed through Galileo's telescope once more, the astronomer coolly measuring and noting Satanic effects and recording the detritus of that first visitation in his *Letters on the Solar Spots* (Rome, 1613).

The contemporary and historical instances of human life since the Fall are invariably deployed by Milton as analogues to, or similes for, Satan and Satanic activity. There are practically no similes in Heaven, and Raphael's to Adam are short, simple and few. It is Satan who attracts similes like a magnet, and that he should do so is in part a requirement of the convention of epic writing in which the hero regularly trails extended similes behind him. But Milton's treatment of his material is no cliché of homiletic method; on the contrary, he generates deliberate confusion. This confusion depends on our natural tendency to associate, as in some kind of illustrative collusion, the two parties to the simile – Satan, and his human or 'natural' counterparts – and to see them as mutually reinforcing, the one amplifying the other. Thus Satan is like (and vice versa) Leviathan (I, 200ff.) or a Jesuistical wolf (IV, 183) or a thief (IV, 188) or the Egyptian Busiris (I, 307). But are the fallen angels also, and in the same sense of the word, *like* the 'Autumnal Leaves that strow the Brooks / In *Vallombrosa*' (I, 302–3), or 'Bees / In spring time' (I, 768–69)? Is Satan really like 'the Sun new ris'n' (I, 594) or the Plowman of IV, 983? Is his experience of Eden really like that of the seamen and the '*Sabean* Odours' of IV, 159ff.?

In the unique scenarios of *Paradise Lost*, the meaning of the word *like* is bound to be intensely problematic. Granted his extraordinary subject-matter, the logic implied in Milton's brief as a poet is subtle and inexorable. It begins of course in the necessary imaginative and dramatic rehearsal in material forms (that is, forms appropriate to an epic poem) of abstract spiritual ideas: Sin and Death, spiritual wickedness in high places / Goodness and Creativity and obedience, enacted by a vast population of incorporeal beings having no humanly accessible dimensions or shape. This transformation, or translation, of this recalcitrant 'material' is the very life of the poem as a poem, and it gives Milton every opportunity for all kinds of delicate or ironic discriminations in the epic mode itself. But until the Creation occurs, or more properly until the Fall occurs, it also means that all the material which makes up this poetic substance is strictly after the event. This fact, as several commentators have noted, allows Milton both broadly and in the minutest details of the poem, to ring the various changes inherent in this *post hoc ergo propter hoc* situation: Satan is not like Turnus or a vulture or a comet or Leviathan or Pharoah, but it is Turnus, vultures, comets, Leviathans and Pharoahs which are like Satan. Or, by slightly different strategies, it is not Eden which is like the '*Nyseian* Ile' (IV 268–9, 275) but it is, fragmentarily, suggestive of Eden. Or it is not Eve's 'wanton ringlets' (IV, 306) that are wanton, but ours. So many of the allusions and comparisons are (to use a favourite word of Bishop Henry King) 'preposterous', back-to-front. As far as Satan is concerned, this means very often that what he is being compared with does not, at that moment in the poem's time, yet exist; it only comes to exist through the effect – an effect opposite to that intended by Satan – of God's creativeness which brings about, with a perpetual and therefore easily ignored or forgotten irony, those things, whether good or evil, with which Satan may be compared. There is a continuously running visualised commentary tempering the otherwise abstract assertions that *nothing* happens except 'by sufferance of supernal Power' and that *all* acts are performed in God's service, whether voluntarily or involuntarily. The similes reveal the 'success' of Satanic operations as both very evident and very contingent; they reveal too, more often than is good for Satan's morale, that his labour 'out of good still to find means of evil' (I, 166) is in fact turned to an occasion to 'rejoyce / Much more, that much more good thereof shall spring' (XII, 475–6).

The substance of the Miltonic simile may thus be seen as expressive of the main impulses and direction of the poem. For with respect to such a temporal / logical situation, the longstanding arguments about the relevance or irrelevance, the 'organic' or the 'decorative' status of long-tailed comparisons, seems to miss the point: in a sense, the longer the tail the better. The fact that they are there, and are thus possible and available, whether of eclipses, storms at sea, polar winds and the hooves of Tartar horsemen, or whether of summer air, Sabean odours, harvest fields or shepherds, has a subtle cutting edge. If we think they all document and illustrate Satan's successes, we might recall some words of Rabindranath Tagore:

If existence were an evil, it would wait for no philosopher to prove it. It is like convicting a man of suicide, while all the time he stands before you in the flesh.[14]

I do not mean, however, to suggest absurdly that Milton does not distinguish between good and evil – as if, in some oriental mood, he were indifferent to all but the fact of existence. There are of course the patterns not only of the wider emblems of dark and light, heroism and humility, slavery and freedom, disobedience and loyalty, but also, as Dennis Burden has shown, clear distinctions between 'the right and the wrong sort of song, and the right and the wrong sort of pastoral'.[15] Nor do I mean to ignore the overbearing weight imposed by the last two books of the poem, whose bleakest perspectives show us 'what miserie th'inabstinence of *Eve* / Shall bring on men' and depict that 'sad, noisom, dark . . . Lazar-house' of our world (XI, 476–7, 478–9). But even when we acknowledge that, by contrasting our world with Eden, these books strategically direct our attention to the wilderness through which we, like Adam and Eve, must wander with the aid of faith, they cannot grub up by the roots the poem's fundamental nostalgia – a paradoxically *energetic* nostalgia. We may further acknowledge that it may not have been Milton's purpose in writing *Paradise Lost* to show us *how* we can recover what we have lost but only how we can run our race 'not without dust and heat'. But we may still find our own powerful response of nostalgia, encouraged by the rest of the poem, resisting the formal artist. Though the vision of the 'saints everlasting rest' in a purely spiritual paradise may be Milton's final emphasis, the poem is full of significant moments when enduring insights and intimations of what Eden embodies are present even on the 'subjected Plain' we inhabit. The Attendant Spirit's dismissive view of

> the smoak and stir of this dim spot
> Which men call Earth, and with low-thoughted care
> Confin'd and pester'd in this pin-fold here,
> Strive to keep up a frail, and Feaverish being,
> (*A Mask Presented at Ludlow-Castle*, 5–8)

coming from a youthful and zealously reforming Milton, is a part, but only a part, of the view of *Paradise Lost*. Our striving to survive, however frail and feverish, is shown in *Paradise Lost* to be assisted by what Edwin Muir, in his poem 'One Foot in Eden', called memory's 'treasure trove'.[16] Milton himself makes this point in moving moments of autobiography. The present world out of which the poet writes seems to hold Eden like a dream

from which we have just awakened: the invocation opening Book
III (that most spare and unmetaphorical book) is, as Anne Ferry
says, full of images

> of the passing year, the cycles of sunrise and nightfall, the
> seasonal changes of foliage and scenery . . . images of light
> falling on 'flocks' or 'herds', or the 'Summers Rose' or the
> 'vernal bloom'.

Such images are 'obviously intended to remind us of pastoral
poetry . . . of existence in the Garden of Eden'.[17] The emblems
of Eden, though they may be simple and conventional in the
invocation, are still available in memory to the blind poet: the
relation seems to be that as the visible world is to the blinded
poet, so Eden is to mankind at large. And its emblems are woven
into the texture of the narrative, by way of simile and comparison,
not only as ironic demonstrations of the *differences* between Eden
and the fallen world (such 'ironic disparity' is of course one of
Milton's most noted effects) but also as demonstrations of the
resemblances, for all Satan's stratagems, between Eden and the
world of here and now. Perception of such resemblances is often
dependent on recognizing that the distinctions or the correspondences we expected to be there in a simile are not always present,
or are not those we had anticipated.

For example (and to return to Milton's thoughts on the discovery of Russia), the extended simile in Book II of Satan's flight
towards the gates of Hell and the fleet at sea is clearly a fine
instance of Milton's skill in maintaining multiple correspondences between tenor and vehicle (it is also a simile which Dr
Bentley impatiently dismantled and discarded as 'spurious'):

> As when farr off at Sea a Fleet descri'd
> Hangs in the Clouds, by Aequinoctial Winds
> Close sailing from *Bengala*, or the Iles
> Of *Ternate* and *Tidore*, whence Merchants bring
> Thir spicie Drugs: they on the Trading Flood
> Through the wide *Ethiopian* to the Cape
> Ply stemming nightly toward the Pole.
>
> (II, 636–42)

William Empson long ago spelt out the correspondences in *Some
Versions of Pastoral*. The ships ply nightly because Satan is in the
darkness of Hell; the fleet is seen 'farr off' and seems to hang in

the clouds, just as Satan is flying; the ships are making for the Pole because Satan is going upwards towards the concave wall of Hell; they are merchants because Satan is like a merchant trading the fragrance of the forbidden tree for Eve's innocence; they carry spicy drugs just as Satan carries confusion of mind; and so on. Such correspondences, and the logical power they demonstrate, are emphatically there. But there are other elements equally present which can extend our admiration beyond the cataloguing of correspondences.

B. A. Wright's note[18] reminds us how intimately Milton himself was involved in such trading ventures, for these voyagers are men contemporary with the poem. In 1623 the English factory at Amboyna, one of the East India Spice Islands, was destroyed by the Dutch, the English shipping sunk, and the traders massacred. In 1652 Milton, as Cromwell's Foreign Secretary, drew up claims for compensation on account of the Massacre at Amboyna. The tragedy lay not in the enterprise, nor especially in the cargo (which would include important spices for preserving meat for winter consumption, ingredients for pharmacy, for dyeing, and a host of other useful commodities), but in sheer human greed. Such journeys, motivated by 'Gaine and Traffic' among other things, were also dangerous and full of labour; for what is also present in the simile is the sense of *effort*, of sailing close to the wind, of plying, that is, of beating against the wind, and of 'stemming' or making difficult headway against tide and current. Despite Wright's comment that all this suggests 'the difficulty and labour of Satan's flight', the sense of effort seems not a correspondence but a contrast to Satan who, on the contrary, 'Puts on swift wings', and who 'scours' 'shaves' and 'soares', 'touring high'. Satan's real difficulties begin when, after a long narrative interval, Milton resumes at the end of Satan's journey the simile made near its beginning. The simile here seems to pick up the same merchants on the same voyage, but it is tonally quite different. The spices are not drugs to confuse the mind but are the very remembrance of Eden; the mariners, 'Well pleas'd', are presented in amazingly genial and mellow terms:

> As when to them who saile
> Beyond the *Cape of Hope*, and now are past
> *Mozambic*, off at Sea North-East windes blow
> *Sabean* Odours from the spicie shoare

Of *Arabie* the blest, with such delay
Well pleas'd they slack thir course, and many a League
Cheard with the grateful smell old Ocean smiles.

                                        (IV, 159–65)

The interest of this total 'articulated' simile lies not only in the
immediate situation in the fable, but in its accumulative resonance. When it has run its course we are made aware not only that
merchants and cheating, acquisitive traders are like Satan, and
their ironically heroic voyages like his awe-inspiring flight, but
also that God's creativity and the hint of Eden's fragrance (a hint
which makes them welcome the delay and forget their profit-
motive) can be part of a merchant's experience too. The simile,
like so many others, begins in correspondences which catalogue
Satan's apparent success in the world and ends in foreshadowing
the survival of nature and the ultimate defeat of Satan. For instance, these sea-faring men also appear in Hell during the infernal debate to point the devils' response to Mammon's speech (II,
284–90), and again what begins as an apparent correspondence
between the devils and 'blustring winds' ends with a ship safely
anchored 'in a craggy Bay' and having survived 'the Tempest':

He scarce had finisht, when such murmur filld
Th'Assembly, as when hollow Rocks retain
The sound of blustring winds, which all night long
Had rous'd the Sea, now with hoarse cadence lull
Sea-faring men oerwatcht, whose Bark by chance
Or Pinnace anchors in a craggy Bay
After the Tempest.

This sort of effect is repeated elsewhere. When Satan, in another seascape and the first of his similes, is like Leviathan de-
ceiving the 'Pilot of some small night-foundered Skiff' (I, 200–8),
it reads like a *nusquam tuta fides* emblem from Quarles or Wither,
and its point is clear enough. There is the sense too of the vulnerability of that fragile craft and its human cargo (the storm, so
early in the poem, might anticipate already Eve 'From her best
prop so farr, and storm so nigh'), the frequency of this predica-
ment (there is an almost Chaucerian naivety in 'oft, as Sea-men
tell'), and the tense and ominous lull, engaging our sympathy,
while the 'wishd Morn delayes'. What is also clear in this opening
simile, which seems to embrace at the same time the end of the

poem (surely the whale-island,'With fixed Anchor in his skaly rinde', will submerge?), is the resonant and emphatically defined creatureliness of 'that Sea-beast' 'which God of all his works/ Created hugest that swim th'Ocean stream'. Milton is putting the unfit or Manichean readers, and Satan along with them, into difficulties from the start. When we meet this sea monster again, rollicking in the newly created oceans of the earth, where

> Leviathan
> Hugest of living Creatures, on the Deep
> Stretcht like a Promontorie sleeps or swimmes,
> And seems a moving Land, and at his Gilles
> Draws in, and at his Trunck spouts out a Sea,
> (VII, 412–16)

we may review our propensity to trust false appearances or illusions of security, but we will properly find responsibility for it not in Leviathan but in ourselves. The sequence in which the repeated lines occur in the poem (mirroring the sequence of the 'plot' but reversing, in the simile's prior appearance, the sequence of 'real' time) challenges us to reconsider the easy and deceptive typology of our initial response. The verbal echo here is undeniable but I do not think it is, as Stanley Fish claimed, 'also irrelevant, at least as statement about the structure of the universe'.[19] On the contrary, the point seems to be (and it is a fundamental point in the poem's 'statement about the structure of the universe') that Leviathan, though he is exploited by Satan (and in a strategic sense by the poet too), remains unequivocally part of that 'high Providence' the poet seeks to defend.

Just as the innocent Leviathan of the creation has become an emblem of deceit, so one of the dominant emotions in *Paradise Lost* is the sense of loss and regret. In the first books it is Satan's regret as well as ours: 'Happy Fields' are exchanged for 'Desart soile', and Satan's first 'bold words' to Beelzebub are not bold at all but pathetically unguarded, still dazzled by the memory of 'him, who in the happy Realms of Light' (why *happy*? – they were supposed to be intolerable) 'Cloth'd with transcendent brightness didst outshine / Myriads though bright' (I 85–7). But Satan shakes off this fatal nostalgia and the mining, construction work and technological development of Hell are put in hand, and the devils' conference predicts ominous things for God's creation. Nevertheless, the logic we spoke of earlier renders the whole perspective ambiguous, for the pictures that furnish Milton's analogues are available to the poet and to us: the whale and the sailors on the North Sea, the eruptions of Etna, the moon, the pine-tree mast, the autumnal leaves (I have in front of me as I write some autumnal leaves from Vallombrosa, sent by a colleague on holiday there, each one, as it were, a shrivelled angel form), the chariot wheels, the locusts, the barbarian hordes, the Dead Sea, Greece, Italy, France, The British Isles (I, 519–21), the sunrise of I, 594, the beehive, the pygmies, the dreaming peasant. If the comparison of Satan's host to the Memphian chivalry destroyed in the Red Sea, or to locusts oddly sent to plague their masters, or similes of the 'Serbonian bog' where the unsuccessful rebel Typhon lay overwhelmed, or of Jason and the Argo, or others like them, all suggest ironically bad omens for Satan's enterprise, so, on the other side and in a more oblique fashion, do those recurring landscape pictures drawn from natural, mundane scenery, places and activities.

It is remarkable how predictably, at critical, pivotal moments in his narrative, Milton suspends the 'story' to offer another story by presenting for contemplation a scene which we all know and can recognise, a scene which is not especially 'literary' or learned or complex or allegorical, though it may have associated with it various 'significances'. For instance, those autumnal leaves seasonally fallen in a sheltered brook in the Arno valley, a natural, rural and available scene, makes its point (Homeric though the comparison may also be) a fraction *before* the typological extensions amplify it for us in a more deliberately self-conscious mode. And this scene, modulating into the Red Sea and the deliverance of the Children of Israel, is strategically inserted between 'he stood and calld' (I, 300) and Satan's by that time vacuous 'Princes, Potentates, Warriors' (I, 315). When Satan stands 'like a Towr' (an epithet at once military and ironic, for Christ is also the Tower) to address the throng once more, the first part of the simile that follows –

> As when the Sun new ris'n
> Looks through the Horizontal misty Air
> Shorn of his Beams
>
> (I, 594–6)

– images a dawn full of potential for the new day. The subsequent eclipses and disasters are appropriate to evil power, but the sun, momentarily veiled in mist and 'Shorn of his Beams', debilitating Satan, is also that sun to which Eve offers praise:

> Thou Sun, of this great World both Eye and Soule,
> Acknowledge him thy Greater, sound his praise
> In thy eternal course,
>
> (V, 171–3)

and which

>   to each inward part
> With gentle penetration, though unseen,
> Shoots invisible vertue eev'n to the Deep.
>   (III, 584–6)

Satan's appropriation of the sun for simile is, like everything else about him, *ersatz*, and catches him in a web of poetic complicity. This is not precisely simile at all, since the point is not likeness but unlikeness, or likeness of a certain limited local sort offered in the same breath as a gigantic disparity.

At the gathering of the Council of Pandemonium, 'Bees / In spring time' appear 'among fresh dews and flowers', suddenly superimposing colour, sweetness and fertility upon the industrial landscape of 'rowling smoak', 'glossy scurf', 'Sulfur' and 'boiling cells'. Their appearance is accompanied by a host of allusions and resonances (Carthage and Rome, Samson and the lion, and so on), but the bees and the flowers are reverberately *there* too; as is that un-Virgilian head-scratching human figure, the 'belated Peasant' who half sees these fairies 'by a Forest side'.

As the Council gets under way, Beelzebub's look 'Drew attention still as Night'. Night we would expect as simile: the devils are consigned to the 'seat of desolation, void of light'. But Milton adds the unexpected alternative, 'Or Summers Noon-tide air' (II, 308–9): precisely that which is, from one point of view, inaccessible to these fallen legions (Satan, under the naphtha cressets of Hell, frankly yearns for 'the brightening Orient beam' and 'soft delicious air'), and which, from another, is the earth's summer stillness the devils are about to vote to destroy. It is almost as if Milton is asking us to take our pick of similes from opposite poles – Night and Noon, dark and light – and as if the ultimate result will be the same. Characteristically, Dr Bentley misses the point, though it bristles at him under his censorious pen. Instead of worrying about the *relevance* of 'Summers Noon-tide air', he indulges a nice pedantry which unwittingly explains the simile's potential with brilliant imperception:

> I suppose that the Poet gave it,
>   *Still as Night*
> Or Summer's noon-tide HOUR.

The *noon-tide Hour*, as IV. 581. *Meridian Hour*. For it was not the *Air*, that made the Silence and Stillness, but the *Hour*: when in hot Countries, the Sun shining fierce, both Men and Animals retire to Shade and Rest.

Satan actually visits the sun, his poetic *Doppelganger*, in Book III, and gazes round him at its splendour, 'all sun-shine', 'as when his Beams at Noon / Culminate from th'*Aequator*' (III, 616–17). As in the earlier simile, so here and on several other occasions in the poem, the hands of Milton's clock point to noon as the time of divine judgement.[20] That devilish attention still as 'Summers Noon-tide' can be reinforced symbolically to deflate Satan – 'As the Sun, when in the centre of his orbit, that is to say, at the midday point is hottest, so shall Christ be when He shall appear in the centre of Heaven and earth, that is to say, in Judgment'[21] – but its simple glance at a pastoral stillness holds its own more tacit reply to Satan's machinations.

At the end of the conference the fallen legions worship Satan 'as a God' and 'thir doubtful consultations dark' conclude in rejoicing. What Milton uses as an amplifying, explanatory simile for their sudden clarity of purpose is a spectacularly luminous landscape:

> As when from mountain tops the dusky clouds
> Ascending, while the North wind sleeps, orespread
> Heav'ns chearful face, the lowring Element
> Scowls ore the dark'nd lantskip Snow, or showre;
> It chance the radiant Sun with farewell sweet
> Extend his ev'ning beam, the fields revive,
> The birds thir notes renew, and bleating herds
> Attest thir joy, that hill and valley rings.
>   (II, 488–95)

This beautiful moment derives not from the Pandemonium that surrounds the devils and in which environment Satan may seem 'as a God', but from the creation the authentic God has furnished despite Satan. Occupying the centre ground of the painting are the reviving fields and the flash of sudden sunlight. And we hear voices, after storm, of birds and sheep that 'Attest thir joy'. (The best Bentley could do with this was to grumble that it ought to be FLOCKS: '*Herds* is a Word proper to Cattle, that do not *bleat*'. There is perhaps a nice irony in the possibility of such dispute, granted the narrative moment in hand.) That all this is a simile apparently amplifying the revival of the fallen angels is both sinister, in that it exposes the vulnerability of this pastoral world to the concerted efforts of the infernal powers now on the move, and at the same time curiously defeating of Satanic ambitions. The simile over, Milton then comments on this accord of 'Devil with Devil damnd' and turns to address the reader in a straightforward piece of moralizing which places responsibility for the destruction of pastoral landscapes squarely on the shoulders of fallen man (II, 496–505).

As if intent on producing a simile of truly surpassing incongruity and irrelevance, Milton offers at the end of Book IV, at the critical moment of Satan's encounter with Gabriel and his patrol, a 'correspondence' which, together with the situation it undertakes to illumine, has repeatedly given readers a difficult time:

> While thus he spake, th'Angelic Squadron bright
> Turnd fierie red, sharpning in mooned hornes
> Thir Phalanx, and began to hemm him round
> With ported Spears, as thick as when a field
> Of *Ceres* ripe for harvest waving bends
> Her bearded Grove of ears, which way the wind
> Swayes them; the careful Plowman doubting stands
> Least on the threshing floore his hopeful sheaves
> Prove chaff.
>
> (IV, 977–85)

What is that Plowman doing there? Bentley crosses him out ('where's the least Similitude?'). Christopher Ricks calls the simile 'beautiful but digressive'; Empson roundly objects that scenery is unimportant when man's Fall is at stake; Stanley Fish says, mysteriously, that its point is its 'indeterminateness'; for John Peter it is 'inappropriately debilitating' of the angels.[22] Without adding further hypotheses (Alastair Fowler's full and excellent notes do much to unmask Milton's 'intentions' here), one can stress again that the central image which remains in control of the encounter is of a wheatfield and a Plowman, standing on the surface of 'this pendulous round Earth with ballanc't Aire / In counterpoise' (IV, 1000–1). The great issue of the poem may be seen at this point as not so much Satan's judgement or the fate of angels, but rather the issue of whether man and the earth can stand, 'though free to fall', and whether, having fallen, they can stand again. Along with escatological images of threshing and of divine judgement, there is the purely human doubt of the Plowman about this year's harvest: the human observer who is Adam, Abel, Galileo, the Peasant, the Plowman, the reader, both doubtful and hopeful, and who eventually, though fallen, stands to contemplate (in the words of *Areopagitica*) 'the field of this world' in which 'good and evil . . . grow up together almost inseparably'. The iconography of these repeated landscapes-with-figures is endorsed by Michael in the penultimate book, when he plainly says to a superstitous Adam:

> Surmise not then
> His presence to these narrow bounds confin'd
> Of Paradise or Eden . . .
> Yet doubt not but in Vallie and in Plaine
> God is as here, and will be found alike
> Present.
>
> (XI 340–51)

Milton reserves one of his richest and most glowing similes for the critical confrontation between Satan and mankind. (It is also one that left Bentley, for once, speechless.) Eve is 'half spied', 'Veild in a Cloud of Fragrance', and as Satan hones his wit to accost her, the scene dissolves into a rural landscape with figures: a tourist-townsman out for the day in the countryside, and a country girl. Satan is

> As one who long in populous City pent,
> Where Houses thick and Sewers annoy the Aire,
> Forth issuing on a Summers Morn to breathe
> Among the pleasant Villages and Farmes
> Adjoind, from each thing met conceaves delight,
> The smell of Grain, or tedded Grass, or Kine,
> Or Dairie, each rural sight, each rural sound;
> If chance with Nymphlike step fair Virgin pass,

What pleasing seemd, for her now pleases more,
Shee most, and in her look summs all Delight.
                                        (IX, 445–54)

By this stage (Book IX) of the poem we may have grown ac-
customed to Milton's dismissive or negating or ironically inappropriate use of simile, and be ready to conclude that this must be
another such use. Christopher Ricks, contrasting the motives of
the townsman out to enjoy the countryside with those of Satan,
suggests that this instance reminds us that 'we cannot do without
a sense of disparity as well as of similarity in Milton's similes'.[23]
James Whaler had also cited this simile as an example of the way
in which 'by ignoring motive in the comparison of two situations
or actions the poet can emphasise a contrasting picture of peace
by setting it in the midst of terror or peril', and stressed the
difference between the city-dweller and the Arch-fiend.[24] Yet in
this case it seems more likely that Milton *is* concerned with
correspondences, not unlikenessess. The axes of the simile are
pastoral ones: Hell is like a city, and both Satan and townsman
issue from the sewers of cities, while Eden, veiling Eve in fragrance, is like the country nurturing the fair virgin in 'The smell
of Grain, or tedded Grass' ('So thick the Roses' surrounding Eve
possibly anticipating 'Where Houses thick' surround the townsman in his native milieu). By the end of the simile Satan appears
to be dissociated from the townsman seeking, apparently, healthy
pleasure – 'But the hot Hell that alwayes in him burnes . . . soon
ended his delight' – and we may wish to emphasise a man who,
unlike Satan, has come for love, not hate. But things are not
always what they seem, and it is difficult to ignore a sense of
impending exploitation. Within the simile (as outside it) the stage
seems set for a seduction scene; 'each rural sight, each rural
sound' is forgotten, 'for her now pleases more, / Shee most, and in
her look summs all Delight'. The *loucherie* of the townsman is
only a step away from Alec D'Urberville seducing Tess in a
country lane.

Milton's radical refurbishment of the conventional epic simile
involves not glorification and celebration of the epic hero or epic
gestures, but their placement and deflation. In this instance the
epic hero is in alien and yet easy territory, a pastoral garden; and
for a moment he is no more than an urban tourist, apparently as
innocent as we should like to think ourselves to be in such a

situation. Indeed, he is something of a connoisseur of pastoral. But what Milton invites us to contemplate is not only the occasioners of the simile but also the substance and resonance of the simile itself. So often Milton inverts simple narrative functions: the simile is not to amplify but to diminish its nominal subject, and in so doing to amplify itself. What survives this particular simile is neither the townsman nor Satan. But neither is it Eve, nor the country girl. What survives is the 'Summers Morn' itself, the created world, the landscape in which our moral choices act out their own drama.

NOTES

1. See William Empson, 'Milton and Bentley: The Pastoral of the Innocence of Man and Nature', in *Some Versions of Pastoral*, London: Chatto & Windus, 1935. Bentley's edition is reprinted in facsimile, New York: AMS Press, 1974.
2. Quotations from *Paradise Lost* are from Helen Darbishire's old spelling text, *The Poetical Works of John Milton*, London: Oxford University Press, 1958.
3. An instance of the sort of reading I have in mind may be illustrated in Elizabeth Ely Fuller's *Milton's Kinesthetic Vision in Paradise Lost*, Lewisburg: Bucknell University Press, 1983, a study bristling with reader-responsive antennae. Interestingly, Professor Fuller dissociates herself from Stanley Fish's pioneering *Surprised by Sin: The Reader in Paradise Lost* (London: Macmillan, 1969), largely because Fish disguises, or buttresses and protects, his reader-response interpretation with historically plausible reference to Puritan literature and to authorial design.
4. Hester Piozzi (Mrs Thrale), *Anecdotes of the late Samuel Johnson*, ed. S. C. Roberts, Cambridge: Cambridge University Press, 1925, p. 66.
5. See Roland Mushat Frye, *Milton's Imagery and the Visual Arts: Iconographical Tradition in the Epic Poems*, Princeton, New Jersey: Princeton University Press, 1978, pp. 226–7.
6. This point is well made in G. K. Hunter's *Paradise Lost*, London: Allen and Unwin, 1980, p. 108, where he takes F. R. Leavis to task for failing to see the *point* of what Leavis called the 'laboured, pedantic artifice of the diction' (Leavis, *Revaluation*, London: Chatto & Windus, 1936, p. 49.)
7. J. B. Broadbent, *Some Graver Subject: An Essay on Paradise Lost*, London: Chatto & Windus, 1960, p. 184.
8. *Paradise Lost*, ed. Alastair Fowler, London: Longman, 1971, p. 208n.
9. See R. M. Frye, *Milton's Imagery and the Visual Arts*, pp. 221–7.
10. *Brief History of Moscovia*, published 1682 but 'writ by the Author's own hand before he lost his sight'.

11. For example Blake's famous remark: 'Milton wrote in fetters when he wrote of Angels and God and at liberty when of Devils and Hell . . . because he was a true poet and of the devil's party without knowing it', *Marriage of Heaven and Hell*, 1790, plates 5–6; William Empson, *Milton's God*, rev. edn, London: Chatto & Windus, 1965, *passim*.
12. *The Complete Prose Works of John Milton*, ed. D. Bush *et al.*, New Haven: Yale University Press, 1953–, I, 571.
13. J. B. Broadbent, *Some Graver Subject*, p. 72.
14. Rabindranath Tagore, *Sadhana*, London: Macmillan, 1913.
15. Dennis Burden, *The Logical Epic: A Study of the Argument of Paradise Lost*, London: Routledge, 1967, pp. 58–64.
16. Edwin Muir, *One Foot in Eden*, London: Faber, 1956. The title poem concludes:

> What had Eden ever to say
> Of hope and faith and pity and love
> Until was buried all its day
> And memory found its treasure trove?
> Strange blessings never in Paradise
> Fall from these beclouded skies.

17. Anne Davidson Ferry, *Milton's Epic Voice*, Cambridge, Mass.: Harvard University Press, 1963, p. 37.
18. B. A. Wright, *Milton's Paradise Lost*, London: Methuen, 1962, p. 111.
19. Stanley E. Fish, *Surprised by Sin*, p. 151.
20. See Alastair Fowler, *Paradise Lost*, p. 182, 482.
21. Pierre Bersuire, *Dictionarium seu repertorium morale*, Nuremberg, 1489, iii. 194r; cited in E. Panofsky, *Meaning in the Visual Arts*, New York: Doubleday, 1955, p. 262.
22. See Christopher Ricks, *Milton's Grand Style*, Oxford: Oxford University Press, 1963, p. 130; William Empson, *Milton's God*, pp. 112–13; Stanley Fish, *Surprised by Sin*, p. 174; John Peter, *A Critique of Paradise Lost*, London: Longman, 1960, pp. 24–5.
23. Ricks, *Milton's Grand Style*, p. 131.
24. James Whaler, 'The Miltonic Simile', *PMLA*, 46 (1931), pp. 1034–74.

7

CONVENTIONS OF GENRE
Playing the field in *Paradise Lost*

Is some blaspheming soldier to own these acres
I have broken up and tilled so well – a foreigner
to reap these splendid fields of corn?
Virgil, Eclogue I, 'The Dispossessed'

It has sometimes been remarked how the progress of *Paradise
Lost* may be seen as a *generic* conflict between pastoral and epic
modes, the values and associative symbols of each constantly
weaving in a pattern of opposition through the narrative. The
'epic' gesture (the assertive prowess, the inflated chest, the flash-
ing eye, commonly fuelled, in this poem, by a wounded pride and
sense of pique) is embodied, as it were, in Satan, repeated in
Adam and Eve, and finally corrupts the pastoral garden world of
Eden. We can say with equal sense that *Paradise Lost* is an epic
poem and also a pastoral poem. But Milton is not offering a novel
hybridized genre of pastoral-epic or epic-pastoral; on the contrary,
he is confronting each with the other so that both become transformed by the contact.

There was in fact ancient precedent for introducing quasi-
pastoral elements into epic – a precedent out of which Milton
constructs a crucial axis of meaning in his poem more resonant,
because its implications are even more critical, than, for instance,
the recurrent tension in Virgil's *Aeneid* between city and country.
For example, Homer lovingly presents the natural life of the
farmer in the description of Eumaeus, Odysseus's faithful pigman
(especially the opening of *Odyssey*, Book XIV). Homer's epic also
offers the idealised demi-paradise of Phaeacia, whose inhabitants
are freed from the usual cares and constraints, whose time is
spent in feasting, playing games, dancing and listening to poetry,
and where the timeless pastoral wonderland is touched by magic,
like self-steering ships and the never-failing gardens of their king
Alcinous (*Odyssey*, Book VII). But Phaeacia passes Odysseus on to
the 'real' world of Ithaca and, like Milton's Eden which sends

Adam and Eve out into human history, itself becomes, for ordinary mortals, a paradise lost.[1] The pastoral glimpses given in
Virgil's *Aeneid* include Aeneas's visit to Evander and his Arcadians
at Pallanteum, the simple rural community that inhabits the site
of future Rome (*Aeneid*, Book VIII). The epic world of warriors
from one city destined to found another is contrasted with the
virtuous poverty of the rustic world into which they come and
which they virtually destroy. Cattle low in what will be the forum,
and browse in what was to be the fashionable Roman district of
the Carinae: Charles Martindale even suggests that the adjective
Virgil uses, *lautus* (1.361), meaning chic or smart, is a word which
'jarringly raises the question of his emotional allegiance'. The
adjective is not, however, necessarily pejorative: it means literally
'well washed', that is, kempt and tidy, and could be registered as
another instance of Virgil's simultaneous admiration for the simple rural life *and* the glories and golden towers of the great city.
Emotional allegiance is further complicated though, for the
author of the *Eclogues* and the *Georgics*, by the moment when
Aeneas sees the ruined heaps of yet older cities built by Saturn
and Janus.[2] If Virgil does not make it entirely clear that he prefers
cows to the Carinae, or vice versa, there seems to be very little
ambiguity in Milton's treatment of the idea of the military
metropolis.

In Milton's exercise of generic transformation, in which the
heroic is shown to be unheroic and the apparently merely weak or
pretty is shown to be strong and essential, the polarities are partly
those of city and country, of Pandemonium and Eden, Carthage
and bees in spring time, townsman and country girl; but there is
also an apparent, and perhaps not surprising, energy with which
Milton lights on the ambiguous word *field* and liberally punctu-
ates his narrative with this poetically fruitful *coincidentia op-
positorum* of a word. A pattern begins perhaps with Satan's
interesting question: 'What though the field be lost?' (I, 105).
The jaunty phrasing is characteristic of Satan, the military
metonymy both apt and routine. (Alastair Fowler suggests that
Milton is perhaps amplifying the speech of Satan in Fairfax's
translation of Tasso's *Gerusalemme liberata*, IV, 15: 'We lost the
field, yet lost we not our heart'.)[3] Yet something more subtle is
disclosed by the immediately preceding line, 'In dubious Battel
on the Plains of Heav'n', and reinforced a little later in Satan's
regretful 'Farewell happy Fields / Where Joy for ever dwells' (I,

249–250). What makes Satan's 'What though the field be lost?' interesting is that he recognises that he has forfeited both the military field and the celestial-pastoral 'happy Fields'. In his question he *means*, of course, the battlefield, but Milton registers, and has Satan acknowledge, precisely what other kind of field has been lost too.

Christopher Ricks once wrote that the *lie/lie* homonym is 'simply the most important pun in the language'.[4] Milton's *field* may be another candidate, not perhaps for top 'importance', but for its equally curious potency and its suggestive verbal miscegenation. The *OED* maps out the territories occupied by the word: the field as cultivated enclosure, as the surface upon which harvests come to fruition, 'The feld' as 'fundament of the flouris'[5]; and the field as battlefield, the 'tented field' of *Othello* (I.iii.85) where, as in Dryden's translation of the *Georgics*, 'They . . . strew'd his mangled Limbs about the Field'.[6] The word, in either of its primary significations, attracts associated nouns: Field Marshal and field-gun, field-naturalist and field-notes, representative of diametrically opposite human ambitions and activities. Its derived figurative phrases point consistently to some kind of competitive arena: to keep the field (continue the fight); conquer the field (gain one's point); to hold the field (not to be superseded or displaced); to leave the field (to give up the contest or argument); to play the field (to secure one's own advantage on the best possible terms); and so on.

A third area of the word's circumference appears in the paradoxical combinations of the two primary arcs: field-sports are catered for in *The Field*, and cricketers and baseball players go out to field, as if in these cultural images the opposing battlefield (epic) and the harvest field (pastoral) are reduced and accommodated in the hunting of deer, fox, or hare across cultivated rural landscapes, and gladiatorial contests are softened and joined with the green outfield, the immemorial elms, the shaded bower of the beer marquee. And of course the cultivated field itself is also a battlefield, as any farmer will tell us or as Ted Hughes's 'Thistles' ('Every one manages a plume of blood') so vividly depicts: 'Their sons appear / Stiff with weapons, fighting back over the same ground'. This curse of the labourer follows upon the Fall: in Milton's original garden-field its substance and its imagery cannot apply, either logically or chronologically, but are functions of the infection of pastoral by epic.

It would be surprising if Milton was the first to spot, and exploit, the rich potency of this homonym. Is it possible to see Chaucer's images of the field, in the skirmish of Theseus against Creon that precipitates *The Knight's Tale*, as *significant* multiple repetitions? Theseus, in threatening intimidation, sports his 'white baner large', 'That all the feeldes glyteren up and down' (976–7),[7] until they come to Thebes 'and alighte / Faire in a feeld, ther as he thoughte to fighte' (983–4). After the slaughter is over 'Stille in that feeld he took al nyght his reste' and, ominously, 'dide with al the contree as hym leste' (1003–4). Emily appears in a garden, gathering flowers (1051); Arcite, remembering his 'observaunce to May', goes to gather flowers and 'Is riden into the feeldes hym to pleye' (1503): a field of play that is rapidly transformed into a battlefield as Palamon and Arcite 'Up to the ancle foughte they in hir blood'.

The word can also be used transitively as a verb 'to fight with', and intransitively 'to fight' or 'to take to the field' (*OED*). Thus Spenser, in Book II of *The Faerie Queene*, has the passionately wrathful Cymochles assault Sir Guyon,

> Who soone prepard to field, his sword forth drew
> And him with equall value countervayld.
>
> (II.vi.29)

The curious thing is that Spenser's archaism, *to field*, is specifically set in a landscape of fields: Cymochles's encounter with Phaedria lures him, like Odysseus's encounter with the Lotus-eaters in *Odyssey*, IX, into ease and sloth. Phaedria deliberately ignores the sentence of toil on Adam after the Fall and instead she misapplies Matthew 6:28 ('Learne, how the lilies of the field do growe: they labour not, nether spinne'); she shows Cymochles 'The flowres, the fields, and all that pleasant growes' and 'laid him downe upon a grassie plaine' (II.vi.14, 15):

> The lilly, Ladie of the flowring field,
> The Flowre-deluce, her lovely Paramoure,
> Bid thee to them thy fruitlesse labours yield
>
> (II.vi.16)

But, despite this 'seduction', Phaedria is not all bad: she is in part too a good Venus Pandemos or Venus Genetrix, for

> all though pleasant, yet she made much more:

The fields did laugh, the flowres did freshly spring,
The trees did bud.

(II.vi.24)[8]

The 'battel fierce' is waged by Cymochles and Guyon in these allegorical fields, and their destructive anger is only overcome by Phaedria's appeal to the reconciling story of Mars and Venus.

Possibly even more subtle are Marvell's delicately laconic paradoxes of the Mower poems, or his sharp releases of the pun's potency in *Upon Appleton House*, the garden of the general (Field Marshal?) Fairfax, where

> Flow'rs their drowsie Eylids raise,
> Their Silken Ensigns each displayes,
> And dries its Pan yet dank with Dew,
> And fills its Flask with Odours new.
>
> (XXXVII)

As the *Governour* goes by the flowers let fly their 'fragrant Vollyes' in salute. But what has gone wrong?

> Unhappy! shall we never more
> That sweet *Militia* restore,
> When Garlands only had their Towrs,
> And all the Garrisons were Flowrs,
> When Roses only Arms might bear,
> And Men did rosie Garlands wear?
>
> (XLII)

But the original garden is now irrecoverable:

> What luckless Apple did we tast,
> To make us Mortal, and the Wast?
>
> (XLI)

so that even the scything of the hay can become a vivid visual metaphor for the field's transformation:

> The Mower now commands the Field;
> In whose new Traverse seemeth wrought
> A Camp of Battail newly fought:
> Where, as the Meads with Hay, the Plain
> Lyes quilted ore with Bodies slain.
>
> (LIII)[9]

In *Paradise Lost*, the plains of heaven are exchanged for the landscapes of Hell, 'yon dreary Plain, forlorn and wilde' (I, 180), and the distinction, so important to the poem, between reigning and serving, egoism and obedience, is made partly in the context of different conceptions of the function of a *field*. Satan's speech at I, 242,

> Is this the Region, this the Soil, the Clime . . .
> That we must change for Heav'n,

acknowledges the loss of joy yet goes on to insist on the possibilities of the new field, the battlefield created by the rebellion and which can hopefully be reconstructed and repeated elsewhere: 'Here at least / We shall be free . . .', 'Here we may reign secure'. In the authentic field whose paradigm is heaven, the moral life is one of service and obedience; in the military heroic field the values are to be those of power and dominance. The activities of Satan's twelve disciples are clear enough: they destroy pastoral and productive landscapes. The 'watry Plain' of Rabba, the 'pleasant Vally of *Hinnom*', the 'flowry Dale of *Sibma* clad with Vines', the 'fertil Banks / Of *Abbana* and *Pharphar*' are all lost, and the 'Summers day' corrupted. The defeated rebels flourish the new tools of cultivation and perform impressive ceremonies of power to ease 'Thir painful steps ore the burnt soile':

> All in a moment through the gloom were seen
> Ten thousand Banners rise into the Air
> With Orient Colours waving: with them rose
> A Forrest huge of Spears.
>
> (I, 544–7)

What is remarkable here is the subtle way that Milton involves them with landscapes beyond Hell: the forest of spears (at the close of the book we are to join that very human peasant 'by a Forrest side' watching the demonic antics), and the 'Orient' banners waving like Traherne's 'orient and immortal wheat'. When the legions set about organizing their environment and constructing Pandemonium, Milton's imagery is of anatomical dissection of 'thir mother Earth' – 'Soon had his crew/ Op'nd into the Hill a spacious wound' (I, 688–9) – and also of military and mining activity. The same sort of excavations had been made into the field of heaven, 'the Celestial soile' of VI, 510, to provide ammunition for the rebellion. But here their search for metallic ore attracts a simile derived from our own present human activities, the trenching of a field for war:

> As when bands
> Of Pioneers with Spade and Pickaxe armd
> Forerun the Royal Camp, to trench a Field,
> Or cast a Rampart.
>
> (I, 675–8)

Its language of siege and battery is that of Shakespeare's

> When forty winters shall besiege thy brow
> And dig deep trenches in thy beauty's field,
>
> (Sonnet 2)

and adds to the growing number of references to the two significances of a *field* – another of which is inserted parenthetically into the account of the devils thronging the 'spacious Hall' for conference:

> (Though like a coverd field, where Champions bold
> Wont ride in armd, and at the Soldans chair
> Defi'd the best of *Panim* chivalry
> To mortal combat or career with Lance).
>
> (I, 763–6)

Heroic encounters, even in chivalric defence of the faith, provide in Milton's poem an inevitable simile for Hell and its inhabitants. The arena is again the field, but the 'op'n field' of Eden (IV, 245) transformed by the epic mode into the *champ clos* of judicial combat. And yet the authentic, uncovered and undefiant field of pastoral values artfully reasserts itself in the subsequent complex and satanically diminishing simile of springtime, bees, flowers, elves and the dreaming peasant which prefaces the devils' 'great consult'.

It is also at this moment that Milton, not for the first time in his poetic career, offers a subdued but disturbing commentary on his own artistic fictions. Just as the animated, sympathetic pastoral flowers, so carefully gathered in 'Lycidas', are ironically dismissed or revalued by

> For so to interpose a little ease,
> Let our frail thoughts dally with false surmise,

so here Milton reminds us that his usefully anti-satanic, pastoral analogies may be no more than poetic devices. For the book ends with the sense that what was *really* going on is imaginatively inaccessible to us:

> But farr within
> And in their own dimensions like themselves
> The great Seraphic Lords and Cherubim
> In close recess and secret conclave sat.
>
> (I, 792–95)

'But farr within' suggests not only deep inside that infernal hall but also far beyond our organizing mythologies; the offer of a simile ('in their own dimensions like . . .') is simultaneously withdrawn to register instead the impossibility of simile ('like themselves'); and while allowing the irony of their recessed and secret hiding from God, Milton also acknowledges their untouchability by human figuration and human art.

During the conference, Mammon finds what comfort he can in this 'Desart soile', and his plea for peace provokes a gale of applause: 'for such another Field / They dreaded worse then Hell' (II, 292–3). When the debate concludes the devils' new sense of purpose is likened, with complex irony, to reviving fields where 'bleating herds / Attest thir joy' (II, 493–5): the simile is suddenly luminous with a fertile earthly reflection (if momentary) of those 'happy Fields / Where Joy for ever dwells' which Satan and his crew have just in fact lost. Instead, the devils make do with *'Pythian* fields' across which to race each other, or 'rend up both Rocks and Hills' for the sheer hell of it, while others, more assiduously miming the lost pastoral pursuits, retreat to a quiet valley to sing, of course, 'Thir own Heroic deeds' or to 'a Hill retir'd' wander in mazes of dialectic imitative of the angelic 'mazes intricate' and the irrecoverable 'song and dance about the sacred Hill' (V, 618–27). And to remind Satan again of his question, 'what though the field be lost?', Sin, temporarily barring Satan's way on the journey to infect Eden, rehearses the recent rebellion in which 'Warr arose / And fields were fought in Heav'n' (II, 767–8).

While Satan continues his flight towards Eden, Milton prefaces our entrance to the *'Elisian* Flours' and 'Celestial Roses' of Heaven with an invocation to light that is full of earthly allusions and emblems. At the conclusion of the parallel 'debate' in Heaven, the focus shifts again to Satan, alighting 'upon the firm

opacous Globe / Of this round World' (III, 418–19): 'Here walkd
the Fiend at large in spacious field'. To make sure we recognize
what kind of field Satan thinks it is, Milton repeats himself:'the
Fiend / Walkd up and down alone bent on his prey' (III, 430,
441). Pausing at the stairs which lead up to the portal of Heaven,
and finding himself compared with Jacob dreaming in a field

> when he from *Esau* fled
> To *Padan-Aram* in the field of *Luz*,
> Dreaming by night under the op'n Skie,
> And waking cri'd, This is the Gate of Heav'n,
> (III, 512–15)

Satan gazes down on 'all this World at once' and is further compared, in an apt but subdued simile encompassing notions of
military conquest, with a scout.

The comparison of Satan with Jacob is full of Milton's characteristic allusive shorthand. Alastair Fowler has noted the relevance of the simile to Jacob's situation, for like Satan Jacob has fled
from retribution after cheating Esau out of his father's blessing
(as Satan is bent on cheating mankind), and Jacob could still (and,
as the story unfolds, does) repent – unlike Satan. His vision upwards has too its counterpart in Satan's contemplative survey of
the earth. But where Satan sees in prospect the gates of Hell,
Jacob sees the gate of Heaven, implying that the entrance to
Heaven is through repentance and meditation on, not corruption
of, created nature: Jacob's ladder was usually identified with
Homer's golden chain which Zeus let down to the earth, the *scala
naturae* of generative sequence. Jacob's journey to Padan-aram is
also undertaken at Isaac's order: Jacob must take a wife from the
daughters of Laban so that God may 'make thee fruitful, and
multiply thee' (Genesis 28); and after his dream (in which it is
promised that 'in thee shall all the families of the earth be
blessed') he continues his journey to arrive at last where 'he
looked, and behold a well in a field', from which moment Jacob
embarks on his astonishingly energetic and fertile career as a
begetter of children. Milton's phrase 'the field of *Luz*' is perhaps
unexpected; in the biblical story Jacob merely 'lighted upon a
certain place', and it is associated with a city rather than a field:
Jacob renames the place Bethel, 'but the name of that city was
called Luz at the first'. But Milton has, significantly, 'the field of
Luz'. Repentance, fertility and generation are again opposed to

heroism, aggression and destruction, and Milton locates the opposition once more in a field.

In Satan's journey, the life of other worlds 'Amongst innumerable Starrs', those 'happy Iles' and 'Fortunat Fields', do not, for the moment, attract his attention. But when, inquisitive, he lands on the sun (to which he is so often and so ironically compared in the poem), the narrator steps in to interpret Satan's view of that world 'beyond expression bright', and introduces an ambiguous tone which turns on the word *here*, meaning either 'here in the sun' or 'here on earth':

> What wonder then if fields and regions here
> Breathe forth *Elixir* pure, and Rivers run
> Potable Gold, when with one vertuous touch
> Th'Arch-chimic Sun so farr from us remote
> Produces with Terrestrial Humor mixt
> Here in the dark so many precious things
> Of colour glorious and effect so rare?
>
> (III, 606–12)

The moral of the Arch-fiend's encounter with the Arch-chimic Sun is clearly made to Satan's disadvantage, and offers future hope to those 'fields and regions here' which are about to suffer, and endure 'here in the dark', epic infection.

The rural nature and the rural values of Eden are of course obvious. It is, at its creation, expressly incomparable with 'That faire field / Of *Enna*'

> where *Proserpin* gathring flours
> Her self a fairer Floure by gloomie *Dis*
> Was gatherd
>
> (IV, 268–71)

– though it is soon to become so, and the fruitfulness of the pastoral fields rendered, at least partially, barren. At the centre of Milton's perspective on Eden lies symbolically as well as topographically the as yet 'op'n field', a landscape which

> not nice Art
> In Beds and curious Knots, but Nature boon
> Powred forth profuse on Hill and Dale and Plaine,
> Both where the morning Sun first warmly smote

The op'n field, and where the unpierc't shade
Imbround the noontide Bowrs.

(IV, 241–6)

The whole of Eden breathes the authentic 'smell of field and grove'. At the close of Book IV, at Satan's confrontation with Gabriel and his patrol, the image which Milton allows to work in his reader's mind is of 'a field / Of *Ceres* ripe for harvest' (IV, 980–1), used as an 'occasional' simile for the ported spears of the angelic guards and suggesting the eschatology of judgment and threshing, both of Satan and of the harvest eventually to be reaped from this 'pendulous round Earth'. The encounter has its narrative significance – the battle has already been fought in Heaven and is not to be repeated here – but equally it gives Milton a further opportunity to underline a fundamental opposition of imagery: the pastoral simile of the rural, productive *field*, represented by the good angels and finding reflection in the earth, opposed by the epic gesture (Satan's intimidating dilation, his spear and shield) of the battlefield.

Morning breaks in Eden. The first *aubade* is sung: 'Awake, the morning shines, and the fresh field / Calls us' (V, 20–1). Though Eve's dream has taken her 'up to the Clouds' and the 'fresh field' has momentarily been seen, as Satan the scout first saw Eden, as an 'Earth outstretcht immense, a prospect wide' (V, 88), ripe for exploitation, her weeping is stilled by Adam and her tears are kissed away: 'So all was cleard, and to the Field they haste' (V, 136). Already the fresh field of Eden has, both to us through our foreknowledge and to Adam and Eve, taken on the character of a moral battlefield. When Raphael descends to converse with Adam, he comes into 'the blissful field' amid the odours and perfumes that were characteristic of imaginative descriptions of the Elysian fields, home of the blessed, and which Milton uses as a model for Paradise. Eve gathers the fruits of the field:

and from each tender stalk
Whatever Earth all-bearing Mother yields . . .
She gathers, Tribute large,

(V, 338–9, 343)

an activity implicitly contrasted with the 'impious hands' which 'Rifl'd the bowels of thir mother Earth' in Book I.

Milton turns our attention away from Eden for an interlude to view, through Raphael's narrative, the recent exploits of the rebels upon the 'plaines of Heav'n'. That landscape itself, though perhaps metaphorically, is attacked and dismembered and the 'blissful field' which gives meaning to Paradise becomes, as night falls on the battleground of Heaven, 'the fought'n field' (VI, 410). Yet, as the narrative moves into the account of the Creation, the ability of the blissful fields to reassert themselves is never in doubt. The fallen legions take their corruption with them, while the new earth 'Brought forth the tender Grass, whose verdure clad / Her Universal Face with pleasant green' (VII, 315–16). In this creation each

> Plant of the field, which ere it was in the Earth
> God made, and every Herb, before it grew
> On the green stemm; God saw that it was good.
> (VII, 334–8)

The only innocent mime of vegetable heroism might lie in 'the cornie Reed / Embatteld in her field', echoing Virgil's precisely observed *tumulus, quo cornea summo / virgulta et densis hastilibus horrida myrtus (Aeneid*, III, 22), and already given a significance by the memory of the ported spears of Gabriel's angels, like corn blown in the wind in defence against the truly epic menace.

The rich field of the new Eden is celebrated throughout the seventh book, from the 'cattel in the Fields and Meddowes green' (VII, 460) to the divine gesture which 'sow'd with Starrs the Heav'n thick as a field' (VII, 358). But the generic list of 'beast of the field' becomes, as the catalogue of animal life closes before the creation of man, ominously specific. Raphael, coincidentally as it were, mentions the serpent last of all: 'suttl'st Beast of all the field' (VII, 495). The epithet is repeated at intervals throughout what follows. 'The Serpent suttl'st Beast of all the Field' appears early in Book IX (86). Eve, stumbling over what she can recall of Raphael's account (and confirming herself in Milton's judgment that 'still they knew, and ought to have still rememberd'), exclaims: 'Thee, Serpent, suttl'st beast of all the field/ I knew, but . . .' (IX, 560–1). To this the serpent replies, tossing the word *field* back at her and investing it with his own special meaning:

> I was at first as other Beasts that graze
> The trodd'n Herb . . .

> Till on a day roaving the field, I chanc'd
> A goodly Tree farr distant to behold.
>
> (IX, 571–6)

Satan had looked for Eve in her rural surroundings – 'In Bowre or Field he sought' (IX, 417) – and on finding her had for a moment been stopped short, trapped in one of Milton's complex similes celebrating 'The smell of Grain, or Tedded Grass, or Kine / Or Dairie' (IX, 450–1): that rural scene upon which the epic ego will seek to 'trench a field'. Playing on Eve's response to a country romp, he lured her on; she 'minded not, as us'd / To such disport before her through the Field / From every Beast'. At the Fall itself, the pastoral field seems lost, and it is the Earth, 'all-bearing Mother', which suffers first: 'Earth trembl'd from her entrails, as again / In pangs' (IX, 1000–1), and the curse of the labourer falls on Adam and Eve:

> And thou shalt eate th'Herb of the Field
> In the sweat of thy face shalt thou eate Bread.
>
> (X, 204–5)

'With delight' Satan 'snuff'd the smell / Of mortal change on Earth', and in a rush of eager, breathless punctuation the victorious simile now takes its triumphant place:

> As when a flock
> Of ravenous Fowl, though many a League remote,
> Against the day of Battel, to a Field,
> Where Armies lie encampt, come flying, lur'd
> With sent of living Carcasses design'd
> For death, the following day, in bloodie fight.
>
> (X, 272–8)

It is ultimately a hollow victory, for the hissing of the serpents, ruled now by 'a greater power', renders the devils' hopeful 'issuing forth to th'op'n Field' (X, 1101) which they appear to have won, only mocking and absurd – though we notice how subtly Milton has transferred the epithet 'op'n' from one kind of field to the other. Adam and Eve begin the journey towards regeneration in a penitential image of restored fertility, 'with tears / Watering the ground' (X, 1101), and in an acceptance of the only terms on which the pastoral world can be restored: 'the Field / To labour calls us now with sweat impos'd' (XI, 171).

But the once paradisal field will always remain ambiguous, with a potential resonance of either toil and harvest, or war and destruction. Adam endures the vision of Cain's slaughter of Abel,

> His eyes he op'nd, and beheld a field
> Part arable and tilth, whereon were sheaves
> New reapt,
>
> (XI, 429–31)

and this lesson showing the transformation of the rural field into the competitive arena of violence and murder is writ large as Michael, in a passage of sombre resonance, shows Adam war itself:

> He lookd and saw wide Territorie spred
> Before him, Towns, and rural works between,
> Cities of Men with lofty Gates and Towrs,
> Concours in Arms, fierce Faces threatning Warr,
> Giants of mightie Bone, and bould emprise;
> Part wield thir Arms, part curb the foaming Steed,
> Single or in Array of Battel rang'd
> Both Horse and Foot, nor idely mustring stood;
> One way a Band select from forage drives
> A herd of Beeves, faire Oxen and faire Kine
> From a fat Meddow ground; or fleecy Flock,
> Ewes and thir bleating Lambs over the Plaine,
> Thir Bootie; scarce with Life the Shepherds flye,
> But call in aide, which tacks a bloody Fray;
> With cruel Tournament the Squadrons joine;
> Where Cattel pastur'd late, now scattered lies
> With Carcasses and Arms th'ensanguind Field
> Deserted.
>
> (XI, 638–55)

Here Milton gathers, in a poetic *tour de force*, those strands of imagery he has been deploying through the poem, and a kind of despair is registered as, pendant upon the finality of the 'ensanguind Field', the adjective 'Deserted' hangs over the huge precipice of the line ending.

The significant issue here is not, as some might think, whether or not Milton was (anachronistically) a pacifist. He clearly knew all about armies, was himself preoccupied during the Commonwealth with furthering the aims of Cromwell's militaristic foreign policy, and approved, or acknowledged the necessity of, just wars fought by the right people in the right cause.[10] His depictions of human warfare in *Paradise Lost* (including the account of the war in heaven) are not offered as practical views, thinly disguised in cosmic imagery, on soldiers and armies and the causes they may serve in his own day, but are reflections of general human wickedness and greed consequent upon the Fall.

But there is political mythography here too. In the future of mankind and the chosen people, related in the last books of the poem, there is a universal paradigm figured in different forms throughout history. The temperate use of nature and proper respect for the field of the earth leads to a people's prosperity. Adam watches Cain and Abel in pastoral sacrifice, and sees the moment destroyed by jealous murder. After the Flood there is a time of pastoral prosperity under 'paternal rule' in which men

> fearing the Deitie,
> With some regard to what is just and right
> Shall lead thir lives, and multiplie apace,
> Labouring the soile, and reaping plenteous crop,
> (XII, 15–18)

until destroyed by the 'proud ambitious heart' of Nimrod the Hunter '(and Men not Beasts shall be his game)'. After the captivity in Babylon there is another spell of prosperity under kings, the result of godly and 'moderate' living (XII, 350–2). Michael offers these brief, admonitory moments in history, fleeting though they are, as bearing hope and as crucially dependent on the right viewing of the field of this world.

As the poem closes, the 'spacious Plaine' of Eden has become the 'subjected Plaine' (XII, 640) of our mundane world. Yet, as Milton's phrase 'subjected Plaine' carries with it implications not only of subjection and defeat but also of submission and obedience on the part of Adam and Eve (no epically aggressive 'what though the field be lost?') so too the final emblem which crowns the recurring pastoral / epic confrontations is of Mary, one of whose figures in traditional Christian iconography is that of a field, seedbed or garden. Told of the virgin mother and of those pastoral figures, 'simple Shepherds, keeping watch by night' to await the paschal Lamb, Adam responds:

> Now clear I understand
> What oft my steddiest thoughts have searcht in vain,

Why our great expectation should be calld
The seed of Woman: Virgin Mother, Haile.
(XII, 376–9)

Flora, Juno, Ceres, the Eve of the Garden, have been lost or
mutilated; but we have gained Mary so that 'disciplined / From
shadowie Types to Truth, from Flesh to Spirit' (XII, 302–3) we
may see the 'seed of Woman' in Mary the virgin field on which
the dew of 'God most High' will settle and from which life and
food will be produced. Or as Charles Fitzgeffery had earlier
offered, in a frankly typological summary:

> Behold a field which nere by man was tild
> Wheat whence is made the bread of life doth yield.
> Thus ere the heavens did showres on earth distil
> A mist her pregnant wombe did fill . . .
> And thus from Mary's wombe, a Plant proceeded,
> Which neither planting, neither watering needed.[11]

NOTES

1. See Charles Martindale, *John Milton and the Transformaton of Ancient Epic*, Beckenham: Croom Helm, 1986, pp. 84–5.
2. Martindale, pp. 85–6, 148.
3. *Paradise Lost*, edited by Alastair Fowler, London: Longman, 1971, paperback edn, p. 50n. All quotations from *Paradise Lost* here are from the old-spelling text edited by Helen Darbishire, London: Oxford University Press, 1958.
4. Christopher Ricks, *Critical Inquiry*, 2, 1 (Autumn) 1975; reprinted in *The Force of Poetry*, Oxford: Clarendon Press, 1984, p. 371.
5. Cited in *OED*: Reginald Pecock, *The repressor of overmuch blaming of the clergy*, c. 1449.
6. Dryden, *The Works of Virgil: containing his Pastorals, Georgics, and Aeneis*, London 1697.
7. *The Canterbury Tales* in *The Works of Geoffrey Chaucer*, ed. F.N. Robinson, 2nd edn, London: Oxford University Press, 1957. Robinson reminds us that this means 'rather the lands over which they marched than the "grounds" of their banners (as understood by Skeat)'.
8. Spenser, *The Faerie Queene*, ed. Thomas P. Roche, Jr, Harmondsworth: Penguin English Library, 1978.
9. *The Poems of Andrew Marvell*, ed. Hugh Macdonald, London: Routledge, reprint 1963.
10. See Robert T. Fallon's *Captain or Colonel: The Soldier in Milton's Life and Art*, Columbia: Missouri University Press, 1985.

11. Charles Fitzgeffery, 'The Blessed Birthday', 1636, in *Poems*, ed. A. Grosart, Manchester: Manchester University Press, 1881.

8

CONVENTIONS OF TIME
Foreknowledge and freedom in *Paradise Lost*

> Necessity relieves us from the embarrassment of
> choice.
> Vauvenargues, *Reflections and Maxims*, 1746

Dryden printed in 1674 (the year of Milton's death) the libretto of
an unperformed opera called *The State of Innocence and Fall of Man*
in which, in the words of an admirer Nathanael Lee, he refined
what Milton 'rudely cast and roughly drew'. Dryden himself, in
his 'Apology' of 1677 prefixed to the libretto, hoped readers
would not compare the two, 'the original being undoubtedly one
of the greatest, most noble, and most sublime poems which either
this age or nation has produced'. However, Dryden's treatment of
Milton, while it does not actually parody or mock, does draw out
what Dryden obviously saw as the comic aspect, hopefully disguised beneath Milton's grandeur, of Adam's dilemma at the
moment of the Fall, the absurdity of the Catch-22 situation in
which Adam is invited to prove to himself that he has free will,
thus bringing about his Fall. Dryden responds to what appears as
the impossible, and hence potentially comic rather than tragic,
situation in which a posited free will finds itself in a universe in
which the future inferred by God is in any case bound to come
into existence.

It is to the at least partial extrication of Milton from such (to my
mind) frivolous responses to the relation between God's knowledge and man's will that this final chapter is dedicated – for, as
Dryden rightly put it (though he was talking in fact about some
lines of Cowley): 'How easy 'tis to turn into ridicule the best
descriptions, when once a man is in the humour of laughing, till
he wheezes at his own dull jest'. ('Apology' to *The State of Innocence*.) And the foundation of my account of Milton's strategy lies
in his creative poetic revision, or dialogue with, our logical conventions of time, history, sequence and cause.

Of course, the reader of *Paradise Lost* who ventures into the

mazes of determinism and free will can only do so with an awareness of the labyrinths of 'Providence, Foreknowledge, Will and
Fate, / Fixt Fate, free Will, Foreknowledge absolute' (II, 559–60)
and of Milton's reservation of such endless discussions to fallen
angels.[1] Nevertheless, its author is constrained, by the very subject of his poem, to risk joining them, and although *Paradise Lost*
is a poem and not a dialogue on liberty and necessity, Milton
shows himself intimately acquainted with all the subtle, devious
and baffling philosophical and logical problems his material en-
tails. In *Christian Doctrine* he is strenuously concerned with the
issues that need to be untangled if what for him is an inviolable
principle can stand: for without true freedom of the will, 'liberty
will be an empty word, and will have to be banished utterly not
only from religion but also from morality' (*CD* I, iii)[2] Milton's
casuistry continues to generate speculation and new studies devoted to precisely this aspect of Milton's thought have recently
appeared.[3] What I wish to rehearse here are only *some* of the
philosophical puzzles, and those most evident even to the non-
professional-philosopher reader. The emphasis is also, however,
on Milton's artistic and poetic deployment, or embodiment, of
these puzzles in action and plot, and his 'solution' to them which
depends upon a resonantly ambiguous handling of the phe-
nomenon of *time* in the poem. But we need, too, to get the nature
of some of the puzzles as clear as possible.

It will be readily acknowledged that at the heart of the middle
books of the poem lie questions of freedom, causality, determinism – and hence of responsibility – questions to which both
Milton as poet and we as readers are forced to offer various shifts
and stratagems. One of these characteristic questions is that if
Adam's fall is in any sense caused (whether by external events or
by his own actions is indifferent here) then it logically cannot be
avoided; if something is caused, it cannot not happen. If we, or
Milton, were to argue in response, recoiling from this idea of
necessity, that Adam's choice is not caused, then the only alternative seems to be that it is an arbitrary event, an accident, for
which no more responsibility can be adduced than for a necessitated act. Either way, we do not have what the poem seems to
demand: a clear conception of free will acting with full responsibility and accountability.

It may be, of course, that we are looking for the wrong thing; a
clear conception may not be possible. Adam's free will may be

both an insurmountable logical problem and at the same time an article of belief – which is after all a perfectly familiar theological position. When St Augustine speaks of free will, the impression emerges that it is, in Adam's case, a kind of minimal theological requirement, a technicality sufficient to allow the apportioning of blame, but not to constitute the freedom to have chosen differently.[4] One mode of argument, like that of St Augustine, would be to attribute to free will only the exercise of *rational* choice ('for reason is but choosing,' as *Areopagitica* has it, and thus choosing is the act of reason); this argument would suggest that Adam is free only to act rationally or in proportion as he acts rationally. Adam's 'half abasht' response to Raphael's lecture on love, reason, and passion contains the defence that:

> I to thee disclose
> What inward thence I feel, not therefore foild,
> Who meet with various objects, from the sense
> Variously representing; yet still free
> Approve the best, and follow what I approve.
> (VII, 607–11)

It is however a defence with ominous echoes, both of St Paul and of Medea's: 'I see the better, and I approve it too: / The worse I follow.'[5] Raphael's farewell to Adam picks it up a little later: 'take heed lest Passion sway / Thy Judgement to do aught, which else free Will / Would not admit' (VIII, 635–6). The difficulty with the view that Adam is free only to act rationally (which is what Raphael appears to be saying here) is that it invites the problem that one cannot, in the same sense of the term *free will*, argue that it is by free choice also that he acts irrationally; otherwise one would be saying that Adam can freely will that which, should he ever will it, would not be freely willed.

Together with such logical conundrums regarding the moral position of free will lies the equally intransigent issue of causality. The moment one asks *why* Adam did this or that (whether it be a morning hymn to the Creator or the eating of the fruit), one seems to be talking about unavoidable acts in the sense that, if they have those causes, they must occur; there is only the possibility of other and different acts if there are other and different causes. Consequently, we have been encouraged to take up various positions toward Milton's narrative. The simplest is to acquiesce in the illogicality, admit the impossibility of the posited free will, and relish the comedy of the situation.[6] Another encourages us to shut our eyes to causes in the poem, or at least to recognize that Milton only offers 'causes' as they come to hand, none of them sufficient or decisive. Milton, it is argued, is highly sensitive to the problems of causation, and hence of necessitated acts, and offers us free will *without* causation.[7] Yet others have persuaded us to recognise that Milton *stresses* the causes, plots the Fall from the beginning, offers us an unfallen Adam passionately fixated and an Eve petulantly contrary, but, at the same time, promotes the 'official' view of a paradisal innocence with which these actions are subtly at variance. The object is to present moral freedom, which Adam forfeits, as provisional, relative, and contextual, depending on his acting within the scope of his true stature and not contrary to his higher knowledge and sense of moral obligation.[8] In the first strategy we are asked merely to see the joke; in the second we are asked to pretend not to have noticed and are (paradoxically) invited to be surprised by sin; in the third we are asked to untangle, or at least to endure, the riddles of Adam being in one sense free to sin or not to sin, but in another sense not free should he sin.

In the face of such difficulties, defenders of the doctrine of moral freedom from Plotinus and Boethius to Kant have characteristically acknowledged that true freedom cannot be conceived except outside of time. A dominant theological form of this acknowledgment stresses, as St Augustine did, that freedom is proportional to our ability to escape from worldly and temporal processes and can be approached only through contemplation of the eternal and the immutable – that is, God.[9] Adam's excessive response to Eve and the critical confusion of loyalties of which Raphael sharply warns him make one significant strand in Milton's dramatisation of events and may be numbered among the 'causes'. But another response to the possibility timelessness offers for escape from the riddles of freedom and causality is in a sense more searching and equally germane to Milton's treatment of the Fall.

One of the most poignant dimensions of the poem is its nostalgia for what might have been, for what is lost irrecoverably in time. It renders a particular time inaccessible and past in a peculiarly definitive way. It is, too, full of conditionals and second thoughts, which are, of course, the necessary conditions of acts of remorse and repentance. The sense of time is also the necessary condition for the exercise of free will and of choice itself: to choose involves deliberation; deliberation implies time as its condition. But is choice then an illusion? For time is also the necessary condition for causation; there can be no cause without sequence, and causation seems to contradict free choice. Where every action or event occurs in time, determined by the past and determining the future, freedom must seem a figment, for things can only be as they are or as they will be. Milton's approach to this dilemma involves two strategies: one is to assume a crucial difference between causal necessity and logical necessity, the other is to assume and demonstrate a God who is non-temporal and, despite his temporary descents to the grammar of the human mind, knows all actions and events without 'before' and 'after'. The first strategy challenges us to distinguish between 'this must happen' and 'this will happen' and see where our distinctions may lead; the second enters into combat with yet another celebrated conundrum regarding Adam's freedom and responsibility (a conundrum to which the form of Milton's poem gives unavoidable exposure), the relation of man's will to God's foreknowledge. To both of these issues Milton's treatment of time is critical.

In *Surprised by Sin: The Reader in 'Paradise Lost'*, Stanley Fish has persuasively conducted the reader of Milton's account of the Fall through the minefields of possible misunderstanding that Milton lays in his path. The ever-present tension between Adam's and Eve's innocence and our own foreknowledge is delicately invoked in Milton's instruction to the reader and in moments of poignant dramatic irony. While this effect unquestionably poses possibilities no imaginative writer could ignore, there may be a more rigorously philosophical questioning involved at the same time. When we have followed the course of Eve's and Adam's temptation and fall, have recognised that they, unlike us, canot know the end of the story, and have recognised too that what we have thought 'necessary' or 'inevitable' has not been so to the protagonists at their moments of action (those actions have been more 'free' than we may have supposed), there still remains a confusing nexus of riddles involving the multiple senses of the terms *necessary* and *impossible*. We may find ourselves wondering whether, if the Fall was not then 'necessary' (in the sense that nothing may have 'determined' it but our own foreknowledge), was it also therefore possible for Adam and Eve to have acted differently? We may have to conclude, accepting the argument from causation, that it was not for the overwhelmingly simple reason that the Fall occurred. So that although we may have avoided committing ourselves to the proleptical view that the Fall 'must' occur, we have no answer to the assertions either that it will occur or that it has occurred, and, consequently, cannot have been otherwise. The upshot may seem to be that Adam and Eve had no other choice and, therefore, no choice.

One of the assumptions involved here is that if it is logically necessary for the past to be what it has been and for the future to be what it is going to be (if it is logically impossible for the future not to be what it is going to be), then it follows that there is no point in doing anything about it or in speaking of free will. Whatever Adam has done must have happened anyway, and whatever Adam and Eve have not done could not have happened anyway, even if they had tried to make it happen. From this position, the possibility of a Miltonic freedom seems to vanish without trace, despite the poet's formal and repeated protestations of its reality.

And yet logical determinism, which asserts no more than that things are as they are and cannot be otherwise, need not involve us or Milton in causal necessity. The sense in which things 'cannot possibly be otherwise' because they are what they are greatly differs from the sense in which things 'cannot possibly be otherwise' because other things – Adam's uxoriousnes, Eve's wilfulness, Satan's 'glozing lies', or even the absence of free will – cause or compel them to be what they are. To say that the future is logically determined is not to say that it is causally determined. Logical determinism is not fatalism; nor is logical necessity causal necessity. Milton presents a Fall in which a posited free will, though not compatible with fatalism, is perfectly compatible with a determinism which proposes that for everything that ever happens there are conditions, given which, nothing else could happen. I think that, despite the aggressively defensive stance and the desire to make sense of the issue in terms of God's 'decrees', this awareness lies somewhere at the centre of *Christian Doctrine*, where Milton discusses the paradox that 'man fell, though not unwillingly, yet by necessity' (I, iv).

It may be true that all paradises are paradises lost, and the peculiar sense of loss in the poem depends in part for its effect on the possibility that although the future cannot be changed from what it is to be, it may be 'altered' from what it might have been *if* our first parents had not taken the actions they did. The real moral issue here, of course, is not whether the future will (tautologically) be what it is to be, but whether *what* it is to be owes anything to our future or present efforts and activities. Fatalism asserts a present causally discontinuous with the future, in which all events occur by accident or by chance and in which free will is illusory.

This, at any rate, is Satan's view of the matter. Milton characteristically invites us to consider events in the poem as happening by chance, a word almost inevitable in introducing similes in which Satan participates: Leviathan is discovered 'haply' (by chance) 'slumbring on the Norway foam' (I, 203); the devils' new sense of purpose is like a 'Bark by chance' anchoring in a 'craggy Bay' (II, 288–9); the illuminated landscape of Book II ocurs 'if chance the radiant Sun' (492); Satan approaches Eve by chance, both in the simile 'if chance with Nymph-like step fair Virgin pass' (IX, 452) and in his mental picture of a universe in which events occur only by necessity or by chance – 'He sought them both, but wishd his hap might find / Eve separate, he wishd, but not with hope / Of what so seldom chanc'd' (IX, 421–3). Milton even springs a little trap for the reader in his exclamation 'hapless Eve', inviting us to think of her as a victim of bad luck caught in an accident (IX, 404). Milton's God, on the other hand, assigns chance only to Chaos, to which he chooses not to extend his form-giving goodness: 'Necessitie and Chance / Approach not me and what I will is Fate' (VII, 172). In Milton's usage 'fate' means not fatalism, but 'only what is *fatum*, spoken by some almighty power' *CD* I, ii). Replying to Belial's optimistic yet deterministic hope of what 'future days might bring, what chance, what change / Worth waiting,' Mammon perceptively rebukes him: 'him to unthrone we then / May hope when everlasting Fate shall yield / To fickle Chance, and Chaos judge the strife' (II, 231–3).

That is, if 'everlasting Fate' should ever yield to chance, the result would be chaotic, for 'Chance governs all' only in Chaos (II, 910). The alternative is an eternal providence which is logically determined, and logical determinism tells us no more than that the future will be what it is to be and cannot be otherwise. It tells us nothing, in other words, about free will's relation to the apparent alternatives of chance and causal necessity; it can be invoked without implying either of them.

As we read Milton's account of the Fall, both our own foreknowledge of events and our difficulties in distingishing logical determinism from causal necessity and from fatalism may interfere with our understanding of his assertions of man's freedom. Much more intractable an issue, however, is raised by the presence in the action of the poem of a God who knows all events, a God who has to be presented as in a sense 'neutral' (noninterfering, not-determining) with regard to man's actions and yet whose defined attributes of omnipotence and omniscience seem to render such neutrality logically impossible. And it is clear from Milton's wrestling with free will and divine foreknowledge in *Christian Doctrine* that he was sharply aware of all the devious and complex implications of these problems.

Paradise Lost embodies the end-in-the-beginning of an accomplished theological as well as poetic structure. That the Alpha and Omega who knows all truths from the beginning of time presides over its action gives a powerful imaginative appeal to the suggestion of a determinism militating against free will's operation in time. One response to the paradox is to pretend that it isn't there and to fall into the trap of incoherence about the concept of 'the future': 'The relation between cosmic time and human time depended upon Adam's action and God's response to it; now the outcome of the Fall has altered the future of all human history'; 'this is the final purport of all Michael's teaching'[10]. This view appears to suggest either that God has a number of possible futures up his sleeve and selects the right one for the circumstances, or that he just got it wrong.

Let us look a little more closely at the nature of this problem. At noon on the thirty-second day of the action of *Paradise Lost*, Eve reached for the forbidden fruit, 'she pluckd, she eat' (IX, 781). Prior to noon on the thirty-second day, God knew that Eve would eat the fruit at that precise moment. It would therefore seem, from our general theological and logical assumptions about the nature of God – his eternity, omnipotence, omniscience, and infallibility – that at the time of the action Eve was not able, it was not within Eve's power, to refrain from eating the fruit. Eve's eating of the fruit cannot be accounted a voluntary action since, it seems safe to assume, no action is voluntary if it is not, at the time, within the power of the agent to refrain from its performance. From this blunt statement of affairs, which Milton must handle in his account of the Fall, it is perhaps necessary to get the details of the issue as clear as possible. Among the assumptions

central to the nature of God are first, the claim that God is infallible and second, the claim that God knows the outcome of human
actions in advance of their performance. Related to these claims
is the assumption of God's omniscience, that God knows all facts,
and that it is conceptually impossible for an individual who is
God to hold a false belief or to be mistaken; also crucial is the
assumption of God's eternity, that God has always existed and
will always exist, and that he extends indefinitely both forward
and backward in time. To suppose, therefore, that Eve could act
in such a way as to render false a belief previously held by God or
an item of knowledge previously known by God would be to
suppose that at the time of the action Eve was capable of something having a conceptually incoherent description, namely,
something that would render false an item of knowledge held by
God, who is infallible. Of course, the same argument holds had
Eve *not* eaten the fruit.

What then is Milton to make of this situation? Of the claim that
God knows in advance the outcome of human actions, Milton
writes: 'God has complete foreknowledge, so he knows what
men . . . will think and do, even before they are born and even
though these thoughts and deeds will not take place until many
centuries are passed' *(CD* I, ii). But into the hiatus I have exca-
vated here Milton drops the words – in this context, I think,
inconsistent words – 'who are free in their actions'. He also takes
up the issue of infallibility. Concerning God's decrees, he argues
that they may be merely contingent: 'God makes no absolute
decrees about anything which he left in the power of man, for
men have freedom of action' (*CD* I, iii). Hieronymous Zanchius
provides a classic text revealing the interior of the problem
Milton is probing: 'Now if God foreknew this, He must have
predetermined it, because His own will is the foundation of his
decrees, and His decrees are the foundation of His Prescience;
He therefore foreknowing futurities, because by His predestination He hath rendered their futurition certain and inevitable.'[11]
Briefly acknowledging the host of adherents on each side of this
issue, Milton appeals to human common sense ('if it is allowable
to apply the standards of mortal reason to divine decrees') and
tilts at the paradox, about which the Reformed theologians themselves appear to have been sensitive, of absolute predestination,
which seemed to conclude that what was necessary for eternal life
was not any human will or exertion, 'but only some sort of fatal

decree' (*CD* I, iv). God made his decrees conditional, Milton argues, 'for the purpose of allowing free causes to put into effect that freedom which he himself gave them'; freedom is destroyed, 'or at least obscured', 'if we admit any such sophisticated concept of necessity as that which, we are asked to believe, results not from compulsion but from immutability or infallibility. This concept has misled and continues to mislead a lot of people' (*CD* I, iii). He then offers as plain a statement of affairs as possible: 'The divine plan depends only on God's own wisdom. By this wisdom he had perfect knowledge of all things in his own mind and knew what they would be like and what their consequences would be when they occurred' (*CD* I, iii). But then comes the question, 'how can these consequences which, on account of man's free will, are uncertain, be reconciled with God's absolutely firm decree?'[12] Milton says simply that God does not always absolutely decree; he points out that the decree in Genesis 2:17 – "do not eat of this, for on the day you eat it you will die" – 'itself was conditional before the Fall' (*CD* I, iv). He draws a distinction between things happening of necessity and God foreknowing that they will happen, and he argues that Adam's fall was certain but not necessary (*CD* I, iii).[13]

It is of course evident that *Christian Doctrine* keeps to the context of Arminian-Calvinist oppositions over the doctrine of free will. Milton conducts his argument entirely in terms of that debate. He frequently refers, at times in a rather weary way, to the nature of the language being used in this sort of discourse about God, who is, in one of Milton's listed attributes, incomprehensible (cf. *PL* III, 705–7; VII, 112–14); he warns, for example, that 'when we talk about God, it must be understood in terms of man's limited powers of comprehension', and he shows exasperation with such debate: 'but really, if we must discuss God in terms of our own habits and understandings.' In this treatise his defence of man's free will and God's noninterference rests upon two basic arguments, contingency and human analogy, both of which remain within the terms of formulations about God's foreknowledge.

The argument from contingency, as offered by Milton in *Christian Doctrine* and, in another form, by Leibniz in *Theodicee*,[14] contrasts 'necessary' to 'conditional' or 'contingent' and also opposes 'necessary' to 'voluntary'. To say that Eve's eating of the fruit is true or certain (because it is foreknown by God), but not *necessarily* true or certain, does not salvage the issue of free will. St Augustine, as the Reformers well knew, says that if God fore-knows actions, then they *are* necessary in the sense that they are not voluntary. The conditional or contingent response does not solve the problem that, if Eve's action were only contingently necessary, and if Eve were able, contingently, to refrain from eating the fruit, then either she was able, contingently, to act in a way which would have falsified an item of God's knowledge or she was able, contingently, to act so that God held not that item of knowledge, but some other. Neither of these possibilities is acceptable; each fails to touch the issue in hand.[15] The argument from human analogy, also espoused by St Augustine as an ap-proach to this question, suggests that since our own human pres-cience of another's actions does not involve compulsion, then neither does God's[16] God knows in advance, it is argued, that a given person is going to choose to perform a certain action at some specific time in the future. And yet this argument, too, is not without its problems, since God is required to know both that Eve will eat the fruit at noon on the thirty-second day (an item of knowledge which cannot be other and is therefore necessary, not free) and also that she acted freely. God is thus discovered hold-ing a false belief. In other words, the human analogy is not a parallel to God's foreknowledge in relation to determinism, for the crucial difference is that human foreknowledge, unlike that of a being who is God, is not infallible. St Augustine therefore pro-ceeds to attack the notion of infallibility, while on another front, both he and, later, Boethius attack that other assumption in-volved in the complex, the notion of God's knowing in advance.[17]

In Part 5, section iii, of *The Consolation of Philosophy*, Boethius said, like St Augustine, that if God is infallible and knows the outcome of all human actions in advance of their performance, then no human action is voluntary.[18] At the same time, Boethius held that some human actions are voluntary. He was therefore obliged to deny either that God is infallible, or that he knows beforehand how human beings will act. Boethius chose to deny the second. He denied that God can have temporal extension. A timeless being cannot know the outcome of human actions in advance of their performance, since the cognition of such a being is not located in time relative to the action in question. In Section vi of the fifth book he offers the view that it is not possible to speak of a timeless being knowing prior to, at the time, or after.

God's knowledge is present tense only and cannot involve time-qualified predicates. This attack on assumptions about the nature of God's duration would seem to reach the heart of the issue, for, without locating God's cognition in the past relative to the actions it knows, there appears to be no way of formulating the problem of divine foreknowledge.

We should now return to *Christian Doctrine*. At one or two moments, Milton seems about to break out of the charmed circle of predestinarian debate. At one point early in the discussion, he observes that 'It is absurd . . . to separate God's decrees or intention from his eternal resolution or foreknowledge and give the former chronological priority. For God's foreknowledge is simply his wisdom under another name, or that idea of all things which, to speak in human terms, he had in mind before he decreed anything.'[19] His hint here that the very notion of foreknowledge is merely a human mental fabrication and has nothing to do with God's perception (for with God there is no latter or former, no 'chronological priority') and that foreknowledge for a being who is God is simply knowledge is, surprisingly, not developed or incorporated into the discussion. Following St Augustine's concept of eternity, where 'nothing is flitting, but all is at once present,'[20] Boethius' celebrated formulation of God's *interminabilis vitae tota simul et perfecta possessio* (simultaneous and complete possession of infinite life'),[21] and Aquinas' 'nunc stans' other commentators saw the crucial issue readily enough, though they may have made very different things of it. For Luther, 'there is no Dinumeration of tyme with God,' for whom 'all thynges are lapped up as it were in one bundle.'[22] Even for Calvin, God 'holds and sees' all things at once 'as if actually placed before him.'[23] For Sir Thomas Browne, there is in eternity 'no distinction of Tenses'; with God there is 'no prescious determination of our Estates to come,' for 'what to us is to come, to His eternity is present, His whole duration being but one permanent point, without Succession, Parts, Flux or Division.'[24] Why then does Milton give no prominence to such views in *Christian Doctrine*, and why does he appear to ignore the Augustinian and Boethian solutions to the problems of determinism?

It has been noted that Milton was 'one of the few great writers of the Renaissance to depart from the traditional view of time.'[25] Where for St Augustine time did not exist before the Creation ('the world was made with time, and not in time'),[26] Milton counters that 'there is certainly no reason why we should conform to the popular belief that motion and time, which is the measure of motion, could not, according to our concepts of 'before' and 'after', have existed before this world was made' (*CD* I, vii). In *Paradise Lost*, Raphael makes it clear to Adam that time reaches behind the Creation and that there is time in Heaven, though it differs from human time:

> As yet this World was not, and *Chaos* wilde
> Reignd where these Heav'ns now rowl, where Earth now rests
> Upon her Centre pois'd, when on a day
> (For Time, though in Eternitie, appli'd
> To motion, measures all things durable
> By present, past, and future) on such a day
> As Heav'ns great Year brings forth.
>
> (V, 577–83)

A possible explanation for Milton's lapse from orthodoxy (or his original adaptation of it) may be that in *Paradise Lost* a timeless stasis before the Creation would make action utterly intractable, eliminating or rendering inconceivable of execution any dramatic or narrative possibilities depending upon suspense, movement, and sequence. Milton may have other issues on his mind in *Christian Doctrine*, where his antitrinitarianism, the subordinate position of the Son and the Holy Spirit and the Son's generation *in time*, requires not timelessness, but duration in eternity.

While there may be special reasons for Milton's tactics in *Christian Doctrine*, it may be admitted that *Paradise Lost* is not a poem which gives great prominence to antitrinitarian views (though they may be there) or to theological novelties generally. Milton's insistence on time before the Creation and in Heaven (until for Milton, as for St Augustine, time will cease and, after the Last Judgement, 'stand fixt')[27] has the curious and paradoxical effect not of trapping his God in time but of liberating him from it. To argue that Milton's God, unlike the God of the scholastics, is time-bound and that this position 'makes [Milton's] unqualified assertion of divine omniscience and creaturely freedom difficult to sustain'[28] may be true of *Christian Doctrine*, but the sense of what 'time' means and of what God's relation to it might be is a matter on which the poet of *Paradise Lost* employs some of his most energetically enigmatic language.

As we have seen from Milton's manipulation of simile in the poem, there is a sense of a God who is neither centred in locality nor located in time but whose omnipresence, in signs and traces, may be registered and recognised in past and in present, in Eden and out of it, in Abdiel or Galileo, in Leviathan or North Sea whales, in Abel or in seventeenth-century seamen returning from the East Indies. Unlike the human inability to know a place except at a time or a time except at a place, God is all times and all places. Milton invites us to explore the ironic paradoxes (ironic, that is, for Satanic ambitions) of introducing poetic material for simile and comparison derived from a world surviving the anarchy-threatening event in hand and mutely signing its defeat. He invites us to recognise through classical, biblical and seventeenth-century analogues the simultaneity of an action in which sequential ordering is merely a deceptive narrative convenience, where the present is in the past, the past in the present, and where 'before' and 'now' and 'after' may be conflated in one continuum. Uriel, for instance, glides down Bentley and Empson's notorious sunbeam to the newly created Earth and is transformed into a shooting star observed by both an Homeric and a seventeenth-century mariner (IV, 555–60). The sun, as significant symbol, measures time relentlessly as it passes and signals crisis and judgement, yet remains a static archetype, emblematic, out of time. While he pays detailed attention to measurements of time, to precise chronology, to significant sunrises, noons and sunsets, Milton also indicates simultaneous (as it were) dimensions where 'time and place are lost' (II, 894). Events constantly repeat themselves. We begin and end the poem with a picture of the sea swallowing Pharoah / Satan 'with all his Host', God crazing 'thir Chariot wheels', and the 'Sojourners' surviving to 'gain thir shoar' (I, 304–11, XII, 190–215). Man's fall and Satan's decline are presented in perspectives which make them appear to occur continuously, from the time when seamen moor alongside Leviathan in the opening epic simile to the time of Adam's capitulation to 'what seem'd remediless'. Time is necessary for the rendering of narrative and dramatic action, both terrestrial and extraterrestrial, but Milton seems to order his perspectives vertically rather than sequentially (and hence causally) – that is, there is a 'mythic' use of times within times. As we read we grapple with the stratified accumulations of a sequence of events complicated by flashbacks but unfolding in time, with the

relation of these to historical time and to a vividly present contemporary time (what is Galileo doing itemising Satan's armour?),
and with the relation of all these to the time of the reading
experience itself as we turn the next page. We are reminded of at
least two things: that a world without time is a world that cannot
be redeemed, and therefore a world ultimately without meaning;
and also that our sense of time, and with it of place, is both acute
and confused, relative, uncentred (except upon ourselves), and
finally mysterious.

What then, we may ask, is God's relation to these stacked and
various time-worlds of the poem? For all these times are further
complicated by another cosmic time that exists in Heaven, sur-
mounted by a God who views all times simultaneously from a
point altogether outside time. In *Paradise Lost*, if not in *Christian
Doctrine*, Milton poetically energises the Boethian view and all its
implications. Time and place are lost not only in Chaos but also in
God's empyrean where he sits in an eternal present indicative,
'Wherein past, present, future he beholds' (III, 78). In one sense
Milton's God is a character in the story, and one with a tenden-
tious speaking part. In another sense he is not *in* the story at all
but is the ultimate author of the story, so that Satan, Adam and
Eve, and we ourselves, are part of God's story. His authorial
'actions' within the story's time are veiled in temporal mystery
even while Milton is pretending, as it were, to the greatest preci-
sion. God's actions are in any case protected, or mediated, by
Raphael, who descends for the purpose into metaphor: the momentous account of the Son's generation, which 'when on a
day . . . on such day / As Heav'ns great Year brings forth' (V, 579–
83) announces, is prefaced by Raphael's

> what surmounts the reach
> Of human sense, I shall delineate so,
> By lik'ning spiritual to corporeal forms,
> As may express them best.
> (V, 571–4)

The narrative 'event' of the Son's generation is enclosed in time
(to protect it from eternity) and yet resists the question 'when?',
despite its temporal indicators – 'Heav'ns great Year' or the *annus
magnus platonicus* when the cycle of the heavenly bodies is complete and they simultaneously return to their original positions, is

a moment, as Alastair Fowler informs us, 'variously estimated (e.g. by Servius at 12,954 natural years, by Macrobius at 15,000, by Plato himself probably 36,000).[29] Yet all this is in any case a red-herring since the event clearly antedates the time and place 'where these Heav'ns now rowl'. The actual event narrated is equally obscurely rendered, and is in fact neither event nor narration, for God is not seen to act but only to announce an action already effected:

> This day I have begot whom I declare
> My onely Son.
>
> (V, 603–4)

In terms of narrative sequence the event appears to belong to a period subsequent to the creation of 'Th'Empyreal Host' assembled to witness it (and which of course they do not) but, as William Myers points out in discussing this passage, 'Satan and Abdiel will be arguing before the dawning of the next 'day' about whether the newly-begotten Son was instrumental in their own creation'. Myers concludes that 'in his most momentous act, neither the acting God, nor the moment of his efficacy is textually present in Milton's account'.[30] Perhaps the text is like the text of Eve's dream (V, 28–93), which appears to tell us that Eve did *this* and at *this* o'clock, but which in fact tells us nothing of the sort.

Similarly, Raphael's account of the Creation is equally mysterious in its relation to God's 'time'. The alert Adam asks a question about divine motivation and wonders

> what cause
> Mov'd the Creator in his holy Rest
> Through all Eternitie so late to build
> In *Chaos* . . .?
>
> (VII, 90–93)

The interesting thing here is Adam's inability to escape from the terms of Raphael's metaphor which has rendered textually possible 'Great things . . . Farr differing from this World' (VII, 70–1), 'Things above Earthly thought' (VII, 82). Why should Adam suppose that God had acted 'so late'? 'So early' would have made no less and no more sense. The Creation as an act of God both is and is not time-related: in Book VII, 176–7 we are told, following 'So spake th'Almightie', that

> Immediat are the Acts of God, more swift
> Than time or motion, but to human ears
> Cannot without process of speech be told,
> So told as earthly notion can receive,

just as we were earlier informed that the agency of the 'Word, begotten Son' will create the world 'in a moment' (VII, 154). Phrases like 'more swift / Than time or motion' and 'in a moment' suggest a view of time not unlike the geometrician's view of a mathematical dot, that is, as an event paradoxically occurring and yet not occurring in time. So that both God's 'actions' in the poem and his 'knowledge' are eternally *there* and eternally *known*. God is both the ultimate author and also the ultimate reader of the story of the book of the Creation.

But God's descent to character, notably in Book III, raises some difficulties. As Milton scholars often note, Milton's God articulates the essentials of the foreknowledge-and-necessity issue like an inspired summary of *Christian Docrine*,[31] and such discussions are not limited to a single section of Book III, though elsewhere (as in V, 535–8) they may be mediated by Raphael. Both the speaking God of *Paradise Lost* and the customary theological language – whether of 'foreknowledge', 'prevenient grace' or 'the promis'd seed' – that embodies such time-qualified perspectives exist in the poem simultaneously with a timeless Boethian God and a poetically realised disintegration of temporality.

In his discourse on predestination in Book III, Milton's God propounds a liberal anti-Calvinistic view which, like that expressed in *Christian Doctrine*, is so defined as to hope to exclude 'necessity' or 'determinism.' Whatever the problems and limitations of that particular nexus of arguments, Milton also indicates the timeless being who is dramatically rendering such a discourse. He does this in part by assigning to God a totally random us, of tenses which allows the Fall to be at some points future ('till the, enthrall themselves,' 125), at others present ('They trespass, Authors to themselves in all / Both what they judge and what they choose,' 122–3), and at others past ('they themselves decreed / Thir own revolt,' 116–17). When the Son responds to offer 'life for life,' Milton again presents a supratemporal view, a timeless present *sub specie aeternitatis*, without precise chronological sequence (256–65). Similarly, God's later words deny time's limitations:

So Heav'nly love shall outdo hellish hate
Giving to death, and dying to redeeme,
So dearly to redeem what hellish hate
So easily destroyd, and still destroyes.

(298–301)

God involves us in tenses which could imply that the Fall has already occurred and is occurring; his words sustain the impression created earlier in Book III – 'that he may know how frail / His fall'n condition is' (180–81) – the impression of timeless meditation by a being whose knowledge comprehends many different temporal perspectives and who is not himself 'in' any of them.

Through Satan's misconceptions and confusions, Milton ironically affirms aspects of God's nature, most notably, of course, the omnipotence (which Satan regards as mere potency) and the creativity (which Satan thinks contingent on his own initiatives). In other ways, Satan is equally mistaken: he garbles the Neoplatonic notion of God as an infinite sphere whose centre is everywhere and whose circumference nowhere (IX, 107–09), and he scoffs at an omnipotent God who requires *time* to create 'and who knows how long / Before had bin contriving' (IX, 138–40). We are intended to note these Satanic aberrations and to translate them into alternative propositions.

Milton locates God in his empyrean, but time itself, although it approaches very close to God, is *contained* within a cave 'fast by his Throne', 'where light and darkness in perpetual round / Lodge and dislodge by turns' (VI, 6–7). Although there is time in eternity (there is, in Milton's imaginative view which contradicts both Plato and St Augustine, motion in eternity), it is conceived not as a passage or a process but as a form of relation between events. In Heaven that relation is 'grateful vicissitude', In Satan's mind time conceived as a process provokes the bad theology of a God capable of 'second thoughts' (IX, 101); but more urgently, time is the relation between 'the bitter memorie / Of what he was, what is, and what must be / Worse' (IV, 24–5). In Adam, after the indulgence of despair at a falsely deterministic response to his own foreknowledge of future history (XI, 763), time registers as a form of relation between disobedience and repentance. The moral 'actions' of the poem are narrated in time, or times: the

harangues, rebellions, falls, the discharging of debts, the repen-
tances. The moral 'postures' of the poem – love and hate, obedience and disdain – are expressed as conditions, not as events;
they are not time-related. Conditions or aptitudes realised in action constitute the poem's narrative process, but at the same time
deny process. In other words, *Paradise Lost* is a myth, and like all
myth, it requires a temporal dimension in which to unfold, yet
uses time only to obliterate it.

Milton thus presents events – angelic and human falls – which
take place both within times and outside time. For the human
understanding and the grammar of the human mind, they are in
time; for God, they are outside time. From one point of view
there is causality, suspense, sequence; there is remembrance,
knowledge and foreknowledge. From another there is, in a phrase
with which Jackson Cope has described *Paradise Regained*, 'only
the exfoliation of the eternally given into time'. It is part of
Milton's genius to make demands on his readers' ability to comprehend the length of the narrative with all its recurrent themes,
back-references and parallels, to grasp correctly the whole range
of the story as it is unfolded. But Milton also reminds them that
the story unfolding in their time ultimately works to deny the
reality of time. One of the poem's most ambiguous words is
'now'. Together with its associates 'then', 'next', 'thus', 'forth-
with', and so on, 'now' also gathers up with it every tensed verb in
the poem's grammatical web.[32] It is, for instance, instructive to
look again at so familiar a passage as the autumnal leaves, the Red
Sea coast, the deliverance of the Hebrews, and the voice of Satan
in Hell (i, 301–13) and to ask where, if anywhere, is the 'now' of
this shifting temporal kaleidscope? In such a mythic utterance
(and despite Milton's failure to resist the temptation of a literary
tour de force which temporarily traps his articulate God in the toils
of human grammar), the presiding Boethian God lies outside
time, causality, sequence, or proleptical decrees. In the poetic
universe of *Paradise Lost*, the fact that Satan's or Adam's, Mulci-
ber's or Abraham's, Charles I's or Galileo's 'future' actions exist
in the space-time manifolds observed by God does not mean that
they come to each action independently of what they have done
in the meantime, or that they come fated or despite their wills. In
such a mythic utterance, God's angelic and human creations go
about their business of falling and of standing again, 'known' of
God, but not 'foreknown'.

NOTES

1. All quotations from *Paradise Lost* are cited from *The Poems of John Milton*, ed. Helen Darbishire, London: Oxford University Press, 1958.

2. *Christian Doctrine*, trans. John Carey, in *The Complete Prose Works*, New Haven: Yale University Press, 1973, VI. All quotations refer to book and chapter of this edition.

3. For example Dennis R. Danielson, *Milton's Good God: A Study in Literary Theodicy*, Cambridge: Cambridge University Press, 1982, and most recently William Myers, *Milton and Free Will: An Essay in Criticism and Philosophy*, Beckenham: Croom Helm, 1987. Myers's book is an essay in philosophy rather than criticism and is written at a level of technical specialisation that will deter all but professional philosophers – at whom, one suspects, it is chiefly directed. Milton is frequently left mute in the interrogations of Newman, Henry James, the present Pope, a host of academic philosophers and an equal host of Marxists and deconstructionists. Quirky and always interesting, Myers defends a strong version of free will, though all too rarely does he show us *how* the peculiar energies of Milton's text actually function: often it is *Paradise Lost* minus the poetry.

4. See *De Gratia et libero arbitrio*, XV, 31, in *The Fathers of the Church*, LIX, Washington: Catholic University of America Press, 1968, p. 285.

5. Ovid, *Metamorphoses*, trans. George Sandys, Oxford, 1632, VII, 20–21.

6. See, for example, William Empson, *Milton's God*, London: Chatto & Windus, 1961, and K. W. Gransden, 'Milton, Dryden and the Comedy of the Fall', *Essays in Criticism*, 26 (1976), pp. 116–33.

7. See, for example, Stanley E. Fish, *Surprised by Sin: The Reader in Paradise Lost*, London: Macmillan, 1969.

8. See J. B. Savage's interesting 'Freedom and Necessity in *Paradise Lost*', *English Literary History*, 44 (1977), pp. 286–311. Savage, attempting to accommodate Milton's poem to a compatibilist theory of free will, i.e. that free will does not preclude causal determinism and vice versa, concludes that 'it can make no sense to say that the Fall is freely willed' (p. 295). Dennis R. Danielson, commenting on Savage, continues the pursuit of knock-down logical contradictions in *Imago Dei*, 'Filial Freedom', and Miltonic Theodicy' *English Literary History*, 47 (1980), pp. 670–81.

9. See *De musica*, VI, 11, 29, in *The Fathers of the Church*, II, New York: Cima, 1947, p. 355.

10. Laurence Stapleton, 'Perspectives of Time in *Paradise Lost*', *Philological Quarterly*, 45 (1966), pp. 734–48.

11. *The Doctrine of Absolute Predestination*, trans. A. M. Toplady (1769), London, 1930, p. 91.

12. Cf. Turretinus, *Institutio theologiae elenticae*, IV, 3, 3–4, cited in *Reformed Dogmatics*, ed. and trans. John W. Beardslee, New York: Oxford University Press, 1965.

13. Cf. *Paradise Lost*, III, 111–23, and Milton's *The Art of Logic* (1672), I, 5, in *The Works of John Milton*, ed. Frank Allen Patterson *et al.*, New York: Columbia University Press, 1931–38, XI.
14. Leibniz, *Theodicee*, trans. E. M. Huggard, New Haven: Yale University Press, Part I, sec. xxxvii.
15. Cf. Thomas Hobbes's comment: 'for whatsoever God hath *purposed* to bring to pass by *man*, as an instrument, or foreseeth shall come to pass: a man, if he hath liberty, such as his Lordship affirmeth, from *necessitation*, might frustrate, and make not to come to pass, and God should either not *foreknow* it, and not *decree* it, or he should *foreknow* such things shall be, as shall never be, and decree that which shall never *come to pass.*' *To the Lord Marquis of Newcastle: Of Liberty and Necessity*, in *English Works*, IV, ed. Sir William Molesworth, London: Bohm, 1840, p. 278.
16. *De libero arbitrio*, III, 3, sec. vi, in *Augustine's Earlier Writings*, trans. J. H. S. Burleigh, London: S. C. M. Press, 1953.
17. St Augustine's and Boethius's arguments receive lucid discussion in a study to which I am indebted here, Nelson Pike's *God and Timelessness*, London: Routledge, 1970, chap. 4.
18. *The Consolation of Philosophy*, V, Prose vi, trans. W. V. Cooper, London: Dent, 1902.
19. *CD* I, iii, and Milton's definition of God's eternity, I, ii. Cf. the rather different view set out in his *The Art of Logic*: 'Here among the adjuncts of circumstance is put *time*, to wit, the duration of things past, present and future. Thus also God is named, who is, who was, and who is to be. (*Apocalypse*, 1, 4, and 4.8.) But to God everlastingness or eternity, not time, is generally attributed, but what properly is everlastingness except eternal duration . . .?' (I, xi)
20. *Confessions*, XI, 11, trans. William Watts (1631), ed. W. H. D. Rouse, London: Loeb Classical Library, 2 vols., 1912.
21. *The Consolation of Philosophy*, V, Prose vi.
22. *A Commentarie . . . uppon the twoo Epistles Generall of . . . Peter, and Jude*, trans. Thomas Newton, London, 1581, fol. 158.
23. *Institutes of the Christian Religion*, III, 21, trans. John Allen, Philadelphia: Presbyterian Board of Publication, 1813, II, p. 145.
24. *Religio Medici* (1642), I, xi, in *Sir Thomas Browne: The Major Works*, ed. C. A. Patrides, Harmondsworth: Penguin Books, 1977, pp. 72–3.
25. C. A. Patrides, 'The Renaissance View of Time: A Bibliographical Note', *Notes & Queries*, CCVII (1963), pp. 408–10.
26. *De civitate dei*, XI, 6, trans. John Healey (1610), rev. R. V. G. Tasker, London: Dent, 2 vols, 1942.
27. *P. L.*, XII, 555; Cf. *Ad Patrem*, i, 131, and *On Time*, in *The Poems of John Milton*, ed. H. Darbishire, pp. 413, 551–4.
28. William Myers, *Milton and Free Will*, p. 9.
29. See A. Fowler, *Paradise Lost*, Longman edition, p. 293, n. V, 583.
30. William Myers, *Milton and Free Will*, p. 201.
31. See for example Maurice Kelley, *This Great Argument*, Princeton: Princeton University Press, 1962.

32. *A Concordance to Milton's English Poetry*, ed. W. Ingram and K. Swaim, Oxford: Clarendon Press, 1972, lists 370 uses of 'now' in *Paradise Lost*, many of them temporally problematic, from the first announcing of Satan, whom 'now the thought / Both of lost happiness and lasting pain / Torments' (I, 54–6) to Eve's final words to Adam, 'but now lead on' (XII, 614), introducing the 'now' of human history and also immediately blurring any sense of *place*: 'for with thee to goe / Is to stay here' (XII, 615–16). Interestingly, there are relatively few uses of the basic words of *location*, 'here' (112) and 'there' (102). Where 'there' is not, as it frequently is, neutral in terms of location, most often it indicates Hell ('to bottomless perdition, there to dwell', I,47) and Eden, with a concentration around the activity of the creative Word in a universal 'there': 'Let there be Light' (VII, 243). Curiously too (and for what it may be worth) the word 'never' occurs in a poem about loss, only 40 times.

BIBLIOGRAPHY

Adams, R. M. (1953) 'Reading *Comus*', *Modern Philology*, 51.

Allen, Don Cameron (1954) *The Harmonious Vision: Studies in Milton's Poetry*, Baltimore: Johns Hopkins University Press.

Arthos, John (1961) 'Milton's Haemony and Virgil's Amellus', *Notes & Queries*, 206.

Atkins, J. W. H. (1951; repr. 1968) *English Literary Criticism: Seventeenth and Eighteenth Centuries*, London: Methuen.

Augustine, St (1953) *De libero arbitrio*, in *Augustine's Earlier Writings*, trans. J. H. S. Burleigh, London: SCM Press.

Augustine, St (1968) *De gratia et libero arbitrio*, in *The Fathers of the Church*, LIX, Washington: Catholic University of America Press.

Augustine, St (1947) *De musica*, in *The Fathers of the Church*, II, New York: Cima.

Augustine, St (1912) *Confessions*, trans. William Watts (1631), ed. W. H. D. Rouse, London: Loeb Classical Library, 2 vols.

Augustine, St (1942) *De civitate dei*, trans. John Healey (1610), rev. R. V. G. Tasker, 2 vols, London: Dent.

Babb, L. (1940) 'The background of *Il Penseroso*', *Studies in Philology*, 37.

Barthes, Roland (1970) *Mythologies*, 2nd edn, Paris: Seuil.

Beardslee, John W. (ed. and trans.) (1965) *Reformed Dogmatics*, New York: Oxford University Press.

Bentley, Richard (1974) *Milton's Paradise Lost* (1732), repr. New York: AMS Press.

Bethell, S. L. (1953) 'The nature of metaphysical wit', *Northern Miscellany of Literary Criticism*, 1.

Boethius (1902) *The Consolation of Philosophy*, trans. W. V. Cooper, London: Dent.

Boucher, J-P. (1965) *Etudes sur Properce*, Paris.

Briggs, Katharine (1965) *A Dictionary of Fairies, Hobgoblins, Brownies, Bogies, and Other Supernatural Creatures*, London: Allen Lane.

Broadbent, J. B. (1960) *Some Graver Subject: An Essay on Paradise Lost*, London: Chatto & Windus.

Brooks-Davies, Douglas (1983) *The Mercurian Monarch: Magical Politics from Spenser to Pope*, Manchester: Manchester University Press.

Brown, Cedric C. (1979) 'The shepherd, the musician, and the word in Milton's masque', *Journal of English and Germanic Philology*, 68.

Brown, Cedric C. (1985) *John Milton's Aristocratic Entertainments*, Cambridge: Cambridge University Press.

Browne, Sir Thomas (1977) *Sir Thomas Browne: The Major Works*, ed. C. A. Patrides, Harmondsworth: Penguin Books.

Burden, Dennis (1967) *The Logical Epic: A Study of the Argument of Paradise Lost*, London: Routledge.

Calvin, John (1813) *Institutes of the Christian Religion*, trans. John Allen, Philadelphia: Presbyterian Board of Publication.

Calvino, Italo (1982) *If on a winter's night a traveller*, trans. William Weaver, London: Picador.

Carey, John (1981) *John Donne: Life, Mind and Art*, London: Faber.

Casaubon, Isaac (1614) *De rebus sacris et ecclesiasticis exercitationes XVI. Ad Cardinalis Baronii Prolegomena in Annales*, London.

Chaucer, Geoffrey (1957) *The Works of Geoffrey Chaucer*, ed. F. N. Robinson, 2nd edn, London: Oxford University Press.

Clements, A. L. (1961) 'Donne's Holy Sonnet XIV', *Modern Language Notes*, 76.

Coleridge, Samuel Taylor (1956) *Letters of Samuel Taylor Coleridge*, ed. E. L. Griggs, Oxford: Oxford University Press, 2 vols.

Cox, Gerard H. (1983) 'Unbinding "The hidden soul of harmony": *L'Allegro, Il Penseroso*, and the hermetic tradition', *Milton Studies*, 18.

Crooke, Helkiah (1631) *A Description of the Body of Man*, 2nd rev. edn, London.

Culler, Jonathan (1975) *Structuralist Poetics*, London: Routledge.

Danielson, Dennis R. (1980) '*Imago Dei*, "filial freedom" and Miltonic theodicy', *English Literary History*, 47.

Danielson, Dennis R. (1982) *Milton's Good God: A Study in Literary Theodicy*, Cambridge: Cambridge University Press.

Diekhoff, J. S. (1937) 'The Text of *Comus*, 1634 to 1645', *PMLA*, 52.

Diekhoff, J. S. (1940) 'Critical activity of the poetic mind: John Milton', *PMLA*, 55.

Donne, John (1985) *The Complete English Poems of John Donne*, ed. C. A. Patrides, London: Dent.

Donne, John (1978) *John Donne: The Divine Poems*, ed. Helen Gardner, 2nd edn, Oxford: Clarendon Press.

Donne, John (1966) *John Donne's Poetry*, selected and edited by A. L. Clements, New York: Norton.

Dryden, John (1674) *The State of Innocence and the Fall of Man*, London.

Dryden, John (1697) *The Works of Virgil: containing his Pastorals, Georgics, and Aeneis*, London.

Empson, William (1930) *Seven Types of Ambiguity*, London: Chatto & Windus.

Empson, William (1935) *Some Versions of Pastoral*, London: Chatto & Windus.

Empson, William (1965) *Milton's God*, rev. edn, London: Chatto & Windus.

Estienne, Charles (1545) *De dissectione partium corporis humani*, Paris.

Evans, Maurice, ed. (1977) *Elizabethan Sonnets*, London: Dent.

Fallon, Robert T. (1985) *Captain or Colonel: The Soldier in Milton's Life and Art*, Columbia: Missouri University Press.

Ferguson, Margaret W.; Quilligan, Maureen: Vickers, Nancy J., eds (1986) *Rewriting the Renaissance: The Discourses of Sexual Difference in Early Modern Europe*, Chicago: Chicago University Press.

Ferry, Anne Davidson (1963) *Milton's Epic Voice*, Cambridge, Mass.: Harvard University Press.

Ficino, Marsilio (1975) *Marsilio Ficino: The Philebus Commentary*. ed. and trans. M. J. B. Allen, Berkeley: University of California Press.

Fish, Stanley, E. (1969) *Surprised by Sin: The Reader in Paradise Lost*, London: Macmillan.

Fish, Stanley, E. (1975) 'What It's Like to Read *L'Allegro* and *Il Penseroso*', *Milton Studies*, 7.

Fitzgeffery, Charles (1881) *Poems of Charles Fitzgeffery*, ed. A. Grosart, Manchester: Manchester University Press.

Frye, Roland Mushat (1978) *Milton's Imagery and the Visual Arts: Iconographical Tradition in the Epic Poems*, Princeton, New Jersey: Princeton University Press.

Fuller, Elizabeth Ely (1983) *Milton's Kinesthetic Vision in Paradise Lost*, Lewisburg: Bucknell University Press.

Gosse, Edmund (1899) *The Life and Letters of John Donne*, 2 vols, London: Heinemann.

Gransden, K. W. (1976) 'Milton, Dryden and the comedy of the Fall', *Essays in Criticism*, 26.

Gray's Anatomy (1949) 30th edn, London: Longmans, Green.

Greville, Sir Fulke (1907) *The Life of the Renowned Sir Philip Sidney*, ed. N. Smith, Oxford: Oxford University Press.

Gwynn, Jones, T. (1930) *Welsh Folklore and Folk Customs*, London: Methuen.

Hall, B. G. (12 October 1933) '*Comus*', *Times Literary Supplement*, 691.

Hamilton, A. C. (1969) 'Sidney's *Astrophel and Stella* as a Sonnet Sequence', *English Literary History*, 36.

Hanford, J. H. (3 November 1932) 'Haemony', *Times Literary Supplement*, 815.

Harrison, T. P. (1943) 'The 'Haemony' passage in *Comus* again', *Philological Quarterly*, 22.

Herbert, George (1974) *The English Poems of George Herbert*, ed. C. A. Patrides, London: Dent.

Herman, George (December 1953) 'Donne's *Holy Sonnets* XIV', *The Explicator*, 12.

Hirsch, E. D. (1967) *Validity in Interpretation*, New Haven: Yale University Press.

Hobbes, Thomas (1840) *English Works*, ed. Sir William Molesworth, London; Bohm.

Hopkins, David, and Rudduck, Jean (June 1984) 'Academic sixth-form courses, the library, and perspectives on independent study: a report on a project', *Educational Research*, 26.

Hopper, Vincent (1932) *Medieval Number Symbolism: Its Sources, Meaning, and Influence on Thought and Expression*, Columbia University Studies in English and Comparative Literature, No. 132, New York: Columbia University Press.

Howell, Roger (1968) *Sir Philip Sidney: The Shepherd Knight*, London: Hutchinson.

Hunt, Clay (1954) *Donne's Poetry*, New Haven: Yale University Press.

Hunter, G. K. (1980) *Paradise Lost*, London: Allen and Unwin.

Ide, Richard S., and Wittreich, Joseph, eds (1983) *Composite Orders: The Genres of Milton's Last Poems*, Milton Studies, 17, Pittsburgh: Pittsburgh University Press.

Ingoldsby, William (1973) 'Intramuralia', *Huntington Library Quarterly*, 37.

Johnson, Samuel (1925) *The Lives of the English Poets*, 2 vols, London: Dent.

Kalstone, David (1970) *Sidney's Poetry: Contexts and Interpretations*, New York: Norton.

Kelley, Maurice (1962) *This Great Argument*, Princeton: Princeton University Press.

Kendrick, Christopher (1986) *Milton: A Study in Ideology and Form*, London and New York: Methuen.

Kermode, Frank (1975) *The Classic*, London: Faber.

Knox, George (October 1956) 'Donne's *Holy Sonnets* XIV', *The Explicator*, 15.

Kristeller, P.O. (1943) *The Philosophy of Marsilio Facino*, trans. Virginia Conant, New York: Columbia University Press.

La Branche, A. (1966) '*Blanda Elegia*: the background of Donne's elegies', *Modern Language Review*, 61.

Lanham, Richard A. (1977) '*Astrophil and Stella*: pure and impure persuasion', *Engish Literary Renaissance*, 2.

Leavis, F. L. (1936) *Revaluation*, London: Chatto & Windus.

Le Comte, E. S. (1942) 'New light on the "Haemony" passage in *Comus*', *Philological Quarterly*, 21.

Leibniz, Gottfried Wilhelm (1952) *Theodicee*, trans. E. M. Huggard, New Haven: Yale University Press.

Leishman, J. B. (1951) *The Monarch of Wit*, London: Hutchinson.

Levao, Ronald (March 1979) 'Sidney's feigned *Apology*', *PMLA*, 94.

Levenson, J. C. (March 1953) 'Donne's *Holy Sonnets* XIV', *The Explicator*, 11.

Levenson, J. C. (April 1954) 'Donne's *Holy Sonnets* XIV', *The Explicator*, 12.

Lever, J. W. (1956) *The Elizabethan Love Sonnet*, London: Methuen.

Lévi-Strauss, Claude (1950) *Sociologie et anthropologie*, Paris: P.U.F.

Lewalski, Barbara, K. (1985) *Paradise Lost and the Rhetoric of Literary Forms*, Princeton, New Jersey: Princeton University Press.

Lewis, C. S. (1932) 'A Note on *Comus*', *Review of English Studies*, 8.

Louthan, Doniphan (1951) *The Poetry of John Donne*, New York: Bookman.

Luck, Georg (1959) *The Latin Love Elegy*, London: Methuen.

Luther, Martin (1581) *A Commentarie . . . uppon the twoo Epistles General of . . . Peter and Jude*, trans. Thomas Newton, London.

Marotti, Arthur F. (1986) *John Donne: Coterie Poet*, Madison and London: University of Wisconsin Press.

Martindale, Charles (1986) *John Milton and the Transformation of Ancient Epic*, Beckenham: Croom Helm.

Martz, Louis (1962) *The Poetry of Meditation*, New Haven: Yale University Press, 2nd edn.

Marvell, Andrew (1952; repr. 1963) *The Poems of Andrew Marvell*, ed. Hugh McDonald, London: Routledge.

McCoy, Richard C. (1979) *Sir Philip Sidney: Rebellion in Arcadia*, Hassocks: Harvester Press.

Milton, John (1958) *The Poetical Works of John Milton*, ed. Helen Darbishire, London: Oxford University Press, 1958.

Milton, John (1968) *The Complete Poems of Milton*, eds Alastair Fowler and John Carey, London: Longman.

Milton, John (1890) *The Poetical Works of John Milton*, ed. David Masson, London: Macmillan.

Milton, John (1638) Milton, John, Cleveland, John *et al.*, *Obsequies to the memory of Mr Edward King*, Cambridge.

Milton, John (1972) *A Variorum Commentary on the Poems of John Milton*, eds A. S. P. Woodhouse and D. Bush, London: Routledge.

Milton, John (1972) *A Concordance to Milton's English Poetry*, eds W. Ingram and K. Swaim, Oxford: Clarendon Press.

Milton, John (1931–38) *The Works of John Milton*, ed. Frank Allen Patterson *et al.*, New York: Columbia University Press.

Milton, John (1953–1980) *The Complete Prose Works of John Milton*, ed. D. Bush *et al.*., New Haven: Yale University Press.

Mornay, Philip (1587) *A Worke Concerning the Trewnesse of the Christian Religion*, trans. Sir Philip Sidney and Arthur Golding, London.

Muir, Edwin (1956) *One Foot in Eden*, London: Faber.

Myers, William (1987) *Milton and Free Will: An Essay in Criticism and Philosophy*, Beckenham: Croom Helm.

Nashe, Thomas (1972) *The Unfortunate Traveller and Other Works*, ed. J. B. Steane, Harmondsworth: Penguin Books.

Newton-De Molina, David, ed. (1976) *On Literary Intention*, Edinburgh: Edinburgh University Press.

Otten, C. F. (1975) 'Milton's Haemony', *English Literary Renaissance*, 5.

O'Valle, Violet (1983) 'Milton's *Comus* and the Welsh Oral Tradition', *Milton Studies*, 18.

Ovid (1968) *Ovid's Amores*, text and translation by Guy Lee, London: Murray.

Ovid (1632) *Ovid's Metamorphosis. Englished and Mythologiz'd and Represented in Figures*, G[eorge] S[andys], Oxford.

Panofsky, E. (1955) *Meaning in the Visual Arts*, New York: Doubleday.

Parish, John E. (January 1963) 'No.14 of Donne's *Holy Sonnets*', *College English*.

Patrides, C. A. (1963) 'The Renaissance view of time: a bibliographical note', *Notes & Queries*, 208.

Peacock, A. J. (1975) 'Donne's elegies and the Roman love elegy', *Hermathena*, 119.

Peter, John (1980) *A Critique of Paradise Lost*, London: Longman.

Petrarch (1898) in *Petrarch: The First Modern Scholar and Man of Letters*, eds J. H. Robinson and H. W. Wolfe, New York and London: Puttnam.

Pike, Nelson (1970) *God and Timelessness*, London: Routledge.

Piozzi, Hester (Mrs Thrale) (1925) *Anecdotes of the Late Samuel Johnson*, ed. S. C. Roberts, Cambridge: Cambridge University Press.

Plomer, H. R. and Cross, T. P. (1927) *The Life . . . Of Lodowick Bryskett*, Chicago: Chicago University Press.

Purcell, J. M. (1934) *Sidney's Stella*, London: Oxford University Press.

Puttenham, George (1936) *The Arte of English Poesie* (1589), eds G. D. Willcock and A. Walker, Cambridge: Cambridge University Press.

Richmond, H. M. (1974) *The Christian Revolutionary: John Milton*, Berkeley: University of California Press.

Ricks, Christopher (1963) *Milton's Grand Style*, Oxford: Oxford University Press.

Ricks, Christopher (1984) *The Force of Poetry*, Oxford: Clarendon Press.

Robey, David, ed. (1973) *Structuralism: An Introduction*, Oxford: Clarendon Press.

Roston, Murray (1974) *The Soul of Wit*, Oxford: Oxford University Press.

Rudenstine, Neil (1967) *Sidney's Poetic Development*, Cambridge, Mass.: Harvard University Press.

Sacks, Peter M. (1985) *The English Elegy: Studies in the Genre from Spenser to Yeats*, Baltimore: Johns Hopkins University Press.

Sanders, Wilbur (1971) *John Donne's Poetry*, Cambridge: Cambridge University Press.

Savage, J. B. (1977) 'Freedom and necessity in *Paradise Lost*', *English Literary History*, 44.

Schaar, Claes (1982) *The Full Voic'd Quire Below: Vertical Context Systems in Paradise Lost*, Lund Studies in English, Lund: Gleerup.

Schindler, Walter L. (1984) *Voice and Crisis: Invocation in Milton's Poetry*, Hampden, Conn.: Archon Books.

Shakespeare, William (1980) *Hamlet*, ed. T. J. B. Spencer, introduction by Anne Barton, Harmondsworth: Penguin Books.

Sidney, Sir Philip (1962) *The Poems of Philip Sidney*, ed. William A. Ringler Jr., Oxford: Clarendon Press.

Sidney, Sir Philip (1966) *Defence of Poetry*, ed. J. Van Dorsten, Oxford: Oxford University Press.

Smith, A. J. ed. (1972) *John Donne: Essays in Celebration*, London: Methuen.

Spence, Lewis (1928) *The Mysteries of Britain: Secret Rites and Traditions of Ancient Britain Restored*, London: Rider.

Spenser, Edmund (1912; repr. 1959) *The Poetical Works of Edmund Spenser*, eds J. C. Smith and E. De Selincourt, London: Oxford University Press.

Spenser, Edmund (1943) *The Works of Edmund Spenser: A Variorum Edition*, ed. C. G. Osgood and H. G. Lotspeich, Baltimore: Johns Hopkins University Press.

Spenser, Edmund (1978) *The Faerie Queene*, ed. Thomas P. Roche Jr., Harmondsworth: Penguin Books.

Stapleton, Laurence (1966) 'Perspectives of time in *Paradise Lost*', *Philological Quarterly*, 45.

Steadman, J. M. (1962) 'Milton's *Haemony*: etymology and allegory', *PMLA*, 77.

Stenhouse, Lawrence (1983) *Authority, Education and Emanicipation*, London: Heinemann.

Tagore, Rabindranath (1913) *Sadhana*, London: Macmillan.

Tuve, Rosemond (1952) *A Reading of George Herbert*, Chicago: Chicago University Press.

Vesalius, Andreas (1952) *Vesalius on the Human Brain*, trans. with introduction by Charles Singer, London: Oxford University Press.

Wallace, M. W. (1915) *The Life of Sir Philip Sidney*, Cambridge: Cambridge University Press.

Waller, Gary F. (1982) 'Acts of reading: the production of meaning in *Astrophil and Stella*', *Studies in the Literary Imagination*, 15, 1.

Waller, Gary F. and Moore, Michael D., eds (1984) *Sir Philip Sidney and the Interpretation of Renaissance Culture*, London: Croom Helm.

Watson, S. R. (1940) 'An interpretation of Milton's Haemony', *Notes & Queries*, 178.

Whaler, James (1931) 'The Miltonic simile', *PMLA*, 46.

Wind, Edgar (1958) *Pagan Mysteries in the Renaissance*, London: Faber.

Wright, B. A. (1962) *Milton's Paradise Lost*, London: Methuen.

Zanchius, Hieronymous (1930) *The Doctrine of Absolute Predestination*, trans. A. M. Toplady (1769), London.

INDEX